JX 1952 MAB

New Security Challenges Series

General Editor: **Stuart Croft**, Professor of International Security in the
Department of Politics and International Studies at the University of Warwick,
UK, and Director of the ESRC's New Security Challenges Programme.

The last decade demonstrated that threats to security vary greatly in their causes
and manifestations, and that they invite interest and demand responses from
the social sciences, civil society and a very broad policy community. In the
past, the avoidance of war was the primary objective, but with the end of the
Cold War the retention of military defence as the centrepiece of international
security agenda became untenable. There has been, therefore, a significant shift
in emphasis away from traditional approaches to security to a new agenda that
talks of the softer side of security, in terms of human security, economic security
and environmental security. The topical *New Security Challenges Series* reflects
this pressing political and research agenda.

Titles include:

Brian Rappert *(editor)*
TECHNOLOGY AND SECURITY
Governing Threats in the New Millennium

New Security Challenges Series
Series Standing Order ISBN–978 0–230–00216–6 (hardback)
Series Standing Order ISBN–978–0–230–00217–3 (paperback)

You can receive future titles in this series as they are published by placing a standing order. Please contact your bookseller or, in case of difficulty, write to us at the address below with your name and address, the title of the series and one of the ISBNs quoted above.

Customer Services Department, Macmillan Distribution Ltd, Houndmills, Basingstoke, Hampshire RG21 6XS, England

The Globalization of Security

State Power, Security Provision and Legitimacy

Bryan Mabee
Lecturer in International Politics
Queen Mary University of London, UK

First published 2009 by
PALGRAVE MACMILLAN

Palgrave Macmillan in the UK is an imprint of Macmillan Publishers Limited, registered in England, company number 785998, of Houndmills, Basingstoke, Hampshire RG21 6XS.

Palgrave Macmillan in the US is a division of St Martin's Press LLC, 175 Fifth Avenue, New York, NY 10010.

Palgrave Macmillan is the global academic imprint of the above companies and has companies and representatives throughout the world.

Palgrave® and Macmillan® are registered trademarks in the United States, the United Kingdom, Europe and other countries.

ISBN-13: 978-0-230-22400-1 hardback
ISBN-10: 0-230-22400-8 hardback

This book is printed on paper suitable for recycling and made from fully managed and sustained forest sources. Logging, pulping and manufacturing processes are expected to conform to the environmental regulations of the country of origin.

A catalogue record for this book is available from the British Library.

A catalog record for this book is available from the Library of Congress.

10 9 8 7 6 5 4 3 2 1
18 17 16 15 14 13 12 11 10 09

Printed and bound in Great Britain by
CPI Antony Rowe, Chippenham and Eastbourne

Contents

List of Illustrations

Tables

Figures

Acknowledgements

The present work has benefited from the attention and support of numerous colleagues, from its inception to conclusion, which covered a twelve-year period starting at the University of Wales, Aberystwyth; through Oxford Brookes University; to Queen Mary, University of London. I would especially like to thank Ian Clark who had an enormous impact on the ideas in the book and the overall shape it eventually took. Stuart Croft was integral in getting it published, and I am grateful for his support. I would additionally like to thank the numerous colleagues who read drafts, made comments, discussed ideas, or supported my work in some other way: Barrie Axford, Tarak Barkawi, Chris Browning, Gary Browning, Alex Colas, Mick Cox, Abbey Halcli, Steve Hurt, Ray Kiely, George Lawson, Patricia Owens, Rick Saull, Todd Scarth, Martin Shaw, Steve Smith, Colin Wight, Michael C. Williams, Paul Williams and Richard Wyn Jones. Marjo Koivisto was a huge influence on the work in more ways than she might know, but especially through our conversations on state theory, state power, and the nature of international politics (and beyond).

Portions of Chapter 1 were originally published as 'Security Studies and the "Security State": Security Provision in Historical Context', *International Relations* Vol. 17, No. 2 (2003): 135–51, used by permission from Sage Publications Ltd.

A few passages of Chapter 1 were originally published as 'Discourses of Empire: The U.S. "Empire", Globalisation and International Relations', *Third World Quarterly* Vol. 25, No. 8 (2004): 1359–78.

The book is dedicated to my parents, who have faithfully supported my academic career all of these years, even when it meant a move abroad.

Introduction: The Globalization of Security?

Globalization has been the source of many controversies in contemporary thinking about international relations, in terms of its reality, its content and its potential impacts. Although these debates have mainly been confined to the study of global political economy, there has been an increasing analysis of globalization in terms of its impacts on national and international security. The present study was borne of some dissatisfaction with recent accounts of the relationship between globalization and security, finding limitations in terms of narrowly conceived notions of globalization, and narrowly conceived notions of state power, emanating from all sides of the debates.

The study that follows mainly concerns the interaction of new transnational varieties of threat with advanced industrial states' (mainly in the transatlantic region) ability to cope with such threats, both logistically and existentially. As such, the focus is somewhat broader than just cataloguing new threats and looking at their impacts on the environment of security (or the international system). It entails a fundamental rethinking of the state as a security actor, in terms of state power, combining historical and political sociology with International Relations.[1] The work draws especially on Michael Mann's neo-Weberian account of the sources of social power, looking at power as something that is organized in socio-spatial networks which shift and change over time.[2] The use of Mann's framework allows for greater purchase on the historically contingent nature of state power, but also concerning the conceptualization of globalization and its possible challenge to national state power. While the book takes the strong view that there is some (at least potential) state transformation due to globalization, it is more a working hypothesis that will be tested for plausibility by examining a number of cases.

1

The core thesis is that an ideal-typical 'security state' exemplified the security power of post-Second World War states in the transatlantic region, which is potentially undergoing transformation due to increased pressure from various transnational networks of power. However, this thesis is underpinned by two other proposals: first, that the conceptualization of state power in international relations has been underdeveloped; and second, that the response of the state to globalization is seen best in terms of strategies managing globalization, either through retrenchment of old forms of security provision, or through the transformation of security provision. Therefore, a key part of the analysis is to better provide a historically adequate account of state power in international relations, in order to better understand what the globalization of security may entail.

The key argument of the book is therefore found in the conceptualization of a historically situated 'security state', which better locates the kinds of changes which may occur to the state in an environment of increased globalization. The security state is characteristic of the state of contemporary international relations, possessing a firm demarcation between inside and outside, but also developing a strong infrastructural capacity to provide security: in essence, it has gone beyond the nineteenth-century Weberian 'monopoly of legitimate violence' and provides a *monopoly of security*. A key aspect of the maintenance of security provision is the ability of states to remain legitimate to their citizens. Security provision therefore connects the state with civil society in a significant manner: at least part of the compact between state and civil society is based upon guarantees that the state will protect society from harm. However, key to understanding the development of the security state itself was that it was a product of social change, mainly found in the interaction of states in global war and global economic relations. Thus, the development of a security state was a compromise position that allowed for both internationalization *and* nationalization, by protecting citizens at home. The security state therefore delineates an important connection between the legitimacy of the state and its ability to provide security, which may be challenged and transformed by the advent of conditions of intensified globalization.

By situating contemporary globalization in the broader social dynamics that lead to globalization, the book examines the present state of globalization as it relates to the security of industrialized states in the transatlantic region, in order to better elucidate changes in how security is pursued and obtained by these states. In that sense, to understand the connections between globalization as a condition and security, we need some idea of what the condition of globalization looks like, what precipitates it and what kinds of challenges it holds. The rest of the introduction will discuss the core issues concerning globalization and security in more detail, and delineate the structure of the argument.

The globalization of security: The problem

On the cusp of the twenty-first century, US President Bill Clinton announced that 'there is no longer a clear dividing line between foreign and domestic policy'. He continued on this theme, not only emphasizing the need for domestic social policy to proceed internationally, but also detailing the consequences for international security:

> I believe that the biggest problems to our security in the 21st century and to this whole modern form of governance will probably come not from rogue states or from people with competing views of the world in governments, but from the enemies of the nation-state, from terrorists and drugrunners and organized criminals who, I predict, will increasingly work together and increasingly use the same things that are fuelling our prosperity: open borders, the Internet, the miniaturization of all sophisticated technology ... And we have to find ways to cooperate to deal with the enemies of the nation-state if we expect progressive governments to succeed.[3]

This vision details quite readily what has become a major preoccupation with security threats in the world today: challenges to statehood itself, rather than challenges from interstate rivalry. It also outlines a need to deal with such threats by an appeal to cooperation in the international (or global) community.

Although the preoccupation with rogue states has certainly not vanished, emphasis on 'asymmetric' threats, nuclear proliferation, transnational criminal networks and the environment as a source of threat, as well as global inequality as a threat to 'human' security, have all become of increasing relevance to the discourse of security in the post-Cold War era, and into the twenty-first century.[4] Since 9/11, international and transnational terrorism has also been of utmost importance in the international security agenda.[5] Such concerns are all clearly connected with globalization, not just in its 'economic' variant, but also with the idea of the interconnected nature of social activity, the circulation of goods and people, especially concerning the transnational nature of both threat and opportunity.

Re-articulations of threats to national security are not uncommon in what is increasingly seen as a 'global age'.[6] The globalization of security has become more accepted as part of the discourse of globalization. However, despite an increasing volume of discussion on the subject, globalization and security still seem rather underplayed, as the way in which globalization and security are connected is in the traditional discourse of security studies: mainly in terms of how globalization impacts on the threat environment of nation-states.[7] The studies that have emerged have primarily looked at the changing nature of threats, pointing to the expansion of threats to include the transnational, those that impinge on not only the nation-state, but those that go substantially *through* the state: that is, such threats are not under the control of state actors.[8] In a broader context, a growing literature has assessed the impact of economic globalization on conflict, pointing to a variety of impacts: from the dependence of intrastate war on transnational financial networks to the impacts of economic inequality and under-development on conflict.[9] There has also been a further recognition of the development of global threats, which threaten not only individual states themselves but pose threats to a larger global system.[10] This would include weapons of mass destruction, and also less conventional areas of security such as the environment.

Although an expansion of threat and sources of insecurity provides an important starting point, it does not cover all the complexity conveyed by the diverse writings on globalization. The broader ways in which globalization has been theorized in and out of the discipline of International Relations (IR) tend to be overlooked,[11] especially in terms of the challenge of globalization to the state itself.[12] Additionally, many IR analyses deal with globalization as an essentially economic phenomenon.[13] Although economic power has a central place in the study of globalization, the concept is not synonymous with economic liberalization. This view also tends to marginalize the role of the state in globalization by depicting all states as victims of globalization, instead of looking at the interaction between the states *and* globalization. The danger here is that other aspects of globalization and the restructuring of power on a global level are overlooked. Much of the literature on globalization has shown a trend towards the transformation (especially) of the industrialized states of the North, and such trends are not well engaged with in the literature on security and globalization.

As such, there is a need for developing a better conceptualization of the globalization of security. The relationship between globalization and security needs to be rethought, in line with both the burgeoning literature on the phenomenon of globalization, and with the changing debate in security studies about the nature of security. Overall, the globalization of security needs to be seen as occurring in a number of spheres – economic, military and political – and as intimately connected with changes in the structure and purposes of contemporary states. Furthermore, the globalization of security needs to be coupled with a historical analysis of the changing nature of both state and security to understand contemporary changes in the international system.

To the extent to which security is becoming globalized, we should see the development of substantial global networks of security provision that draw states together in ever-increasing interdependency; in reality the institutionalization of transnational security provision. Such a provision need not be modelled as a top-down hierarchy as in traditional state forms, but such networks would conform more and more with the global governance of security, increasingly blurring the borders of traditional nation-states. As such, the fears of new threats posed by networks of globalization may also be realized as potentially transforming the *pursuit* of security.

The focus in what follows is mainly on the states that make up the industrialized North – mainly Western and Northern Europe and North America – partially because of the importance of those states in pursuing globalization strategies. The narrowing of the focus is to provide analytic clarity, and not to minimize the importance of the connection between globalization and security elsewhere in the world. In fact, as mentioned above, there is a burgeoning literature on the impact of globalization on conflict in the developing world that is in many ways in line with what is being argued here. However, such studies tend to ignore the possibly less obvious impacts on security in the developed world, and this is the main justification for focusing attention in this area.[14] Despite this, the argument still proceeds on the basis of making a point from a global perspective: the 'industrialised North' is not seen in isolation from the rest of the world.[15]

Despite all of these issues with conceptualization, a further examination of globalization is crucial. As the concept becomes evermore present and meaningful in describing the contemporary world, it becomes more important to generate conceptualizations that chime with a variety of changing social conditions. Importantly, globalization also needs to be seen as a condition, not a cause (or process) in its own right, and one that is not of necessity historically novel.[16] Despite what more radical proponents of globalization may claim, globalization is best seen as manifesting a propensity towards time–space compression, of increased interconnectedness, and trends towards global governance. The cause of these conditions is underpinned by changes in social relations more generally, not the other way around. Globalization requires, in Justin Rosenberg's words, 'a theory of globalization and not Globalization Theory'.[17] This means that we need to see the globalization of security in broader trends of changes in social relations: the globalization of security is not a discrete social phenomenon.

Rethinking the state

Though the book is mainly about globalization and security, the key theoretical and conceptual concern is with rethinking state power in international relations. At the centre of the argument is the role of the state in both globalization and the process of providing security. A common theme in the literature on globalization has been a questioning of the future of the state, and it remains an important theme which deserves further investigation. The problem with the common conceptualization of globalization is often seen in terms of its supposed effects on the state: that economic liberalization is effectively hollowing out the powers of nation-states, leaving them prey to global market forces.[18] Many have put this debate in stark terms – either globalization threatens the end of the state or globalization is meaningless.[19] This is a narrow view of the possibilities and problems of globalization, as the either/or characterization of the impacts of globalization is too clear-cut.

The all-or-nothing view on the state and globalization has dissipated, especially as the predictions of radical globalizers in the 1990s have not come to fruition, but also due to the seeming re-articulation of state power that has been seen in international relations after the terrorist attacks of 9/11. In this context, as Ripsman and Paul have rightly noted, 'the key question to be addressed by scholars of globalization and national security is not whether the new challenges of globalization will overwhelm the state but in what ways they alter the state and what mechanisms the state will use to adapt to global social forces while retaining its centrality'.[20] However, even in their analysis the state remains a fairly static container with traditional goals, and methods to achieve them. The need to rethink the state is paramount, as most studies of globalization and security take the state very much for granted as a unit of analysis.

A more dynamic view of the state needs to be taken, drawing on state theory and historical analysis, in order to form a historical sociology of security and the state that is better capable of viewing the interconnections and impact of the globalization of security. Such a perspective is inherent in Kaldor's articulations of 'new wars', which highlight the historical changes in the dual institutions of war and the state, and the link between war, state breakdown and economic globalization.[21] However, as stated previously, the literature on new wars is limited geographically, failing to make a thorough analysis of the connections between globalization and security in developed states. Furthermore, despite the historical logic involved in the work, the literature suffers from a presentism that overstates stark changes between periods.[22]

In order to better deal with state power, the analysis draws on the historical sociological literature on state power, in order to better elucidate the development of state power in time.[23] Such a view complicates the 'newness' of globalization and the challenge to the state. The basic premise of the argument is that there has been a global system for some time, and one of the main sources of changing configurations of state power is through linkages in this system. Some of the sources may be broadly domestic, but many are international (or inter-societal), the paramount example being inter-societal interactions and transactions found in war and economy. Such a view complicates the idea of state power as well. Instead of a transhistorical conception of what states are (e.g. power-maximizers, or followers of the 'national interest'), this view looks at states as being formed through their relationship with extant networks of power. As Randall Collins describes this view: 'the problem isn't to explain the global networks so much as to explain the conditions which determine the kinds of local units crystallizing within them'.[24] As Mann conceives it, the institutionalization of various strands of social power is what makes up social reality at any given time. These constellations may be enduring, but they also change throughout history, mainly through successfully competing arrangements.

As such, the book aims to contribute to the growing literature of international historical sociology by putting both globalization and security in the context of state power. What follows should not be read as a normative injunction that state power *should* shift as a response to globalization, but as an analytic perspective on the historical bases of state power.

Plan of the book

Chapter 1 develops the historical sociology of security and state that is so important for the rest of the study. The chapter starts by examining ideas about change in IR, analysing the lack of a development of a theory of the state in IR. The chapter then examines the neo-Weberian state, taking a historical perspective on the structure of the state, particularly in terms of the security relationship between state and society. The core argument, as stated previously, is the post-Second World War period saw the advent of the 'security state' in Western Europe and North America, the main features of which were the development of a much broader remit of security, a continued stark contrast between outside and inside, but a stronger concession to internationalism than previously conceived. A core part of the argument is that the security state was a compromise between the forces of internationalism and nationalism, a need for states to become more integrated internationally as a *means* of maintaining national power. The compromise entailed a stronger remit for security provision between state and society as well. As such, the chapter challenges much of the present literature on the globalization of security in terms of developing a historically situated understanding of the relationship between state, society and security.

Chapter 2 looks in more detail at the link between globalization and security. The chapter starts off by defining globalization in terms of the condition of social power being organized at the global level: for example, in political terms through the institutionalization of power from states to other scales of political organization (e.g. global governance). It then delves broadly into how far this has been achieved today. The chapter argues that globalization is presently very unevenly achieved; such impacts need to be placed in historical context in order to better understand current happenings. For example, the economic power of the North is increasingly integrated and most clearly globalized in terms of finance; however, political and military power are still much wedded to the state, despite some moves towards the global.

The chapter then examines the specific elements of a globalization of security, by looking at how various aspects of globalization have potentially impacted the way national states provide security. This is done through conceptualizing three facets of the globalization of security. First, the expansion of the scope of threat describes the extent to which threats are no longer solely the purview of *inter*national relations: for example the development of global environmental degradation, transnational terrorism, the impacts of migration and the impacts of global financial instability are all transnationally mediated. The development of networks of social power that provide new sources of threat are the crucial causal factor in the potential development of security globalization. Second, the growth of thinking about security in 'global' terms identifies the development of an ideology of globalism, which begins to conceive global solutions to global security problems. Such ideology is mainly conceived as a reaction to transnationalization, but can also facilitate transnationalism by supporting it. To the extent to which it is 'transcendent' (or transformative) there is a real potential to broadly shift how states conceive of security. Finally, a third facet represents the development of ways of institutionalizing transnational networks of power and can be seen in the development of substantially integrated security provision, from effectively transnational alliances such as NATO to the privatization of military power.

The development of these three facets is the core of the theory of security globalization proposed in the book. To the extent to which the interactions of these facets result in institutionalizing new networks of political power, we will start to see a transformation of state power. However, such a transformation is not assumed. Chapter 2 firms up the theory by describing two potential outcomes that are reactions to transnational sources of threat: either the retrenchment of state power or the transformation of state power.

The focus of the study is therefore centred on questions of how the security state – where aspects of military, political and economic power were concentrated in the state itself – has possibly been untangled. At the centre of the security state arrangement is the role of infrastructural power defining security relationships. The question remaining is in what sense the functional transformation of modern nation-states affects their ability to 'bind' societies when aspects of security provision are being renegotiated. The extent to which security as a legitimating function of contemporary states is being parcelled off is of crucial importance, both in terms of how security will be provided, and also in terms of how this affects other states in the international system.

The second part of the book features the examination of three case studies, in order to judge the potential scale and scope of the transformation of security as part of globalization. This is accomplished through the examination of the transnationalization activities, development of global ideological factors, security provision and legitimacy in three areas: nuclear weapons and the globalization of threat; arms industry globalization; and globalization and migration.

The approach to cases taken in the book demonstrates a compromise. Using the three facets developed above as a framework of analysis, the cases represent an application of the analytic framework to issues that are important to security as whole, and that may be seen as contributing to a globalization of security. Looking at issue areas instead of individual states allows the analysis of differential impacts of globalization, and therefore presents a wider view than looking at the impacts on single states. It also follows more clearly from the account of state power used throughout the study: that states historically should not be conceived as 'bordered power containers', and as such, examining the potential globalization of security on a national basis would misconceive the spirit of the project.

Chapter 3 examines the role nuclear weapons have played in destabilizing the traditional model of the territorial state. Looking back at the work of the early nuclear strategists, and the ways in which nuclear weapons and strategy were seen to impact on state structures (especially in terms of military preparedness and the creation of 'nuclear interdependencies' through the doctrine of extended deterrence), nuclear weapons are understood as a military technology which produced a truly global threat, which should have complications for security provision and state legitimacy. The history of nuclear weapons and nuclear strategy, however, leaves several paradoxes. Nuclear weapons make the territorial state more 'permeable', and as such, challenge the traditional 'hardness' of state boundaries. This would seem to make the state's claim to secure its population tenuous, especially if deterrence is used as a strategy. On the other hand, nuclear weapons have also come to be seen as status weapons that affect legitimacy in terms of state strength and additionally ways of providing security and national power. Despite such paradoxes, nuclear weapons have certainly become part of the discourse of a globalized sense of security and have important impacts on security policymaking and the provision of security itself.

Chapter 4 focuses on the privatization of security, through an investigation of the contemporary arms industry. Such a focus represents a merging of traditional military issues with those of international political economy. The increasingly transnationalized production of armaments has meant that states can no longer be effectively or aspirationally autarkic in their provision of military technology, and are therefore becoming increasingly interdependent in the provision of this fundamental aspect of military security. Such changes are further reinforced by the existence of an ideology of economic liberalization, which has played an important role in supporting claims for arms industry globalization. The chapter argues that the globalization of arms production has helped reinforce the sense of a security community in the transatlantic region and is therefore part of a broader global provision of security. The effects on legitimacy are here again uncertain, mainly due to the fundamentally ambiguous nature of arms production: sitting on the divide between economic and military power, it is often hard for a state (much less citizens) to make claims about the necessity of its nationality. Even in cases where this is done, it often rests more on the perceived economic need rather than security needs. As such, until there is a real legitimacy crisis, the existence of a security community helps to mitigate any potential legitimacy problems.

Chapter 5 examines the impacts of a globalization of migration on state security. The chapter first looks at how globalization has impacted on migration patterns, then delving into the politics of migration. The study of migration as a security issue in IR has mainly focused on the societal impacts, especially in terms of threats to established national identities. Although the impact on national identities is an important aspect, the globalized nature of migration also threatens to shatter old bonds of citizenship, through the development of transnational and global forms of citizenship. These are seen in a positive sense, by the gaining of universal rights, but they also potentially devalue state-bound notions of citizenship, and destabilize the benefits of citizenship in Western states. This connects to security in that citizenship is the signifying security pact between state and society, and as it is disrupted, it raises questions concerning where security will come from. The chapter argues overall that states have been quite robust in maintaining a semblance of control over migration, and as such here we see the greatest sense of state retrenchment against security globalization. Despite the strong state retrenchment, the chapter argues that there are the potential foundations for state transformation in the future.

The book overall provides an examination of the changing nature of security issues, with the background of state transformation under conditions of globalization. As such, it provides an important corrective to studies which see global security issues only in terms of an adverse effect on the state. The globalization of security challenges not only the range of security issues states are confronted with, but also the nature of security provision itself. The possibility of state transformation under conditions of globalization therefore not only represents an important change to the contemporary international system, but also to how states provide security. The intention of the study is not only to theorize (or conceptualize) state power and globalization, but also to examine various trends to illustrate the practical ways in which the globalization of security impacts upon states, which involves asking questions surrounding the manifestations of the globalization of security discussed above. The cases will provide some answers to the important questions surrounding the globalization of security: What kinds of risks are mediated on a global level? What kinds of alternative forms of security provision exist? What are the effects of globalization on the security state's monopoly of security? How is security provision being reorganized? This questioning will help to get to the heart of the matter: the degree to which security has become globalized in the contemporary world.

1
The 'Security State' and the Evolution of Security Provision

Security is at the very heart of contemporary political life. In the developed states of the North, most individuals' security is provided by the state – from protection from the internal and external threat of violence to the provision of basic needs – and is therefore contingent on political relationships, mainly found in the link between citizen and state. The potential impacts of globalization, while not necessarily threatening the life of the state itself, are bound to have an influence on this vital area. However, the state itself is a historically constituted entity that has undergone changes throughout its history. The importance of this recognition is that the development of a theory of the globalization of security cannot be properly analysed without some idea of the interaction between state change and security in international relations.

The debates that the critical agenda for security studies have developed – such as where security resides, and who the 'subject' of security is – are important. However, there remains a crucial question concerning how the provision of security has historically changed with the development of the state. A historical sociological analysis of the development of linkages between state and citizen will assist in this process, by supplying a historical analysis of the state, in order to better articulate its continuing relevance to political life and security, its relationship with individuals and society, and the complexities of contemporary citizenship. Such an approach also helps to centre security as a political practice, where the provision of security itself is the focal point of state–society relations, profoundly connected to ideas about state legitimacy.

During the period of total war at the beginning of the twentieth century, a particular configuration of state–society security relationships developed in Northern states where the state increased its power over society, but also in return gave a bundle of social goods to its citizens as a means of providing security. This model is here referred to as the 'security state'. The increase in domestic security provision was a compromise for a greater internationalization of the state, and provided a distinctive separation of external and internal security. As such, security became more than just the external–internal divide: security was broadened out to include economic hardship and other forms of social protection. Though this is often divorced from discussions of security, as 'domestic' concerns have been relegated by definition to the margins of *international* security studies, this development indicated a particular change in state–society relations. However, the processes which created the security state were a combination of national and international, domestic compromises that were mainly caused by war and economic dislocation. Seen in the context of the emergence of states from the impacts of two World Wars and the Great Depression, the security state was about greater internationalization *for* national autonomy. The interaction between these two factors was in many ways the defining dynamic of twentieth-century international relations.[1]

   In order to accomplish this analysis, five steps will be taken. First, the role of change and the state in security studies and International Relations (IR) more generally will be examined to highlight some of the deficiencies in analysing state power. Second, an introduction to the potential contribution of neo-Weberian historical sociology to security studies will be given, in order to show how security provision is embedded in the state–society complex, through the concept of citizenship. Third, an overview of the development of a security relationship between state and society in the European state-building process will be developed, demonstrating the increasing intensity of state–society bonds that were partly maintained by the granting of protective rights to citizens. Fourth, an analysis of the development of the security state in the twentieth century will provide the background for a historically constituted state–society security complex, with the possibility to incorporate change. Finally, the development of the security state will be put in the context of its post-war environment, where forms of internationalism buttressed the national autonomy of the security state.

Security, the state and change

International political change has become one of the most important concerns of International Relations. The long-standing debate concerning the role of historical study in the development of theories of international relations progressed steadily since discussion in the early 1980s.[2] However, that growth has not had much of an impact on the debates in security studies.[3] The end of the Cold War sensitized theorists and practitioners of security to the existence of a diversity of threats, and much attention has been paid to the expansion of the issue areas of security studies and the deepening of the conception of referents of security.[4] The major changes that have impacted the international system as a result of the end of the superpower conflict, and the increasing recognition of the importance of globalization in international politics, provide an opportunity for a re-examination of the basis of post-Second World War security, especially in terms of the major security actor: the sovereign state.

Though much notice has recently been paid to notions concerning a changing environment of security, less has been connected to changes in the structure of contemporary states. This omission can be explained by the relative inattention those studying security (and International Relations more generally) have spent dealing with theories of the state and its historicization.[5] The state is given an implicit definition that is used transhistorically. The problem with the avoidance of state theory manifests itself in the inability to incorporate changes in state configurations, and the conceptualization of the state takes on an isomorphic character. When the state is seen as a static, transhistorical institution, change is either ignored or only postulated in terms of a radical break from normal practices. This can be seen, for example, in the often-polarized debates concerning the impacts of globalization on the state, between those who deny change, and those who claim radical transformation.[6] The possibility of a change in the state and its functions becomes difficult to hypothesize, and the only possibility for states faced with change is the 'end of the state'.[7]

The problem of transhistoricism is most apparent in the way the state is utilized in International Relations (and, by extension, security studies), where the contemporary state is seen as unchanged from its 'emergence' in 1648 (or, perhaps better put, the early modern state is seen as equivalent to the contemporary state).[8] This tendency overestimates the coherence and capacity of early modern European states, as well as ignoring the tendency for the state to transform.[9] The idea of 'equivalence' is a symptom of the general reluctance of scholars of international relations to devote much effort in analysing the state itself. The state has generally been viewed as a national-territorial totality, where, as Halliday notes, 'the state provides in conceptual form what is denoted visually on a map'.[10] The state in international relations is, due to this, often under-theorized, and often conceptualized in a static manner. The static state is especially clear in the debates about the impacts of globalization on the state which posit the end of the state: it is clear that the state being discussed is highly particular, and ignores the development of the state over time.

Contrasting a new 'age of globalization' with the 'Westphalian era' makes the present look more novel than it necessarily is. Although the importance of the sovereign nation-state is not questioned, the lack of historical perspective on the origins and development of the sovereign state make comparisons with the past difficult. As Hobson has noted, the mainstream of International Relations theorizing, especially that of neo-realism and neo-liberalism, has been susceptible to an ahistorical attitude: that history only exists inasmuch as it reflects present conditions, and as such denies novelty and change.[11] This is not to deny the reality of the Westphalian paradigm (though certainly suggesting that it was not born at the Peace of Westphalia), but to highlight the contingent origins of particular constellations of state power, and to argue that such constellations change over time. Due to an increasing recognition of both the durability of the state and the possibility of changes within the state, the long sterile debate between those who saw the 'end of the state' under the onslaught of globalization against those who minimized or dismissed the importance of globalization entirely, has been rather muted of late.

Security studies has suffered from similar problems with regard to the state and historical change. In the traditional realist approach to security studies, the state has been unquestioned in its historical structure.[12] The traditional model of security is primarily based on the idea that security should be, first and foremost, defined as national security. This can be seen, for example, in Herz's attempt to situate security and the state in the context of territoriality: that the security and legitimacy of the state has been based primarily on its impenetrability, the creation of a 'hard shell' around the state.[13] National security is provided by the protection of the nation-state from threat.

Symptomatic of this, security studies has mainly focused on changes in emphases caused by globalization and the end of the Cold War, ignoring possible changes to the state and security provision itself.[14] Meanwhile, critical scholars have done much to interrogate the assumptions of traditional approaches to security, but their views on the state have mainly questioned its role as the object of security (i.e. a criticism of the *national* focus of security studies) and the state as a security provider (i.e. against the assumption that states act in their citizens'

best interests).[15] This questioning has been valuable in c
the state as *the* provider of security, but has ignored tc
the formation and historical role of states in the securit'
the historical mutability of particular forms (or crystalliz.
power.[16]

In security studies, the state has primarily been discussed, if at all, in
terms of its relevance as an actor in the security process.[17] Though these
debates are important, the terms of the debate encompass the security
provision by Western states in the latter half of the twentieth century.
There is little sense that states have developed particular security relationships with their constituent societies over time, other than those
that embrace notions of the state and a liberal social contract. The result
of this is a situation where the arguments have mainly hinged around
the promotion or dismissal of states as security actors.[18] Though this is
not a problem in the sense that the questions that these debates have
raised are indeed important, it does seem to limit the possibilities of
examining the future of both the state and security provision. As such,
it is necessary to more clearly articulate the historical development of
state power through a theory of the state.

Security and the neo-Weberian state

A dynamic model of the state is crucial in the analysis of globalization, as it assists in getting past the narrow and problematic view of the
relationship between the state and globalization as a zero-sum game,
and shows important ways that the two can be and must be entangled.
'Dynamic' primarily means a view of the state as a mutable institutional
form, a political entity that can and has changed over time. The manner in which the state has changed has primarily been to do with the
relations between the state and the society it governs, and is ostensibly
supposed to protect. The means by which security studies has characterized the state–society relationship have generally been guilty of
having a rather poor model of the state–society relationship, which has
hindered the possibility of analysing the importance of globalization.

The international context of security must presume some kind of
relationship between states and their domestic societies, as states have a
domestic (societal) role in addition to their international commitments.
This could, theoretically, go along a continuum from the idea that states
themselves act completely in their own interests, without regard to their
domestic constituencies, to the idea that national security is primarily
determined by domestic constituencies, at least in the abstract sense

that the 'national interest' embodies the collective interests of domestic society. As McSweeney points out, 'it is implicit in most studies of national and international security ... that the ultimate reference is people ... It is from the human need to protect human values that the term "security" derives its meaning.'[19] Not developing a firmer relationship between state and society causes a problem for examining change that occurs on a societal level, which does not just involve whether or not states are 'strong' or 'weak' according to the level of political cohesion.[20] Buzan's 'maximal' state model of security, for example, contains such problems as a consequence of theorizing society as an adjunct of the state, giving it the same bounded characteristics of the state.[21] As Shaw notes, 'it refuses to acknowledge autonomous social relations as a factor in international relations distinct from the state, and incorporates society into international theory only as an adjunct of the state'.[22] State–society relations can affect a state's international role, just as much as international relations can impact on the state and society itself. For example, the development of more intensified state–society relations in the period coinciding with the development of nationalism and capitalism (in the eighteenth to nineteenth centuries) certainly helped to put to an end to the primarily dynastic forms of international relations seen in the era of European absolutism, and as a result an alternative emphasis on an abstract conception of the 'national interest'.[23] As much was the key argument for a historical sociology of international relations: states, societies and international relations are in a dynamic, causal relationship.[24]

Those working within historical sociology have contended with the problems of studying the state historically, the relevance of state–society relations and developing various models of how changes in state structures, international relations and state–society relations occur.[25] As such, they have done much to help clarify the state as an institution, separating the state (as a socio-political institution) and society (as social relations in general), for the purpose of examining the context of relationships between the two. The merits of this approach are that it helps to clarify state–society relations, and importantly, allows for and substantively examines the state as a historically constituted and dynamic institution, providing for the possibility of change in the institutional framework of the state itself. The position here develops the neo-Weberian view on the state in order to better conceptualize the state in international relations and its relationship to security. There are of course competing approaches to the state found in what Collins refers to as the 'conflict school' of sociology – the approaches of Marx and Weber – both of which have their merits for what is being attempted here.[26] The neo-Weberian position is preferred for one main reason: it better incorporates military power into the purview of state power without it becoming a mere extension of state (or more reductively, economic) power.[27] Additionally, neo-Weberian approaches have incorporated an international dimension to their theorizing from the outset, exemplified in the work of Giddens, Mann, Skocpol and Tilly.[28]

The definition of the state by Weber, as 'that human community which (successfully) lays claim to the *monopoly of legitimate physical violence* within a certain territory',[29] provides the starting point for these theories and an implicit theoretical basis for many International Relations scholars.[30] Neo-Weberians have updated this definition to more clearly delineate states in historical context, analytically dividing the definition into discrete components. In this perspective, Mann provides an excellent neo-Weberian institutional definition of the state:

> i) the state is a differentiated set of personnel ii) embodying centrality, in the sense that political relations radiate to and from a centre, to cover a iii) territorially demarcated area over which it exercises iv) some degree of authoritative, binding rule making, backed up by some organised physical force.[31]

Mann's definition is important as it emphasizes a whole array of factors, pointing to the state as a broad institutional arrangement, more than just government.

The crucial idea that derives from such an approach is the concept of state autonomy. Though in realist IR thought autonomy has generally been placed in the context of the international realm, in that states are autonomous from one another, in this context it also refers to the way the state relates to society (or societies). The state should be seen, as Poggi notes, 'as itself constituting a distinctive social force, vested with interests of its own, which affect autonomously, and sometimes decisively, the state's own arrangements and policy'.[32] This is important because it describes a relationship between states and societies that goes beyond the liberal, social contract fiction of the state as a mere outgrowth of individual desires. However, the autonomy of the state from society is never total, as states often rely on their constituent societies for certain types of social action, exemplified by the role played by resource extraction.[33] Additionally, such accounts more generally would see the sources of change impacting on particular configurations of state–society relations over time. In Mann's terms, it would be wrong to specify a singular 'society', rather than discussing socio-spatial networks of power in particular historical contexts. As such, nationalized state–society complexes are particularly modern institutions, the development of which will be discussed in more detail in the next section.[34]

In the modern state, the concept of citizenship should be seen as specifying a type of compact between state and society, as a part of increasing infrastructural power: seen as the ability of the state to penetrate society and organize social relations.[35] Citizenship is both relational and reciprocal, and it therefore is not simply the case of a beneficent state giving rights to citizens. It also outlines the obligations of the individual within civil society to the state, and individuals' legitimate claims and expectations of the state: 'infrastructural power is a two-way street'.[36] As the state increases infrastructural power, the possibilities and potentiality of civil society rise, and is expressed through the duties and benefits of citizenship. Giddens' account of the relationship between the development of surveillance as a form of administration and struggles concerning citizenship reflects this dynamic relationship between infrastructural power and the rights of citizenship.[37] This is not to say that the state–society relationship is benign, but that it is inherently conflictual: citizenship rights and duties represent a compromise between state and society.

Citizenship, therefore, is the key to examining security relationships between state and society, in that citizenship rights and duties describe the necessary functions of the state in órder for it to remain legitimate. However, the relationship between security and citizenship can be further related to the concept of legitimacy. In Weber's definition, the state must hold a monopoly on legitimate violence to be a state. Though legitimacy in this sense refers to force *itself* being legitimate, the existence of such a monopoly also serves to further legitimize states' claims to provide forms of protection to their citizens. As Tilly states, 'a tendency to monopolize the means of violence makes a government's claim to provide protection ... more credible and more difficult to resist'.[38] As such, the development of a state security apparatus reinforces legitimacy to the extent to which it citizens are protected, or even feel secure.

Weber saw his institutional definition of the state being drawn from the contemporary state, as it represented the 'full development' of statehood.[39] As he stated, 'the monopolization of legitimate violence by the political-territorial association and its rational consociation into an institutional order is nothing primordial, but a product of evolution'.[40] As seen in the definition above, Mann (along with

Giddens) has questioned Weber's position on organized violence as part of the state, who both point out that it is only the modern state that has been actually able to claim a monopoly on legitimate violence.[41] As such, they question the inevitability of the contemporary nation-state, which is a crucial modification. The state should be seen as a flexible institution, whose relationship with the means of violence is open to change. More broadly, the idea of what security provision is, and how it is provided, is open to development and modification.

The analysis of the connections between infrastructural power and the development of citizenship give theoretical background to looking at the building of a security state in practice. However, it also needs to be complemented with the development of a juridical notion of statehood in international society, which has existed in tandem with the development of the state *de facto*, and is crucial in understanding contemporary debates about state and change, especially in the debates over globalization. At the centre of the 'idea of the state' is the international recognition of juridical sovereignty, a concept which is at the heart of the theory and practice of contemporary international relations. This is particularly clear in English School accounts of IR, where sovereignty in legal terms is put at the centre of international society.[42] The juridical notion of sovereignty also contains within it a normative vision of the state itself, one that gives significant prominence to the security state: that sovereign states are ones that are also able to provide security for their citizens. As much is clear in contemporary debates about the rights of sovereignty, particularly found in issues surrounding humanitarian intervention, and the rights of states against the duties of states.[43] As such, there remains a tension between this idea of the state and any social forces which modify aspects of state power: the overall tension between the continued importance of the ideology of statehood and the ideology of globalization.[44]

As such, the development of changed state–society relations goes beyond mere domestic politics. International relations is constitutive of statehood, in terms of how broad social changes influence the content of international relations, and how inter-societal interactions change state–society relations and configurations of state power. Giddens' account of the development of nation-states through the reflexive practices of international relations is one argument along these lines.[45] Similarly, Justin Rosenberg's recent invocation of 'combined and uneven development' as a core historical theory of the international also points to the development of particular forms of state power through international relations themselves.[46] Overall, the changing compacts of the state tend to be part of broader sets of inter-societal interactions, found especially in war and economy.[47]

Taking the 'security state' for granted creates a difficulty in analysing the possibility of change in the state, both because the state is taken as a static institution, and because the array of contemporary security functions and relationships are also taken for granted. The slow development of citizenship rights and duties is an important part of the growth of security compacts between state and society, demonstrating the dynamic nature of the state itself, and also pointing to the possible further evolution of the state and its relationship with broader international processes. The benefit of a historical sociological approach to the state is found in the recognition of the functional autonomy of the state itself, manifested in the concept of infrastructural power. The development of infrastructural power goes along with the development of citizenship and the binding relationship between state and society, and therefore provides a crucial corrective to the analysis of the state in both security studies and International Relations.

The evolution of security provision

The history of the development of the state is one that has been told a number of times from various angles, but primarily in the context of how elite war-making eventually led to the development of states, both for the advancement of socio-political order and the need for the formation of an infrastructure for extraction to finance the evermore costly means of warfare.[48] The development of the state, therefore, was as a means to power – it was not an end in itself.[49] In the context of citizenship and infrastructural power, there had to be the arrival of the state as an end in itself, something that was not properly seen until the late eighteenth century and the French and American revolutions,[50] in order for the kind of security provision associated with the contemporary state to develop. At this point, citizenship and the state became intimately connected, and the infrastructural power of the state increased enormously, through a slow process of development of material infrastructure.

Along with the eventual development of the rights of citizenship, we see a gradual change in what those rights and duties consist of, that moves from the relative disinterest early states and rulers saw in their subjects (except as sources of revenue), to the relatively compassionate governance seen in contemporary states. This goes along with a change in state security provision itself – from the early emphasis on social order and lack of violence (at least against the state) to the contemporary welfare state. Although this story can be told in developmental terms – that is, a switch from mere state despotism to enlightened democratic forms of governance – it is essential to examine this through the context of infrastructural power, where benefits were trade-offs in some sense for the further penetration of state into society.[51] It is essential because such trade-offs between state and society inform the content of security compacts, and as such, are still vital to understanding security provision in the present. The current section provides an overview of the beginnings of the state–society security relationship, followed by a more detailed analysis of the contemporary situation.

The security relationship between states and society has undergone a rather gradual development. Tilly provides an example of an early variant on the development of security relations between states and at least one class actor in civil society, the new bourgeoisie, and the role it played in the development of the state in Western Europe. Tilly describes the growth of the state as a consequence of the development of a 'protection racket', where the pursuit of power and control caused elites to monopolize the control over violence within their territories, while, furthermore, the pursuit of war caused rulers to set up systems of extraction in order to raise capital for these endeavours.

The extraction process, though not excluding outright pillage, importantly included taxation, through the making of promises of protection (of a particular social class). This led to the entrenchment of substantial bureaucracies to regulate taxation, police forces, courts and account keepers, therefore solidifying the existence of exclusive territorial states.[52] Therefore, one of the factors in the consolidation of states was the unintended consequence of the rulers' search for power – that the need for capital to invest in war-making inadvertently led to the elimination of rivals within a given territory, in order to have a greater capacity to extract resources.[53] Overall, a cycle in European state-building centred around the ability of states to extract wealth from their subjects, which further created and reinforced the development of the substantial bureaucratic manifestations of the state, allowing even more intervention in and control over their constituent societies.[54] Importantly this is an international process as well, as the interaction between early state forms – that is, through military competition and war – was a crucial link in the cycle.

The development of such a relationship is borne out by the two major watersheds in the state described by Mann: its increase in size in the eighteenth century, and the increasing extent of its civil functions in the nineteenth century.[55] This can be seen in a number of areas, but one of the most important was the increasing level of bureaucratic management of the state, which increasingly came to be seen as the actual location of rule in the state.[56] This was also accompanied by the development of infrastructures, both material and symbolic, exemplified by the development of roads, railways, postal services, telegraphy and mass education; civilian functions that increased the prosperity of society but further politicized society in the sense that it could not ignore the state.[57]

In terms of civilian expenditures, the average increase over the course of the nineteenth century was about 50 per cent in spending on civilian functions. At the beginning of the twentieth century about 75 per cent of state expenditure was channelled towards civilian purposes.[58] In the nineteenth century, the state's commitment to educating its subjects became an important aspect of its increased civil role. This, of course, was connected to the economic needs of states, and also to the rise of nationalism, and receiving the 'correct' education; education was a product of further democratization, but also contained a strong element of 'parading, flag-saluting, anthem-singing, and hero-worshipping'.[59] Over the course of the nineteenth century, states also started to focus on the conditions of the poor and the sick, and of workers. In Britain, this can be seen through a number of developments, such as the Factory Acts and the eventual establishment of the Ministry of Health in 1919.[60]

The state's control over organized violence also proceeded over this time period. The state became increasingly in control over violence within its territory, which was accompanied by a shift in the status of the military, from a situation where the military was essentially 'embedded' within society, to where the military itself became a bureaucratized arm of the state.[61] It was in the eighteenth century where the distinction between civilians and soldiers became commonplace.[62] By the nineteenth century, national armies and navies had in the main displaced the use of mercenaries and privateers.[63] Along with these changes came a switch in the purpose of armed force, where it became more an instrument of an abstract state, and less an instrument of the rulers. However, the change in the purpose of armed force also accompanied the increased presence of force internally, though eventually through the establishment of police forces as distinct from the military, as the needs of the internal maintenance of order (e.g. controlling mobs) required different techniques to external conflicts.[64]

These watersheds of the state were accompanied by the increased politicization of society in the late eighteenth and nineteenth centuries.

As Mann notes, 'as states transformed into national states, then into nation-states, classes became caged, unintentionally "naturalized" and politicized'.[65] The word 'caging' is of importance, as it describes how the development of nation-states in the period was part of a process of the state bounding social relations within its political territory. The rise of infrastructural power developed the boundedness of the state so taken for granted in traditional accounts of international relations; as Hobden points out, 'traditional international relations theory has portrayed borders as hard shells. A socio-historical construct has become reified into a physical attribute of social relations.'[66]

This boundedness also contributed to the expansion of citizenship, as the combination of nationalism (the result of the process of 'caging') and sovereignty led to the demand for greater national rights for the subjects of the state.[67] As societies were clamped ever tighter within states, the state politicized societies through nationalism and sovereignty. Modern societies therefore reinvented democracy because the state could not be escaped; as Mann puts it, 'in the early modern period people became trapped within national cages and so sought to change the conditions within those cages'.[68] This insight is echoed by Giddens, in his account of the connections between nationalism and the state. As he states,

> nationalism helps naturalize the recency and contingency of the nation-state through providing its myths of origin. But, at the same time, the discourse of national solidarity helps block off other possible discursive articulations of interest. The discursive arena of the modern polity treats what 'politics' is as inherently to do with the bounded sphere of the state.[69]

This tendency can also be seen in conjunction with the changing nature of armed force. The shift from armed force as principally an instrument of the ruling elite to being an instrument of the abstract state was noted above, but with the rise of nationalism, this connection became even stronger. As Howard notes, 'War was no longer considered a matter for a feudal ruling class or a small group of professionals, but one for the people as a whole. The armed forces were regarded, not as a part of the royal household, but as the embodiment of the Nation.'[70]

The overall increase in civilian expenditure and the changing nature of armed force, combined with the increased politicization of society through the development of citizenship rights, point to the development of more advanced forms of security provision. The combination of nationalism and warfare meant that, to a large extent, war was becoming sold in terms of the national interest of the whole population, and therefore could be expressed as providing a form of security. Regarding civilian expenditure, the development of mass infrastructures was all part of increased living standards as part and parcel of citizenship, which should be seen as another aspect of security provision. These two dimensions provide the basis for putting the state at the centre of an internal and external divide that has pervaded the literature on security ever since.

Though this is obviously a highly generalized model of the process, it still provides important insights as an ideal-typical model. The rise of European states was thus founded not only on the development of a powerful state elite and governing apparatus, but also through the development of infrastructural power and through international social interactions such as war. The increased intensity of interaction between state and society was put in the context of protection, which can be seen as a precursor to the more advanced kind of security provision seen through the increased involvement of the state in civil activities. As Hobden points out, 'states did not emerge in terms of contractual arrangement with society, but because of their effectiveness in extracting resources from society, to protect the state as an institution and the population under its jurisdiction. State survival was very closely linked to the protection of a local population.'[71] The end of the nineteenth and beginning of the twentieth centuries heralded a more intensive relationship between state and society regarding security provision. The infrastructural powers of the contemporary state became enormous. The huge rise in infrastructural power has culminated in the post-war security state, which tightened state–society relations much beyond the point of these early state formations.

The security state

The 'security state' therefore represents a situation where the increased penetration of the state into civil society provided the basis for not only more coordination of society by the state, but the reciprocal effect of increased rights and expectations of the citizens of states. Though this is often left aside as irrelevant by international security analysts, as it is seen as a 'domestic' development, associated with the rise of the welfare state, it is in fact an important change in the structure of states, and also requires a transformation in the conceptualization of security. The security state is, basically, a relationship between state and society where the state provides insurance against contingency.[72] In the case of the security state, the contingency is the impact of increasing internationalization, where states were involved in international relations broadly speaking in more and more intensive ways. While the protection from external threat remained a mainstay of state security provision, the development of large degrees of state intervention within states, in order to provide security for its citizens, was a somewhat newer development. The development of a security state also points to the massive increase in intervention in society by the state, in many senses part of an increasing centralization of political (not to mention economic and military) power. This increase in infrastructural power goes in some way beyond the Weberian 'monopoly of legitimacy violence' held by nineteenth-century European states, towards a 'monopoly of security', where the protection from external threat gets bundled together with a variety of other forms of security provision.

The increase in infrastructural power and rights in twentieth-century states had much to do with the rise of industrialized total wars and the increased interpenetration of international economic power, and this context can demonstrate the importance of changing state–society relationships through changes in the rights of citizenship.[73] As stated earlier, the key to understanding the security relationship between state and society is through the lens of citizenship. The need for massive penetration into civil society in order to organize the total wars of the twentieth century had a major impact on the structure of the state, which continued after the end of the Second World War. The First World War of course provides the precedent, where states managed to organize a vast array of market forces in the domestic economy for their own purposes. As McNeill states, 'innumerable bureaucratic structures that had previously acted more or less independently of one another in a context of market relationships coalesced into what amounted to a single national firm for waging war'.[74]

During the Second World War, all of the industrialized nations involved had to organize their economies around mobilization for the war effort.[75] This was usually done through the use of specialized state bureaucracies which organized their economies.[76] In Nazi Germany, economic planning had been divided among the three branches of the armed services and the Schutzstaffel, but under Armaments Minister Albert Speer was centralized to a large degree.[77] The centralization was further recognized in 1943 when the title was changed to the Ministry of War Production.[78] In Britain, a greatly successful war economy was achieved under the auspices of Sir John Anderson, the head of the

Lord President's Committee, responsible for coordination of the wartime economic effort. Measures were also implemented to deal with wartime manpower shortages.[79] The planning introduced many compromises in terms of civil liberties, and in terms of oversight: though ostensibly overseen by the House of Commons, the ability to control the committee was actually quite small in practice, as was its awareness of what went on in the committee.[80] In the US, though in many ways a special case due to its relative isolation from the conflict, wartime production was coordinated through a number of organizations, including the War Production Board, the Manpower Commission, and the Office of War Mobilization. These organizations, facilitated by President Roosevelt's leadership, proved an outstanding success, so that over the period of 1941–1943 the US was significantly out-producing all of the other belligerents in the war.[81] The centralization inherent in this wartime planning inaugurated unprecedented intrusion of the state into society, especially anathema to the long-standing tradition of American anti-statism.[82]

The very immensity of the undertaking of total wars necessitated an increased attention to the needs of people. As the organization of war developed a massive increase in state intervention and discipline, such intervention needed to be complemented with new forms of social compromise.[83] The extensive mobilization of society in the war effort led to a post-war situation where society demanded more from the state, and there was an opportunity for states to meet such demand.[84] As Mazower states, 'it seems as though the war had created – or intensified – a demand for social solidarity, while the economic upswing created the resources to support this change'.[85] However, the total wars not only affected the structure of post-war states, they also affected the relationship between state and society in terms of citizenship.

The post-war arrangements also followed a number of different paths, from the more conservative Catholic policies of West Germany, Italy and France, to the more radical departure of Sweden.[86] In the case of Britain, the 1942 Beveridge report, outlining Britain's post-war social welfare provision, was received with great enthusiasm, and became the best-selling bureaucratic document in British history, selling over 500,000 copies. As Hay points out, 'the fervour with which it was received clearly reflected a deep social appetite for wholesale social reform'.[87] The types of social rights developed in post-war Britain included: full employment, a universal national insurance scheme, a comprehensive National Health Service, free and compulsory education, and an extended state-housing sector.[88]

The US evolved into a more minimalist welfare state compared to the European states, but, despite this, the experience of the Second World War still had an immense impact on both social welfarism and the conception of security overall.[89] During the war, the National Resources Planning Board noted that 'to be worth dying for, a political system must be worth living in'.[90] As Sherry notes, 'in that light, social welfare programs were not "sentimental humanitarianism" but the "first line of national defense"'.[91] In the US example, because of the linkage made between military spending and overall prosperity, the welfare state became folded into the concern with national security.[92] As President Roosevelt pursued an economic bill of rights to be a counterpart to the sacrifice of war, he also stated that the one supreme objective for the future is 'security. And that means not only physical security ... from attacks by aggressors. It means also economic security, social security, moral security – in a family of Nations.'[93] The move towards welfarism also represented a rise in statism: the centralizing tendencies that welfarism required were reflected in other areas of national policy, against the traditional anti-statism of American political culture. Nowhere was this clearer than in the area of national security, with the passage of the 1947 National Security Act, and furthermore, through the vast centralization of control needed to oversee the development of nuclear weapons.[94]

It should be stressed that many of the rights that were developed after the war were general continuations of previous policies designed to promote general welfare, and therefore it would not be accurate to equate the rise of welfarism with the rise or 'rebirth' of liberal democracy in the post-war period: the policies were directly related to the increasing infrastructural power of states. For example, Britain had started much of its domestic reforms in the nineteenth century. The post-war social provision provided by West Germany and Italy was founded on concepts and bureaucratic frameworks developed before the war. The West German 'life ensuring state', as developed by Ernst Forsthoff, was originally approvingly employed in 1938 in the context of the Third Reich.[95]

Despite the recognition that welfarism was not necessarily novel to war or liberal democracy, there was a definite change in the purpose of welfarism. In the nineteenth century, social welfare existed primarily to mollify the lower classes; as Marshall put it, 'the common purpose of statutory and voluntary effort was to abate the nuisance of poverty without disrupting the pattern of inequality of which poverty was the most obviously unpleasant consequence'.[96] After the period of total war, and at least partially as a consequence of it, welfarism took on much more extensive role that, while not necessarily emancipatory, was certainly aimed at relieving an extensive range of social problems. What is particularly notable in this light, is that welfarism took aim at entire populations, not just at 'the poor', or soldiers who had fought in war.[97] Even in the US, where the development of a European-style welfare state was hindered by an anti-statist tradition, there were gains in overall social enfranchisement, as racial and gender barriers began to be broken because of the involvement of women and African-Americans in the war effort.[98]

The various rights that had been consolidated by the period following the Second World War – rights of full employment, unemployment insurance, health care, housing benefits and the like – developed at least partially out of the war effort itself, and the increased pressures put on societies by the war, as well as a number of compromises made by political parties after the war.[99] As such, the provision of such rights were not benign, they were very much a part of state strategies for warfighting, and were a compromise for the increasing reach of the state into the lives of its people, for the purpose of war mobilization. The provision of rights themselves, however, also led to increasing levels of state intervention in social policy and the economy, all in all an illustration of the tension between state and society indicated earlier.

The development of the security state hinges on this elaboration of citizenship and rights which were seen as part of the trade-off in the increased penetration of the state into civil society. The rise of infrastructural power over the past two centuries not only increased the state's involvement in civil society, but increased the expectations of civil society through its politicization, and the recognition of such expectations can be seen in the expansion of citizenship rights.[100] The 'security' that states provide has changed dramatically in the twentieth century, through extended ideas of citizenship in the beginning of the century, to the post-Second World War development of the welfare state and social (or economic) citizenship rights.[101]

Crucially, just as the war effort had shaped domestic society through increasing infrastructural power and through compromises in welfare provision, the war had also fundamentally changed international relations as well. Though the effects of the new nuclear technology have been much commented upon,[102] the internationalized nature of wartime planning had a profound effect on the organization of the international system. The internationalism in the war was most strongly seen in the case of the joint US and British mobilization for the war effort.[103] As McNeill notes, 'thanks to the increasing complexity of arms production, a single nation had become too small to conduct an efficient war. This was, perhaps, the main innovation of World War II.'[104] The legacy of such organization can be seen in the promotion of economic internationalism and integration in the post-war period, and also in the development of more robust institutionalization of international and global security.[105]

The extension of social rights and provision was in part a recognition that the state would have to extend its benefits to citizens in order to participate more intensely in a new international and global environment. The development of more extensive forms of security after the Second World War was part of the post-war consensus of embedded liberalism, the compact giving citizens more security for the trade-off of the state being more integrated into the world economy and military-security system.[106] In the context of the end of a period of total war, which involved the mobilization of society on an unprecedented level, the importance of post-war bargaining as a state strategy becomes clearer. The security state was at least partially the product of the war and the need to participate more intensely on a global and international scale, both by the provision for domestic intervention and the protection from external threat.

The internal–external divide is emphasized in the way that the term 'national security' came to prominence in the period following the Second World War. As Dalby states, 'it was only in the middle of this century that security became the architectonic impulse of the American security polity, and, subsequently, of its allies'.[107] The state had become the prime focus of security, with the US taking the lead in this development: as McSweeney puts it, 'the concept of "national security" serves to focus on the autarky of the state'.[108] Though the stress in these accounts concerns the peculiarity of the state being at the centre of security,[109] at that historical moment, the state *did* become the centre of security: the expansion of infrastructural power and its reciprocal effects had seen both the caging of civil society into the bounded territory of the state and the development of the state as the main security provider, an insurance policy against internal and external contingency. The security state was a way of shoring up the legitimacy of states an era of increasing internationalization. The combination of the highly militarized and centralized state as a form of external protection, and the extension of rights through further enfranchisement and the development of social rights led to the situation where the state was at the centre of security. Protector against external threat and provider of

domestic well-being, the state became the prime guarantor and provider of security.

International dimensions of the security state

The development of the security state as the mediator between two
realms, as a protector from external military threats and as insurer
against domestic malaise, came at a cost. Another transformation
accompanied the development of the security state as part of the total
war era: the need to amalgamate more fully into the international (and
global) realm. The post-war period saw the development of a more
interdependent international system, especially between the Western
allies.[110] Interdependence and integration were not only the result of
the European allies' position at the end of the war, where they were
in need of American financial assistance to overcome the hardships
incurred in conflict, but also the recognition of the importance of an
open international economy. Free trade and enmeshment in a series
of international institutional relationships became the essence of the
post-war compromise: social welfare itself provided the ground for the
increased internationalization of the state.[111] The post-war international
order therefore set the scene for the contemporary discussion of security and globalization, and possible challenges to the security state. The
tensions between internationalizing tendencies and nationalizing tendencies were crucial to understanding power in the twentieth century.
The overall success of the security state was its ability to remain autonomous by *becoming* internationalized. The rest of the section addresses
the increasing internationalization in the Cold War period, and provides some lessons for understanding the state of globalization.

   While the state was always situated at the centre of a national–
international nexus, this nexus was most important and solidified in
the age of nationalism and total war, as described in the previous sec-
tions. Transnational and global forces had always been important, but
the Second World War heralded a new era of global relations, much
more extensive, in terms of reach, than the age of empires.[112] As such,
globalization is not something that is necessarily new, or necessarily
dangerous to states themselves. Reconnecting the post-war order with
the 'security state' will enable a re-evaluation of the state and security
in an increasingly globalized era. A recognition that forms of globalization were the outcome of the creation of the system means that many
of the security challenges that were seen to arise or arrive in the wake
of the Cold War also have links back to the Cold War itself. The aim,

however, is not to merely point to continuities, but to show how the potential institutionalization of security on the global scale was always a possibility in a system of increased internationalization.

A number of commentators have noted that the multilateral liberal international order, promoted by the United States as a grand strategy beside containment policy at the outset of the Cold War, has had a remarkable durability, and remains intact in the post-Cold War period.[113] The recognition of such an order was mitigated by the development of superpower confrontation, but the Cold War itself was hardly based on such ideas: two competing ideological-political blocs, with a powerful state at the centre of each, squared off against one another. The onset of the Cold War made this system exist in the context of inter-systemic struggle between two competing social systems: two ideas or visions of the structure of the international order.[114] However, this should not obscure the growth of a liberal international order during the Cold War period, as it remained the broad outlook of US policymakers throughout the Cold War, and continues to shape the international order in the post-Cold War period. Though the durability of international institutions has been much debated in International Relations, the evidence points to problems with theories which stress the fragility of institutions.[115] The continued durability of the post-war liberal international order is manifested in two important institutional facets which will be discussed here, both based on multilateralism: the economic order and security order.

The post-war economic order devised at Bretton Woods in 1944 established the US demand for a multilateral trading order to replace the bilateral trading order of the interwar period. This was in order to counter the nationalist-mercantilist tendencies that US State Department officials believed were one of the main causes of the Second World War.[116] The intention was to abolish the colonial system and its preferential trading in favour of an open economic order. Thus the pursuit of free trade characterized in the Bretton Woods agreement was for the maintenance of a more peaceful, less militarist world order, enshrined in the principle of national self-determination.[117]

The purpose and principles of the institutions of Bretton Woods shifted (rather radically) over the course of the Cold War, as did the overall economic arrangements of the liberal international order itself, these institutional arrangements, and the principles that underlie them, still guide the international system after the Cold War. The desire for an open international economy, backed up by international financial institutions and trade regimes, provided the background necessary for the development of an increasingly internationalized and globalized economic system.[118] The end of the Cold War allowed for the expansion of this system to the rest of the world, and its further institutionalization, for better or worse.

The military-security dimension of the post-war order was also of great importance. President Roosevelt's insistence for the development of some type of collective security (in the first instance in the 'four policeman' concept) that eventually developed into the United Nations was one part of the institutionalization of security in a global liberal framework.[119] The principles of the UN were very much along these lines, as spelled out clearly in the UN Charter, with the outlawing of aggression and the protection of the rights of sovereign states and national self-determination.[120]

Although the rivalry of the Cold War made the potential for collective security through the UN rather diminished, a more appropriately Cold War security organization was created through the North Atlantic Alliance: NATO. NATO was of course organized against the threat of external aggression, but it gradually developed into a binding institutional arrangement that went beyond a typical alliance. NATO institutionalized a large degree of international cooperation between its members, which bound them to obligations through institutional mechanisms that were much more extensive than the obligations found in other historic alliances.[121] The end of the Cold War demonstrated this durability, as NATO remained intact despite the end of its intended purpose, and also showed the importance of the alliance beyond just the military aspects: the eventual expansion of this Cold War security arrangement to Eastern and Central Europe reflected (and continues to reflect) the importance placed on institutions in providing not only for a strong liberal international order, but for an institutionalization of state power *internationally*.[122]

Military relationships between the Western allies became multilateral in character through the development of security organizations, based on a variety of principles, from the collective defence based NATO to the collective security of the UN. At their most intense, 'security communities' helped to provide a framework for security among the Western allies. All of these relationships were based on degrees of internationalization and globalization, in much the same manner as the global political economy, described above. The UN, although ineffective in its prescribed security role, provided the basis for a collective approach to security. However, it was the Cold War context that solidified such trends, as organizations such as NATO created truly internationalized security provision.

The end of the Cold War strengthened the global appeal of the United Nations, and after the success of the 1991 Gulf War, there was much hope for a new era of collective security. Although this hope was certainly challenged by the varying success of interventions under UN auspices in the 1990s, and the continued politics of the UN Security Council, the principles that the UN stands for are very much the centrepiece of international order.[123] NATO also, surprisingly, still plays an important role in the international system. Though many saw (and some wished) for its demise with the end of the Cold War, seeing its *raison d'être* being destroyed, it has in fact changed into a more political organization: still a military organization, but one whose existence as a security community is more and more pronounced.[124] The expansion programme to members of Eastern and Central Europe is one part of this new reality, as is the improving relationship with Russia, and its recent 'out of area' activities in Afghanistan.[125]

Much of the appeal of the institutions of the liberal post-war order derives from what Ikenberry has described as their 'constitutional' nature. Crucially, the post-war order was based on the ability of the US to engage in 'strategic restraint', to convince allies that it would credibly keep up its commitments to the rules of post-war order and limit its expressions of power.[126] Gaddis and Maier have both noted how this was accomplished not through the 'direct' approach of the Soviet Union in Eastern Europe, but through a form of informal rule: by structuring the autonomy given to new centres of authority.[127] As Lundestad points out, 'the American influence was more pronounced in shaping overall structure ... than in forcing individual policy choices they would not otherwise have made'.[128] What is perhaps the most crucial point to emerge from this discussion is that American leadership is of a special kind, in that it forms a 'liberal hegemony', 'an extended system that blurred domestic and international politics as it created an elaborate transnational and transgovernmental political system with the United States at its centre'.[129] Different American administrations will have had different ways of working within this framework, but it is what made the American-led system so appealing overall.[130]

Although this post-war order is generally portrayed in liberal terms, it also has been described by many as a form of empire, or, at the very least, quasi-imperial. With the US the preponderant power after the Second World War, the decline of Britain as a leading power and the relatively weak post-war position of the Soviet Union (given the costs of the war itself), such a possibility was unsurprising. The use of the term 'empire' had its origins in the revisionist school of Cold War historiography, redressing the balance of scholarship on the origins of the Cold War, by showing the exploitative and expansionist tendencies of US foreign policy.[131] Although these radical approaches were eventually subsumed by the neo-revisionist position,[132] the term 'empire' has regained prominence, not only with Cold War historians, but with more mainstream analysts of contemporary US foreign policy.[133] Though some are critical of America's imperial role, most use the term to signify the enormous guiding role of US power in the international system, while also noting the ways in which it formed a consensual, liberal empire.

Independence in the periphery also provided a crucial basis for the post-war order by providing an alternate outlet for armed conflict which was the result of major changes in the constitution of armed force. As Halliday has pointed out, 'if conflict has been "cold", in the sense of bloodless, in the European theatre, it has cost millions of lives in Asia, Africa and Latin America'.[134] As the borders of violence in the Western core of industrialized states shifted to its edges, conflict tended to become localized through clients in the periphery. Although there have obviously been observers who have noted the importance of conflict in the periphery by Western (and particularly US) clients,[135] the ways in which this constitutes a change has not been much commented upon. However, as Barkawi and Laffey note, 'what is at stake here is not merely the *deployment* of force but more fundamentally the *constitution* of it'.[136]

The development and deployment of transnational military planning was at least in part a reaction to the large scale nature of total war that characterized the World Wars of the twentieth century. Industrial total war necessitates alliances in order to mesh together the economic and social capacities of societies, which gave obvious salience to the development of the large military alliances in the early Cold War period. Nuclear weapons also changed the possibilities for total war, and therefore changed the character of war in the post-war era.[137] As Barkawi and Laffey note, 'the enforced nuclear peace meant that the local forces of clients and proxies became more important instruments for conducting superpower competition. The periphery took on a central importance of the site of armed conflict. The *nature* of war changed – policy-makers found other ways to use force as an instrument of policy.'[138] In instances where relationships were more asymmetrical, as in the relationship with the periphery, it took on characteristics of transnationalism, where direct control of armed force was replaced with varieties of indirect control.

The structure of the post-war international system therefore contained a fundamental contradiction: that while it enshrined sovereignty and self-determination as the most important principles of international order, over the space of the latter half of the twentieth century, these ideas coexisted with increasing state trends towards globalization and integration. In the present international system, as Watson has noted, 'external and internal independence no longer seems to be a monolithic whole', and this has important effects on the structure of the system itself and of the functions of states.[139]

The combination of the open international economy and increasingly internationalized (if not integrated) security institutions provided the backbone for both the post-war order and the further development of internationalized and globalized forms of governance. Both were intended to provide further protection for the security state: the internationalized economy providing global wealth creation and the prevention of economic nationalism that could lead to war and economic depression, and security institutions to provide better foundations for peace. The economic and military orders should not be easily divorced, as both broad trends towards internationalism and globalization were intended to provide security. As Latham points out, the post-war military institutions were all part of the rise of 'embedded militarism' that came at the end of the Second World War, a situation where 'militarization unfolded within and in response to the broader social and political fabric of an international liberal order'.[140]

Overall, the binding institutions of the Cold War period – and after – went some way towards creating a more globalized system. The blurring of the boundaries of statehood, be it through alliance structures or the transnational constitution of force, changed the overall context of international relations and security. In more moderate terms, this meant an increasing interdependence in the security sphere, an increasing conceptualizing of security in global terms, and the development of international security governance structures, as evidenced by global/international institutions such as NATO and the UN. However, there were also the seeds of a potentially more radical political transformation in this institutionalization, a challenge to the nation-state model – and the security state as well. As indicated earlier, the security state was a direct outcome of earlier pushes in this direction, as exemplified in two World Wars and the Great Depression. As such, greater internationalization in the Cold War period does not necessitate an end to the state, or necessitate the advent of increased globalization. It does demonstrate the increased salience of internationalization, but to the extent to which state power is crystallized in ways that combine internationalism with national power, then state transformation is actually resisted (or better put, the security state model is reproduced).

Conclusion

The limitations of post-war security studies manifested themselves in their understandings of the state and its role in security provision. The lack of conceptualization of state power has meant a continued evasion of the evolution of security provision, as well as the overall dynamics of change in international relations. An engagement with state theory, particularly that provided by proponents of neo-Weberian historical sociology, proved useful in elaborating the state as an institution, and a historically constituted actor. The incorporation of a more complex idea of state–society relations demonstrated that the security relationships between state and society have developed over the course of several centuries as the result of a rise in the infrastructural power of the state. In the twentieth century, a further rise in infrastructural power was obtained by the involvement of Western states in two total wars, which led to the development of the 'security state'. This represented a situation where the trade-off for further penetration into civil society was compensated for through increased citizenship rights, which encompassed a large gamut of the provision of social goods, in which should be included not only basic welfare provision, but the whole range of security provision, both 'internal' and 'external': overall, a state monopoly on the provision of security.

The increasing trends for intensified interdependence and internationalism supplied the catalyst for the development of the security state, in terms of the necessity of states to be a part of interdependence as a means to secure state autonomy and capacity. The increased involvement of the state in the international realm also provided the potential seeds for the destruction of the post-war compromise, as it allowed for the further imbrication of transnational social power in the international system. The effect of the total wars of the first half of the twentieth century has given, therefore, the impetus for globalization and for the post-war reorganization of the state. The international aspect of the compromise is thus of crucial importance.

The state cannot be seen as an eternal normative model of political organization, as it is one that has undergone many transformations throughout history in terms of its power capacities. The impacts on the present study are three-fold. First, it challenges overall the way in which international relations itself is examined: 'domestic' forces, transnational challenges and ideas are all crucial in examining the international system as a whole. Second, the very discourse of security itself needs to be substantially expanded to include the domestic compromise, and conceptualizations of state power. Security provision in the nation-state was premised on the idea of the protection of citizenry for the purpose of the retrenchment of state power in a world of intensified internationalism. If we only look at the relationship between the state and the external realm, a crucial part of this compact is overlooked: that contingencies home and abroad are to be protected against. The military component of national security is a crucial component of security provision, but is not the only kind of provision contemporary states are expected to make. Finally, it challenges us to look afresh at the problems and possibilities of a globalization of security. Examining the structure of the state as historically contingent solidifies the case for state transformation: the transformation of the contemporary state is possible because the state has historically adapted to new circumstances.

Glo⅃alization and Security

The previous chapter made a case for a historicized conception of state power, based on a neo-Weberian conception of the state. The security state provides an idealized model of the post-war transatlantic state, which provides a more robust model to examine in the context of increasing globalization. While the previous chapter laid the foundation for a historical understanding of the relationship between state and security, as well as the state and internationalism in the twentieth century, in the main it left out an account of the process of state change in terms of social power. The main argument about change in the previous chapter came from the reaction of domestic social forces to international interactions, found mainly in increasing intensified interstate wars, and an increasingly interdependent international economy.

The present chapter furthers the exposition of the relationship between globalization and security by giving a socio-spatial account of power based on the work of Michael Mann that can inform a theory of globalization and provide a better way of conceptualizing its interaction with the security state described in the previous chapter. The main thesis is two-fold. First, globalization is best seen as an intensification of the institutionalization of social power on the global scale, to the extent to which we begin to see a transformation in the institutionalization of the main networks of social power, away from nation-states. This means that globalization mainly concerns the level of organization of social power, and not necessarily its geographical scope. Second, the linkage with security is in terms of the development of networks of social power that are threatening to the security state, in terms of directly threatening its physical constitution or in terms of the existential threat to the populace. Both of these have in common that the security state begins to have trouble providing security, thus threatening the post-war compromise.

The argument is made that the globalization of security is best seen as having three different facets. The first, providing the main causal power, is the transnationalization of threat. These transnational threats are discrete, but derive their power from broader globalizations of social power. Second, ideas about the nature of the pursuit of security impact on plausible social action. The development of 'ideologies' of global security begin to see such threats in a new light that has the potential to overcome the ideology of the national security state. Finally, the development of global security institutions solidifies the challenge to the security state: however, the development of such institutions needs to be linked robustly with the other two facets, in order to show that such developments are clearly related to changes in state power. The overall theory that is given regards the reaction of states (or state agents) to the development of transnational threats. State agents have two main choices: state retrenchment or the development of global institutions transforming state power. To the extent to which transnational threats are serious, new thinking becomes consolidated and global institutions are developed, we can see the development of a real globalization of security. The chapter pursues the argument by first outlining a conceptualization of globalization in international relations. It then links globalization robustly to Mann's model of social power. Finally, it thoroughly outlines the connections between globalization and security, and the potential transformation of state power.

Globalization and international relations

Globalization provides social scientists with a problem: it is a concept that has become commonplace and is useful to some degree for describing changes in the social and political conditions of the contemporary era, but divides those who use it on many grounds. It has been utilized in various normative fashions, in a prophetic manner, as a form of technological determinism, and, most popularly, as a shorthand for economic liberalization.[1] This is especially clear with respect to popular discourse, which often manifests itself as a debate between traditional (and neo-) liberals extolling the positive aspects of the international or global economy, sceptics questioning its scope and salience, and critics who point out the problems it creates for governance and economic justice.[2] Scholte has described the problem succinctly: 'much discussion of globalisation is steeped in oversimplification, exaggeration and wishful thinking. In spite of the deluge of publications on the subject, our analyses of globalisation tend to remain conceptually inexact, empirically thin, historically and culturally illiterate, normatively shallow and politically naïve'.[3] As such it is necessary to give a critical analysis of the concept before we can adequately understand the connections with security.[4]

Despite conceptual problems, globalization is still a profound description of the present era, and as such it continues to be taken quite seriously.[5] The conceptual (and other) baggage associated with globalization does not minimize its importance. Increasing demonstrations of the impacts of globalization have led to modified claims about its scope, but also increasing study of the variety of the realms of impacts.[6] The basic idea of the development of a condition of globalization, where social relations are increasingly organized at a global level, as opposed to the international, national or local, has had much resonance in the contemporary era. Much of this has been captured in the concept of 'supraterritoriality'. As Scholte states, 'whereas international circumstances involve crossing considerable distance over more or less extended time intervals, global conditions are situated in a space beyond geometry, where distance is covered effectively in no time'.[7] What this involves is a new way of conceptualizing space in international relations, or at least making an allowance for the existence of what Ruggie has referred to as 'non-territorial' regions.[8] While identifying globalization with such transformations in the organization of social space provides a good starting point, it also overstates the kinds of changes associated with the condition of globalization: if globalization is just supraterritoriality, it is difficult to find much of it around.

An associated problem present in trying to form definitions and more general analyses of globalization has been confusion between what is to be explained and the explanation.[9] Many analysts of globalization tend to conflate the two, by expounding a *process* of globalization that actually *causes* a condition of globalization. The issue comes down to whether or not we need a new social theory to elucidate the condition of globalization, or if classical social theory (say of capitalism and modernity) contains more than enough to understand the development of such a condition. While the issue of a 'new' social theory has not been resolved, the force of the argument is coming down on the side of the classical theorists of modernity, to whom globalization as a condition would not be that surprising.[10] Even the most ardent globalizers have had the forces of modernity at the heart of contemporary changes.[11]

Drawing on these insights, we can start off with a definition: globalization (as explanandum) is a condition of the move towards the global spatial scale for the organization of social relations, not a process or force in its own right. It can mainly be explained by a two-fold set of processes: the global spread of the institutions of modernity (particularly the state and capitalism), and the development of systems of thought that both produce and reproduce this spread. As such globalization is not necessarily something new, but a condition that can come about due to a combination of social forces, which begin to organize social power on a transnational and global level. To the extent to which the global organization of social relations becomes dominant, we can say that a condition of globalization has been achieved.

The first aspect, the spread of the institutions of modernity, is one that is at the heart of a number of theories of globalization, particularly that of Giddens. As he bluntly states, 'modernity is inherently globalising'.[12] For Giddens modernity is a juggernaut, 'a runaway engine of enormous power', inexorably moving forward, but often in directions one could not imagine beforehand. As he states, 'the juggernaut crushes those who resist it, and while [it] sometimes has a steady path, there are times when it veers away erratically in directions we can just not foresee'.[13] Such a contention is necessary in order to move away from the idea that globalization is entirely destructive of modernity, or concerns some new era. While there is certainly some overstatement here, and an under-specification of the causal factors driving such expansion, the overall tenor of Giddens' explanation of globalization is correct, and provides a good start to specifying what globalization looks like. If we take the driving force to be the interrelation between three trends in modernity – the global spread of the nation-state (political power), the global expansion of capitalism (economic power), and the extension of systems of coercive force (military power) – there is a rich array of causal forces to draw from to understand the condition of globalization.[14]

The second aspect of globalization described above concerns the development of systems of thought connected to the rise of new forms of social relations. This ideational aspect is important, as it can not only help to underpin the globalization of social relations; it also can, when it gains enough power, drive such changes itself.[15] Ideational descriptions of globalization are quite common in the literature, usually revolving around the role of human consciousness in perceiving the global as a social space. For example, Robertson defines globalization as the 'compression of the world and the intensification of consciousness of the world as a whole'.[16] Scholte directly links consciousness to the chain of causality: 'globality is evident in social activity through global consciousness. In other words, people often think globally.'[17] Beck also refers to 'globality', as a recognition of the existence of a 'world society' where 'the totality of social relationships which are not integrated into or determined (or determinable) by national-state politics'.[18]

However, for Shaw, this emergent global society has at its heart a reorganization of the spatial dimensions of power, which differentiates his view from those that focus more intently on the constitution of a global culture, or on the development of global norms.[19] As such, the development of an awareness of the global scope of social relations is also linked to the development of dimensions of power, which gives content to 'global consciousness'. Indeed, if the dimension of ideational or cultural power is moved beyond just a consciousness of the world, and is about the development of thinking globally, it can easily be described as a form of ideological power. As argued above the prime drivers of any globalization are the three-fold (or four-fold if the ideological component is included) forces of modernity, which will now be discussed in more detail.

As such, social power is at the heart of globalization, and needs to be a prominent part of any analysis. This is recognized by Held et al. when they state, 'globalisation concerns the expanding scale on which power is organized and exercised, that is, the extensive spatial reach of networks and circuits of power'.[20] However, power is rather under-specified in their model, and a more comprehensive account can be found in the work of Michael Mann. Mann's IEMP model of social power – ideological, economic, military and political – provides a powerful way of conceptualizing the socio-spatial organization of power, and can illuminate the ways in which different network of social relations are pushing towards a global condition.[21]

Mann conceives of power in terms of socio-spatial networks of power, which are the basis of the constitution of societies. The four sources of social power that he describes are both 'overlapping networks of social interaction' and 'organizations, institutional means of attaining human goals'.[22] As such, societies are not unitary, and the form of societies will change over time due to the interactions of the sources of power. Key to understanding these forms of power is that they are embodied in networks of people, and particularly through institutions: 'the four sources of social power offer alternative organizational means of social control'.[23] Power comes in three dimensions: distributive and collective; extensive and intensive; authoritative and diffused. Distributive power involves the ability to get 'a' to do 'b', a zero-sum relation of power, while collective power involves cooperation to achieve joint power. Extensive power is the ability to organize large numbers over distance, intensive the ability to organize tightly and achieve high levels of commitment.

Finally, authoritative power is that willed by groups and institutions, while diffused power is spontaneous and decentred.[24]

As stated above, Mann conceives of four ideal typical types of social power: ideological, economic, military and political.[25] Ideological power derives from the organization and control of meaning, which can include both sources of 'ultimate meaning' such as religion, or norms of social interaction. The organizational forms come in two: transcendent and immanent. Transcendent forms are those that are autonomous of other forms of organization; 'human beings belonging to different states, classes, and so forth face similar problems to which an ideology offers plausible solutions'.[26] Immanent forms of ideological power reinforce and enhance existing institutionalized sources of power. Economic power 'comprises the circuits of production, distribution, exchange, and consumption'[27] – as such, it combines intensive power (labour) with extensive power (exchange) and is therefore particularly powerful. Military power concerns the organization of violence for whatever ends (e.g. for the usefulness of aggression or defence and protection of life). Military power exists both intensively (in terms of military organizations) and extensively (in the ability to organize people over extensive areas).[28] Finally, political power 'derives from usefulness of centralized, institutionalized, territorialized regulations of many aspects of social relations'.[29] Political power is therefore organized in the state, but what states actually entail varies in terms of function and the relationship with other networks of power.

It is crucial to understanding Mann's theory that the four sources are seen as ideal types: in the concrete examination of social power, the four sources intertwine, and are, as Mann describes, 'promiscuous'. He gives the example of the capitalist state, which is both a political *and* economic actor. The two forms of power are intimately intertwined in this particular constellation of economic and political power. In this intertwining, Mann's IEMP model can clarify how different networks of power interact and cause change.[30] For Mann, the four sources of social power 'entwine' and interact and change each other's shape.[31] As Mann states: 'in major transitions the fundamental interrelations, and very identities, of organizations such as "economies" or "states" became metamorphosed. Even the very definition of "society" may change.'[32] The different institutions embodying them can undergo changes through the various interrelations of the different sources. As Mann states: 'the sources of social power and the organizations embodying them are impure and "promiscuous". They weave in and out of one another in a complex interplay between institutionalized and emergent, interstitial forces.'[33]

The crucial concept for understanding change is in terms of how power can also undergo transformation through organizational challenges through what Mann refers to as 'interstitial emergence'. As Mann describes it, interstitial emergence is,

> the outcome of the translation of human goals into organized means,...most important of these networks form relatively stably around the four power sources in any given social space. But underneath, human beings are tunnelling ahead to achieve their goals, forming new networks, extending old ones, and emerging most clearly into our view with rival configurations of one or more of the principal power networks.[34]

The socio-spatial organization of power is therefore never entirely fixed: for example, particular crystallizations of state power may have some durability, but they are always up for grabs in terms of the development of new forms of power that may seek to overturn them or subvert them.[35] However, the development of interstitial groupings may never achieve the level of collective power needed to overcome existing institutions. The 'organizational outflanking' of emergent (and extant) groups is therefore an important part of understanding the stability (or reproduction) of particular configurations of power.

Overall, examining the historical development of the various strands of social power can help to better historicize and conceptualize conditions of globalization, and also has much in common with attempts to look at globalization as a network.[36] First, we can examine the different scales on which socio-spatial networks of power develop. The most important here are the national, international and transnational networks. The national networks are those that have maintained stability and institutionalization at the national level, mainly through entwining power within the state. The *inter*-national networks of power are those that are developed between states. Finally, transnational power is that which effectively ignores the state in its relations.

Additionally, a socio-spatial approach to networks of power takes for granted the idea that power has always been entwined at multiple levels of interaction, and the present fixation with a dichotomy between national and global not only misreads the present, but discounts the importance of global interactions in the past. As Collins points out, 'globalization or world-system has always been a central process throughout history, in the sense that local units of social organization are typically structured "from the outside in" by their relationship with long-distance networks of one kind or another'.[37] Indeed, Mann recognizes that, since the industrial revolution, 'we live in a global society. It is not a unitary society, nor is it an ideological community or a state, but it is a single power network. Shock waves reverberate around it, casting down empires, transporting massive quantities of people, materials and messages, and, finally, threatening the ecosystem and atmosphere of the planet.'[38] As such, claims that the globalization of political or economic power have 'transcended' the state, in terms of their location in international institutions or non-state networks of power, have to be put back into historical context.

As the previous chapter argued, the security state was in many ways a creation of intensified globalization, and remains an immensely strong centre of social power. The supraterritoriality described above sounds much like what others describe as transnational relations, and it is questionable how novel or noteworthy such linkages are, and how much of an impact they have on states more generally.[39] As Mann has noted, international and national networks have always developed alongside transnational ones (the main examples being the economic sources of power like industrial capitalism, and also many ideological sources), and it is not necessarily a novelty having the existence of multiple networks of interaction.[40] For example, it is important to recognize that capitalism may form a global network of interaction, but many of its functions are still mediated internationally and nationally. As Mann states, 'what adds up to the global is a very complex mix of the local, the national, the inter-national ... and the truly transnational'.[41]

However, that stated, we can still conceive of globalization within a global system. To the extent to which the transnational scale becomes increasingly important for the organization of social power, then globalization is becoming increasingly entrenched. However, the development of 'global' institutional forms will also never be unchallenged. One way of looking at this is terms of Mann's discussion of the tension between transnational economic power found in classes and the political power of nation-states, which was such an important dynamic in the nineteenth century.[42] That the state was victorious in dominating (and 'caging') classes is indicative of the overall power of the state in the period. However, seeing that the security state unbundled some of this power, both in the economic and military (and the political, in some forms), the increasing globalization can be seen in the ability of transnational social forms to push against the nation-state as the dominating organizer of social power.

If we utilize the IEMP model to look at the extent to which the various power sources have been pushing towards a global condition, or towards the international and global spatial scales, it will begin to lead us to a conceptualization of the impact of globalization on the state and security.[43] A 'pure' condition of globalization could only exist when all of these forms of power intertwined at the global level. However, the current state of globalization is much more mixed, and indeed fragmentary and uneven.

Economic power has been to a great extent globalized, especially through global financial systems.[44] It is mainly in this area that we can talk about globalization, which is very much tied to an ideology of neo-liberalism that underpins it.[45] However, economic power as a whole is divided between the national and global, and also highly differentiated between North and South. The national intersects the global in various ways: by ways in which nation-states continue to place barriers on internationalization, but also through the continued dominance of national economies.[46] The unevenness of globalization in the North and South has been equated with a form of imperialism, and the unequal economic relations between these two 'regions' is crucial for understanding economic power.[47] Overall, the intensification of the global economy is really at the heart of the problem: while other forms of social power remain (seemingly) wedded to the national arena, economic power has become increasingly transnational.[48]

If economic power is pushing towards the global level, the main question is the constitution of political and military power. Political power also remains rather resolutely tied to the national level, although the development of global governance has had some impact on the development of a globalized political power.[49] Overall political power is mixed: in the North strong states have also pooled some sovereignty in other institutions; in the South weak states lack autonomy. Military power has stayed fairly resolutely tied to the state level, and has remained intertwined with political power to a large degree. However, this seemingly nation-state-based nature of military power is also deceptive: the reliance on a global alliance system, the extent to which major powers such as the US actually extend their military power transnationally, the overall development of a Western 'zone of peace' reliant on US military power, and the development of non-state forms of organized violence, are all factors that mitigate against viewing the military as purely state-based.[50] Overall, both these areas are transformed from the nineteenth-century heyday of the nation-state.

And what of ideological power? The prime contender in the nineteenth century would have been nationalism, though mainly on the state level (so ideological and political power would have been fused on a national level), and to some forms of religious belief, though hardly as unifying as it had been.[51] In the present era, there are really only a few strong sources of global ideological power: a transcendent globalism (mainly manifested in neo-liberalism)[52] competing with two other ideologies: transnational religion and the particularism of the nation-state.[53] Globalism and religion are more obviously global, and certainly exist transnationally, though the former does not necessarily challenge political power as it stands (in fact it in some ways reinforces it).[54] The competition with the nation-state as an ideology is still of great importance, and is one of the reasons why it is too early to talk of a 'demise' of the nation-state.[55]

As such, globalization is hardly as entrenched as its strongest proponents would have it, though there are certainly enough indications of the potential for change. The benefit of examining globalization through the IEMP model is that it does not make dubious claims about the timeless nature of how the strands of power are organized (or how political power itself crystallizes), allowing for historical differentiation and evolution. The description of a differentiated and uneven globalization also provides the background for narrowing the study to the realm of security.

The globalization of security

The overall discussion of globalization theory, social power and the state allows for a move into the substantive area of discussion: the relationship between globalization and security. Globalization has primarily been utilized to analyse and describe a form of (sometimes radical) change in international relations. The relationship between change, security and the state is something that has been under-analysed in IR, and needs further elaboration. The move towards a condition of globalization has the potential to transform the nation-state, but it needs to be better specified how.

As stated in the previous chapter, security provision is a crucial aspect of contemporary state power, and with the security state, tied intimately to states' ability to remain legitimate to their citizens. Therefore, security and its connections to transformations in the structure and purpose of states is a vital feature that has been much overlooked in analyses of globalization. The continued popular understanding of security as primarily, or at its core, a military concept, is one important reason why the links between globalization, security and the state have not been better articulated. With military power being the most apparently state-bound dimension of social power in the contemporary world, as national military establishments still remain a paramount part of sovereign statehood, it is hard to envisage this element being globalized.[56]

The view that security is mainly associated with military matters is a narrow one that must be abandoned. As was shown in the previous chapter, the whole rationale of expanding security after the Second World War assumed this expanded conception of what protection entails. So even the development of a 'critical security studies'[57] arguing for the normative expansion of the study of security beyond military force has analytic purchase in the historical development of state power. With the development of the security state, national military security needs to be seen as part of a greater whole, a part of the ability of nation-states to provide security to citizens.[58] Security in this sense becomes about the security of citizens (and collectivities of people more generally), and not necessarily exclusively about the security of states. It is the case that the security of individuals, the 'pursuit of freedom from threat', as Buzan describes it, is intimately tied up with the state itself.[59] As Buzan states, 'the state becomes the mechanism by which people seek to achieve adequate levels of security against societal threats'.[60] From this it does follow that transformations in social power are possibly having an impact on this relationship between state and society found in the security state.[61] As such, globalization has to be seen as a political problem with security at its heart. Such an idea about security is important for the study of globalization and security: linking security squarely with the security of collectivities of individuals gives a better scope for the analysis of globalization and security, by allowing for the possibility that globalization is transforming the relationship between states and the provision of security to citizens.

If globalization truly has impacted upon security, it should be seen in an increasing transformation in the manner in which states provide security to their citizens, as issues, ideas and power structures are institutionalized more diffusely and transnationally. For example, through the development of internationalized (or transnationalized) forms of military power framed as security provision, or in terms of the development of forms of global citizenship. Additionally, this reconfiguration of security provision will have important impacts on state legitimacy, as traditional compacts between state and society are transformed. The analysis of the globalization of security, therefore, provides an opportunity to examine the continuing legacy of the nation-state. As such, the emphasis here concerns the ability of the nation-state to *provide* security. Although this may not please those who see the state as being an inadequate provider of security under the best of conditions, it does have the benefit of looking at the political organization which is in the North traditionally most individuals' focus for the provision of security. The majority of contemporary states pursue a mixture of the protection of the polity and its ideals, which includes the protection of individual citizens. Military power is at the core of such security, but also other forms of protection that have developed over time. The focus on the relationship between security provision, the state and its citizens allows for a better analysis of the potential for state transformation: in what ways is globalization in the realm of security transforming the state? This 'ideal' state and the vision of security contained within it may change, as it has in the past, if global forms of social relations become predominant. Therefore globalization provides a challenge to the idea and reality of the nation-state as a political community, where the social compact between citizens and the state is transformed.

Drawing on the discussion above, and the rather immense literature on globalization, a number of important phenomena can be established as being crucial to globalization. First, globalization has been conceptualized mainly in terms of a spatial transformation: that socio-political relations are becoming more prevalent at a transnational level that tends to undermine or displace (or possibly even complement) the importance of national-territorially bound social relations.[62] Second, globalization also has a complementary idea of what can be termed 'globalism': the tendency to think of the world as one place.[63] This will be referred to as the ideology of globalization. Finally, there is a complementary idea that institutional transformations are also occurring: the development of substantial networks of power and authority beyond the level of the state.[64] These three dimensions map easily on to Mann's conception of power outlined above. The transnationalization of social relations involves the organization of particular (or potentially entwined) networks of power across the transnational scale. The development of globalism as way of seeing the world is a form of transcendent ideological power. Finally, the development of institutions 'hardens' these formations of power vis-à-vis extant institutions (and especially the nation-state). Overall, transnational spatial networks are seen as impacting on social life as a whole. Such networks can be seen to both complement and challenge the state, and in the context of this book, the relationship between the state and the provision of security.

Reflecting on these three dimensions, we can see three important facets to a conceptualization of the globalization of security, which are outlined in Table 2.1. First, the increasing intensity of transnational

Table 2.1   Analytic Components of the Globalization of Security

Facet of globalization	Security impact
Transnationalism	Expansion of the scope of threat: threats no longer exclusively international
Globalism	Global systems of security; thinking of security in global terms
Institutionalization	Global institutionalization of the governance of security matters; decline of state-centred security provision

sources of social power leads to the expansion of the scope of threat. Here forms of transnational social power provide 'threats' to the security state in a variety of issue areas. Second, an overall sense of these interconnections contributing to an increasing social reflexivity, seeing the world as one place, leads to considering the pursuit of security as a global concern. To the extent to which these new modes of thought emphasizing globality are transcendent, they impact crucially on the ways state agents react to globalized threats. Finally, changes in the structuring of provision of security or the structuring of state power leads to the increasing institutionalization of the provision of security at the global level.

The main agent of causation in this account is the development of transnational forms of social power that provide a threat to the security state. The causal relationship will be discussed further below, but it should be highlighted here that the outcome of the interactions between these three facets is basically two-fold: state retrenchment or state transformation. That is to say that despite the development of transnational security threats, they do not necessarily lead to state transformation, as states can also effectively react through attempts to retrench state power. In what follows, each of the three facets will be discussed in more historical detail, before moving on to the potential transformation of the security state.

The expansion of the scope of threat

The first facet is an expansion of the environment of risk and insecurity which has created truly global security concerns that the nation-state has difficulty in managing. In security terms, the key aspect here is the change from the major threats to state security coming from inter-national relations (i.e. military threats from other states) to the increasing threat from transnational sources of power (however, this does not necessitate the demise of *inter*-national threats). The increased interest

in global environmental threats and the threat from an internationalized and transnationalized terrorism are clear examples of the transnationalization of threat: the former pointing to global threats that are
the products of expanded networks of risk, where the actions of particular societies can impact on the entire globe; the latter to threats from
actors other than states.

Such new threats have often been put in the context of the end of the
Cold War. However, the structural context of the Cold War also served
as a mask for disguising salient issues that are now becoming clearer: the
proliferation of arms and weapons of mass destruction, environmental degradation and inequality.[65] While it is not to say that these were
ignored during the Cold War, or that they should have necessarily been
taken more seriously, the Cold War context affected the way such issues
were viewed.[66] As such, many of the important issues that dominate
this new agenda had earlier been seen in the interest with interdependence which developed in the 1970s, as the period of détente brought an
array of new concerns to the agenda of statecraft, perhaps made most
clear during the period of economic crisis in the early 1970s.[67] Economic
issues were brought back to the forefront, as economic linkages between
states made the use of force less likely, but also provided for new kinds
of costs and insecurities.[68] The debate over the expansion of security
threats was not just to do with the narrow focus of security studies and
policy, but interdependence also suggested that states could face other
kinds of threats and crises, problematizing the simple notion of the state
as primarily a military-security actor, suggesting that security could also
involve other issues.[69] This was borne out especially through the problems the United States had as a backer of the post-war financial system
with the abolition of gold convertibility, as well as the Organization of
Petroleum Exporting Countries (OPEC) crisis, not to mention the continued problems of its intervention in Vietnam. Such crises demonstrated
some of the fragility that even leading states could have while involved
in a more internationalized and globalized international system.[70]

With the end of the Cold War, the need to re-evaluate the global security situation became apparent. Although the 'big ideas' of Huntington
and Fukuyama – a 'clash of civilizations' and the 'end of history' – dominated the discourse at the time, a diverse array of alternative threats
were found.[71] The environment, nationalism, nuclear weapons proliferation, 'rogue states', all became a part of the national security agenda.
However, a number of new threats were also more connected with a
globalization of social relations, and increasingly these threats were
identified as being part of the problem of globalization. Writers who see

these kinds of risks or threats as important usually point to a number of specific challenges.[72] The continuing debates concerning the threat of nuclear weapons is a prime example, as the impacts of nuclear weapons go far beyond that of nation-states themselves, and can be seen as a type of global threat.[73] This is also reflected in the problems seen in contemporary patterns of migration, which have causes and effects that emanate from a variety of sources that do not coincide well with national boundaries.[74] Another example of these kinds of global risks is found in the difficulties surrounding environmental degradation and related problems, as they spill over national jurisdictions and require international and global solutions.[75] Other important issues would include terrorism, disease, organized crime and global inequalities in wealth. This clearly represents not only a new environment of security, but also the expansion of the national security agenda from military security to other kinds of threats. The extent to which such issues are also linked to the expansion of institutions of modernity, and as such a part of the extension of the state system is also of importance, in that such threats are part of an overall expansion of a global environment of risk.[76]

Globalism and the expansion of the community of security

The development of ideologies of global security has a long pedigree, from Kant's proposal for a 'perpetual peace' to Wilsonian internationalism that was core to the ideological understanding of world peace in the twentieth century. All such proposals make reference to widening the scope of how security is thought of, and often involves seeing a wider global context for the organization of power. Such an expansion links with the idea of a widening context of human social relations or consciousness, but also the political community itself. If part of globalization is recognized as, in Waters' phrase, 'a social process in which the constraints of geography on social and cultural arrangements recede and in which people become increasingly aware that they are receding',[77] then we also need to envisage the way in which security is impacted by this awareness.

Buzan's distinction between state and international security strategy provides a good way into the idea of a global security community. Buzan differentiates between two policy options: state security strategy and international security strategy.[78] The former is the more traditional approach to state security, with policymakers focusing on minimizing state vulnerabilities. The second refers to attempts to address the causes of insecurity at their core, through making changes in the structure of the international system. While Buzan would emphasize the difficulty of both positions, Held et al. would take globalization to demonstrate a recognition that practices which privilege national security are not adequate to the post-Cold War environment: 'national and international security are considered in some degree indivisible'.[79] For the promotion of a global security ideology, conceiving of a more holistic security strategy is necessary.[80]

The growth of examining 'security communities' of states has not been connected to globalization to any great extent, but has importance to the debate, especially in how it restructures the thinking of policymakers.[81] In a security community, 'a stable peace is tied to the existence of a transnational community'.[82] The transatlantic region clearly takes on these characteristics, especially regarding the dependable expectations of peaceful change. Such communities can also be connected with the idea of the Western alliance forming a 'zone of peace' where the likelihood of armed conflict between these states has almost vanished.[83] Such logic is also a key factor in Wendt's account of international state formation: where collective identities form between states, and are institutionalized at the international level.[84] For Wendt, the formation of collective identities provides a way of solving traditional collective action problems.

The development of a global ideology of security also finds resonance in debates about the 'expansion' of political community.[85] The long-standing debate between communitarians and cosmopolitans is an important facet of the debate, with the cosmopolitans coming out in favour of expanded ideas about what constitutes the boundaries of a political community.[86] The link to the globalization of security concerns the scope of the provision of security: if more insular notions of statehood mainly deal with the provision of security to nationals (though some external 'free riders' may exist), the cosmopolitan ethic would expand the notion to a more global responsibility for security.[87]

Such an approach is found at a more practical, normative level in a number of writers who have tried to visualize a rethinking of security policy in global terms. For example, Paul Rogers looks more broadly at the threats to security – economic divisions, environmental degradation, nuclear and conventional proliferation – and also subscribes to a more globally oriented approach to security policy.[88] A further intervention along these lines is found in the analysis of Michael MccGwire, who believes that the current policymaking paradigm is based on a historical and attitudinal disposition for what he describes as the 'national security paradigm', focusing on an adversarial and exclusive version of security.[89] Prime Minister Tony Blair's 1999 speech to the Economic

Club of Chicago, 'The Doctrine of the International Community', can also be seen as a paramount example of thinking in global terms.[90]

The development of a global ideology of security provides an important complement to the other facets. To the extent to which it relates to solving 'new' security problems and is transcendent, it will help to mobilize the development of new institutional forms. Additionally, to the extent to which it reinforces extant organizational forms (e.g. international institutions such as the UN) it also performs an immanent function, by helping to reproduce these institutions. The overall ideational impact of globalization on security, therefore, is not just a normative rethinking of addressing security issues (or an ideology of global security), but also necessitates security to be seen as part of a broader context than just 'national' security.

The globalization of security provision

The ideology of globalism provides the background conditions for the development of socio-political transformation, but in terms of the way power and authority is organized. The globalization of security provision can be seen as the reshaping of political and military power through the development of internationalized and globalized networks of power and authority that effectively change the way security is governed. Such networks can be found in increasingly institutionalized aspects of the global governance of security, in terms of both formal and informal institutions. The structures of international security institutions have begun to mirror other governance structures created under conditions of globalization. The traditional state-centred security provision is increasingly complemented by other diverse networks of security governance, on a variety of levels: international, transnational, intergovernmental and local.[91] The switch from 'government' to 'governance' has been less analysed in the security sphere, but is becoming more and more pronounced in contemporary security practice.[92]

The possible changes in the organization of security governance and provision can be seen at two main levels. First, through the development of a nascent globalism through international organizations which begin to centralize political power, the substantial 'internationalizing' of security provision, as is mediated through military alliances and organizations such as the United Nations.[93] The development of internationalized systems of security is an important factor underpinning any potential globalization, where security is moderated and legitimated on an international level. Though such internationalization is complicated by the existence of unequal relations within the structure of the UN (e.g. legitimate use of force is mediated through the Security Council), and that leading, powerful states can violate the rules of the system (for a variety of reasons), organized violence is still no longer entirely controlled, monopolized or legitimated within the authority of the nation-state. As Clark notes, 'in so far that this is the case, we are witnessing a diminution of the "go-it-alone" mentality that has been the distinctive hallmark of national security in the recent historical epoch, and a corresponding shift towards what has been called the "transnationalization of legitimate violence"'.[94] The development of international and transnational alliance systems, which substantially internationalize (and transnationalize) the use of organized force, also push the provision of security away from the nation-state, and towards a more globalized framework.[95] Furthermore, there is an increasingly prominent international normative environment where international actions need to be legitimated.[96] This is not to say that states can no longer act alone, or are always forced to work in a collective manner. But it is to say that there are ever greater costs, both in the economics of security provision and international legitimacy, for opting out of internationalized and globalized security networks.

Second, there is the true transnationalization of security, mainly through the organization of networks of power at the transnational level. This aspect is best seen through the substantial 'privatization' of violence, although not just in the sense of being put on the market, but also in the sense of being outsourced from the nation-state.[97] With the transnationalization of security, not only are the networks of power and authority undergoing transformation, but the actual providers of security are potentially changing. The transnationalization of military power is also a way in which empires extend coercive control over peripheral polities. As such, transnational forms of military power have existed throughout the history of the nation-state system. The example of counter-insurgency and civil war is of particular importance, as during the Cold War a variety of civil wars played out the conflicts of the superpowers, as seen in the various interventionary practices in the periphery: in South East Asia, Africa and Latin America.[98] In the post-Cold War international system, this tendency has been overtaken by the push for the international community to promote interventionism for other reasons. This can be illustrated by the interventions in the Bosnian war, and in the NATO intervention in Kosovo, which were nominally undertaken in the name of international justice, instead of power politics.[99] In the main, these restrictions on state power have been the hallmark of states in the periphery, and are the consequence of a variety of tendencies in the power configurations of leading states in the international system.

However, the international institutionalization of security is not necessarily something that effectively transforms the state. Such arrangements have been predominantly international, and have the benefit of enhancing the power and security of nation-states. As such, these reconfigurations of power do not necessarily impinge negatively on extant political power, as found in the security state. Indeed, Waters has noted that globalization has, in some respects, had little effect on the organization of political life: 'the state remains highly resilient, largely sovereign and a critical arena for problem solving. A possible explanation is that politics is a highly territorialized activity and that the organised nation-state is the most effective means for establishing sovereignty over territory that human beings have yet devised.'[100] It is quite difficult to point to areas of organized political life which have been made truly global, especially in the sense of supraterritoriality, an important part of conceptualizing globality.

The institutionalization of the globalization of security can therefore be represented by a variety of impacts in the international system. These vary from formal institutions that shift responsibilities for the provision of security, to the creation of private security, shifting responsibility away from the public sphere, and seeing the development of substantial transnational networks of security provision. As with the other facets of the globalization of security, many of these trends have their roots in the Cold War, and have been strengthened afterwards. The development of more diffused (though sometimes still authoritative) power and governance accompanied the development of the security state. The further entrenchment of international organizations, and the development of increasingly transnational means to organize military power, are quite important correctives to conceiving state transformation.

The globalization of security and the transformation of the state

The detailed discussion of the three facets leaves one major issue remaining: a greater specification of the potential transformation of the state and the globalization of security. It should be made clear that in terms of causal power, the main drive comes from the transnationalization of social power. The other two facets are essentially reactions to such threats, mediated through states. These threats can either be wholly devastating in terms of the 'ontological security' of the state, or about the ability to provide security against the particular threats (here being more about sensitivity to influence). The three facets are also not discrete from broader dimensions of globalization, and the extent to which other areas impinge on security varies by issue area. For example, in terms of the case studies, the globalization of the arms industry is related to broader trends in global capitalism (e.g. the transnationalization of production and distribution), which cannot be reduced to the security sphere. Ideology and institutions are ways of coping with these changes, and are thus outcomes of causal processes. Globalism provides a means to better understanding transnational forces, while institutionalization provides organizationally a means to coping with threats. At the centre of these is the state itself, and attempts by states to act in ways consistent with the security state, or to respond through changed behaviours are integral to understanding the outcomes.

All of the manifestations of the 'globalization of threat' are embedded in concrete social transformations, manifested in the networks theorized in Mann's formulation. For example, global environmental threat is clearly manifested through the expansion of economic power (in terms of the capacity to transform the environment through industry and labour), which also connects robustly with other changes, including migration and the arms industry. The entwining of these sources of power have the potential to burst free from their present institutionalized forms, be they national economies, national polities, national militaries, etc., if challenged by other formations. The current institutional features can create tensions when confronted with expanding networks: for example, economic power moving beyond the state can rub up against state-bound political power. Mann refers to this as 'interstitial emergence', and it is a key source of change over time, and is primarily what the study is an examination into.[101]

The potential consequences for the state arising from the process of globalization (the process being the combination of interactions between three facets)[102] transnationalization of threat can be seen as two-fold. First, the development of transnational forms of threat points to the development of interdependence in the security sphere. In Keohane and Nye's language, the interdependence of security can be seen in increased sensitivity and vulnerability to the actions of other actors.[103] This interpretation implies that states do not always benefit from increased ties with other states. This is clearly the case with the development of nuclear weapons, where the actions taken by one state in terms of nuclear posture would have direct consequences for another. Interdependence can also be seen in the variety of other transnational threats described above: all impact on states' ability to maintain an entirely autonomous security policy.

Second, transnationalism and interdependence also have an impact on state capacity to deal with threats. Although this can be overstated, in terms of 'decline of sovereignty', the issue of state capacity becomes important. The overall impact, as Shaw has noted, is that states become 'one sort of specialized bureaucracy monitoring and attempting to regulate risk; ... they become (but not uniquely: only alongside other institutions) "providers" of security to groups and individuals within society'.[104] This is of course of crucial importance, showing that 'risk management' and provision of security may come through other outlets. To the extent that such risk and insecurity becomes increasingly prevalent, it undercuts the state's central role in security provision, in that it is no longer able to provide against contingency in the way that it had maintained, thus making the state as a security provider much more tenuous.

However, the challenge to the security state is not all or nothing. The security state was developed as an ideal typification of the particular state of the transatlantic area after the Second World War. The security state developed as a means to harness internationalization (and a nascent globalization) in the first place, so to discuss the future of the state in terms of the 'end of the state' is inaccurate. What is really at stake is the potential transformation of the security state, in its relations with transnational social forces. In order to clarify, I distinguish two possible outcomes of the globalization of security: state retrenchment or 'scale shift', outlined in Table 2.2.

State retrenchment represents strategies which resist new understandings and new institutionalizations in favour of reproducing the security state. It has much in common with Mann's notion of 'organizational outflanking', where potential power configurations lack the power to overcome extant ones either because they lack effective collective power, or because the collective power that exists is embedded

Table 2.2   Summary of Outcomes

	Reproductive logic	**Transformative logic**
State response to transnational security threats	State retrenchment	Scale shift
Key processes	Organizational outflanking	Diffusion of governance; development of international state

in already extant institutions.[105] The content of state retrenchment as a reactionary strategy should be quite obvious, in terms of developing strengthened national and international level institutions for coping with increased transnationalism. Elements of these forms of retrench-ment are seen in a variety of state strategies; for example, Weiss's idea of differential state capacity, where states do undergo changes, not in terms of a decline of strength, but in terms of their capacity for trans-formation. States have differential responses to the effects of the pres-sures of economic globalization.[106] A similar notion is found in Cerny's postulation of the rise of a 'competition' state, replacing the welfare state model, providing a switch from the state protecting society from change, to one where society is made more competitive.[107]

'Scale shift' represents a response to changes in social power, and involves a shift in governance strategies to other institutional config-urations.[108] Essentially, there are two interrelated outcomes. The first is a greater diffusion of governance, where institutions embedded in transnational networks of social power do more in terms of organizing collective power. Those analysing the development of global govern-ance in various forms are essentially taking this standpoint, whether analysing the informal and formal governance of global economic relations[109] or the substantial transnational networks formed through transnational civil society,[110] and to some extent historical materialists who conceive of an 'internationalizing of the state'.[111]

The second outcome involves an increasing global centralization of political power, though one which involves multiple power centres, pushing towards what can be described as a 'global' or 'world' state.[112] Wendt has discussed this in the institutionalization of collective iden-tity formation, which is also contingent on a reorganization of the spatial reach of state power.[113] In this vein of thinking, Shaw modifies Mann's definition of the state, in order to get a better sense of what such a transformation looks like. He argues: 'that to be considered a state, a particular power centre must be to a significant degree *inclusive* and *constitutive* of other forms or layers of state power.'[114] This modifi-cation demonstrates how the dominance of other power centres may become inclusive and constitutive of nation-states themselves. It also accounts for how different layers of political rule exist within states themselves, particularly obvious in nation-states with a federal struc-ture, or in states that are substantially decentralized. As Shaw describes it, the international state is 'an integrated authoritative organization of violence which includes a large number of juridically defined states and international interstate organizations'.[115] The potential of scale shift is

best seen as a two-fold process of the diffusion of authority over governance, combined with a centralization of political power.

Finally, any possible re-articulation of the nation-state's role as a security provider should be seen to have important implications for the legitimacy of the state. This is best seen at a very basic level, in changes regarding
the nation-state's overall monopoly over security. As Held et al. have
noted, 'the independent capacity to defend national territorial space by
military means is at the heart of the modern conception of the institution
of modern statehood'.[116] Although security, especially in the contemporary world, concerns much more than military force, it can still be taken as
the bottom line in security. The idea of protection inherent in the concept
of security can be seen in essence as the protection from violence, and as
such, the monopoly on legitimate force plays a large role in the traditional
relationship between state and society in providing security. As Cooper
has pointed out, both armies and laws are behind the legitimacy of state:
'the first duty of the state is to protect its citizens from foreign attack'.[117]

In the context of the globalization of security, it is not necessarily
that legitimacy is being negatively impacted by the changing nature of
organized violence. It is perhaps that states themselves are changing,
and in this context, legitimacy is being reconfigured on a number of
different lines. As Clark has noted,

> the new security agenda is not entailed simply by the declining
> capacity of states to produce security of the traditional variety. It is
> instead revealing of the changing social contracts within states and
> these are, at the same time, part of the changing social logic of state
> functionality in a globalized setting. Neither can be explained in
> isolation from the other.[118]

If the legitimacy of the modern nation-state has been intimately connected to the monopolization of the legitimate means of violence
within its territory, the globalization of aspects of political and military
power should be seen to impact upon on the traditional structure of
security compacts between state and society in contemporary states.[119]
The restructuring of security compacts further raises questions about
the continued efficacy of state legitimacy.

Conclusion

The overview of globalization provided has demonstrated that globalization needs to be seen in a number of distinct (but not discrete)

socio-spatial networks of power, intimately related to the expansion of the institutions of modernity. As such, globalization mainly concerns the spatial organization of power, seeing an increasing transnationalization of power, that has the potential to transform extant nation-state-based networks of power. Therefore trends towards internationalization, to the extent to which they move power beyond a strictly state-bound geography, are intimately tied up with globalization itself. The use of Michael Mann's IEMP model provided a way to better analyse both globalization and the potential globalization of security.

The globalization of security was broken down into three analytic components. First, globalization entails the development of transnational threats: threats which do not just come clearly from other states in the international system, but are derived from a variety of other transnational networks, and have potential effects that go far beyond conventional interstate relations. Second, the globalization of security entails the development of a global ideology of security, which reflects a changing environment of security. The ideology mainly concerns how global threats are dealt with, in that traditional notions of *national* security will not be effective in a global environment. This sense of globalism can, however, change with issue areas, as not all global threats are threatening in the same manner, as will be seen in the case studies that follow. The development of global networks of security provision that move beyond the state provides a final facet. In some ways, these are the mirror image of the ideology of globalism; however, the causal relationship is not straightforward. Rather, both the ideology and development of global networks tend to flow out of the problems of dealing with a more globalized security environment. Postulating these three interlinked facets provides a more comprehensive way of analysing the contemporary globalization of security, without focusing too intently on one causal source: for example, discussing the globalization of security primarily in economic terms.

What remains is to apply the theory to more concrete cases, before finally passing judgement on the potential state transformation indicated above. The three cases that follow focus on 'issue areas' that impact fairly consistently over the whole range of states in the transatlantic area. A more detailed analysis would look for drivers within specific states, but as this study is meant to look at the overall model of the security state, the selection of issues is more appropriate. The issues were selected to exemplify a number of different globalized security trends: a straightforward security threat in nuclear weapons; a threat from interdependence in political economy that straddles the economics and military, found in the globalization of the arms industry; and finally, a 'non-traditional' threat from migration. The cases are all similar in terms of the starting point: a security issue raised by the transnationalization of power. In the case of nuclear weapons the threat emanates from a combination of the interaction between technological change and military power, the increasing relation between destructive power and the extensive reach of power (effectively global in terms of scope). With the arms industry there is a dual entwining of military and economic, as the structure of the arms industry itself is impacted by transnationalizing movements in economic organization, while the military side is also challenged by these developments. Here the sense of threat is derived from the nature of interdependence. Finally, migration is transnationalized through macroeconomic networks of labour mobility (along with micro-networks of support facilitated by technology), and threatens in terms of a variety of issues to do with the movement of large numbers of people into industrialized states. In the end, what brings all of these together is the way that various 'threats' to the security state are derived from changes in the strength and/or constitution of socio-spatial networks of power. The reaction of state agents in terms of thinking and institutions is what is crucial in the outcomes of these threats. Each of the cases will discuss these matters in more detail, looking in turn at the transnationalization of threat, 'global thinking' and institutionalization. Each case will also reflect on the implications for the legitimacy of the security state.

Overall, the three cases that follow are meant as a means of roughly testing the plausibility of the core thesis: that globalization is impacting on the ability of the security state to provide security. The cases help to probe its plausibility in terms of how states respond to challenges of globalization, and also will help to demonstrate the plausibility of this ideal type security state. However, the main causal mechanisms are highly generalized, and for further evidence would need examination in terms of how exactly change has happened.[120] Despite this caveat, the cases will give a sense of the overall future of the security state, as exemplified by the two main plausible outcomes: retrenchment or scale shift – the conclusion will reflect further on the salience of both of these outcomes.

3
Nuclear Weapons and the Globalization of Threat

A common theme in the globalization literature concerns the role of the state in the globalization process – specifically that it is undergoing profound changes due to the effects of globalization. Although much of the literature has focused on the dimension of economic power, there is a growing literature which examines how the social relations of military force have possibly been globalized.[1] Transformations in military technology provide an interesting starting point for the globalization of security, as globalization often has an underlying technological aspect. In this sense, nuclear weapons, through the development of vast destructive capacity with increased speed and reach, have the hallmarks of a globalization of security.

An argument concerning the negative impacts of nuclear weapons on the future of the state does have an early predecessor. In his 1957 article, John Herz declared the end of the territorial state due to the advent of nuclear weapons, a recognition that the destructiveness and reach of such weapons destroyed the previously inviolate boundary between inside and outside the state upon which its legitimacy was founded.[2] As Herz stated, rather extravagantly, 'and as the system of physics so conceived has given way to relativity and what nuclear science has uncovered, so the impenetrability of the political atom, the nation-state, is giving way to a permeability which tends to obliterate the very meaning of unit and unity, power and power relations, sovereignty and independence'.[3] This assertion, made before the analysis of globalization became ubiquitous, was quite novel, if not taken very seriously (indeed Herz retracted much of what he said in a later piece).[4] However, this line of argument is now quite familiar in other areas of social life, and Herz has in fact been revived as someone with profound things to say about nuclear weapons, their effects on the state, and the connection with globalization.[5] This is not to say that Herz was right in every detail, but just to point out that his work was not only extraordinarily prescient in terms of the overall tenor of the globalization debates, but also took the idea of a 'nuclear revolution' out of the realm of strategy and international politics to far deeper social and political transformations.

Although it would be hard to deny the revolutionary aspect of nuclear weapons, in terms of their destructive capacity and global reach, it is characteristic of their paradoxical nature that the claims of Herz and those that have followed him seem overstated. The main problem with Herz's interpretation of the revolutionary argument is that he sees states as a 'hard shell', and that the violation of this shell is somehow indicative of a decline of territoriality. Contrary to this, and as was argued in the previous chapters, the maintenance of the 'hard shell' vision of national security has much to do with the specific development of the post-war security state. For other theorists of the nuclear revolution, their claims have more to do with the nature of strategy than with the focus on the state.[6] This is indicative of the main problem with the Herzian argument: the real possibility is that nuclear weapons simply provided a new way of maintaining the status quo.[7]

Early strategists of nuclear weapons, and those who have continued their legacy, also saw nuclear weapons as revolutionary, albeit on a narrower scale than that hypothesized by Herz. For these theorists, it was primarily the scale of destructive power and speed and scope of delivery which created a contradiction in the purpose of the weapons themselves. In the famous words of Bernard Brodie: 'thus far the chief purpose of our military establishment has been to win wars. From now on its chief purpose must be to avert them. It can have almost no other useful purpose.'[8] This paradoxical maxim was mitigated somewhat by later developments in nuclear strategy, particularly in the attempt of strategists to 'conventionalize' nuclear weapons, so as to integrate them with the broader elements of strategy. However, the original 'revolutionary' approach, associated with not only Herz, but with the 'Golden Age' of strategic thought, has never quite gone away. Even during the 1970s and 1980s when policy was a mixture of deterrence by retaliation and denial, there were calls to return to the old strategy, where nuclear weapons were seen as 'special'. As much is clear in work advocating 'existential deterrence', as well as calls for a policy of 'no-first use'.[9] The end of the Cold War brought much attention away from nuclear strategy.[10] However, recent concerns about proliferation, US pursuit of national missile defence, and the Bush Administration's possible push towards preponderance have all brought the difficulties of nuclear weapons in world politics back to the fore.[11] Despite the move to conventionalize aspects of nuclear weaponry (be it through limited nuclear war or tactical nuclear weapons), the practical consequences of the strategic deterrent have always had broader, revolutionary impacts.

As such, it is important to consider the connection between theories of the 'nuclear revolution' and globalization in more detail. The revolutionary aspects of the weaponry demonstrate that the main feature of nuclear weapons is that they become a part of a global threat that goes beyond the particular borders of nation-states. Although the effects on the state are perhaps less than Herz originally imagined, there do appear to be important consequences for the make-up of states, which are played out in the broader context of post-war 'security state', and its future. The theme of legitimacy, prominent in Herz's work, also plays a crucial role in the relationship between nuclear weapons and the state. The early ruminations of Herz are important to theories of globalization and security, if only to point out an important connection between nuclear weapons and state change.

Overall, the link between nuclear weapons, security and globalization can be examined through the three-fold schema developed in Chapter 2. The following chapter will go into more detail about these three elements, pointing to the profound ways in which nuclear weapons and especially nuclear strategy can be seen as part of a globalization of security. The question remains of the impact on the state, of which Herz was so critical and pessimistic. Nuclear weapons do provide weighty issues surrounding the penetrability of the state due to the difficulties of effective defence, and, as such, the legitimacy of the state as a security provider is profoundly challenged. However, like much to do with nuclear weapons, the impacts on legitimacy have been paradoxical, as states find other ways to shore up legitimacy, and many states have *gained* legitimacy through the acquisition of nuclear weapons, as a means of becoming great powers in the eyes of their people and the international community.[12] As such, the impact on the state is rather more subtle than imagined by Herz, and deserves further comment in its own right. Overall, the impact of nuclear weapons on the provision of security has had a revolutionary impact on states, though nowhere near leading to their demise.

The nuclear revolution: Global threats and the problem of defence

The explosion of two atomic weapons on Hiroshima and Nagasaki as part of the closing moments of the Second World War led to much speculation about the transformative potential of nuclear energy more broadly, and nuclear weapons more specifically.[13] The possibility of radical changes in international relations and strategy due to the advent of nuclear weapons was noted early on, as a generation of strategists identified the revolutionary aspects of the new weaponry.[14] Bernard Brodie's edited volume *The Absolute Weapon* provided one of the definitive early statements, and many of the ideas brought out in those early days were remarkably prescient.[15] The revolutionary aspects most pointed to by the 'revolution' theorists have to do with the possibilities of destructive capability and speed and scope of delivery. The importance of time was made explicit by Brodie, who noted that 'the essential change introduced by the atomic bomb is not primarily that it will make war more violent ... but that it will concentrate the violence in terms of time'.[16] As Jervis further states, 'the possibility that all cities could be destroyed within a period of hours, without any room for negotiations or second thoughts, can deter where the danger of total destruction would not if it had to be carried out a little bit at a time'.[17]

The decisive point of the revolution is that the combination of destructiveness and delivery systems that are far-reaching and fast lead to a situation of mutual vulnerability, or what Jervis describes as 'mutual kill'. Mutual vulnerability affects the possibility of military victory: Brodie's view that military strategy in the atomic age can only serve to prevent wars is an articulation of this new logic. The impossibility of military victory is the key effect of the nuclear revolution, and all of the other presumptions follow from it. When war is potentially nuclear war, the 'conflict of interest' between warring states, as Jervis describes it, becomes irresolvable, as both parties can come out in the end as badly off as each other.[18]

Nuclear weapons can be seen, in Clausewitzian terms, as a lubricant that removes the 'friction of war', the inertia that in normal circumstances keeps the tendency towards total war in check.[19] With the possible use of nuclear weapons, such friction is greatly reduced. As Clausewitz somewhat prophetically noted,

> if war consisted of one decisive act, or a set of simultaneous decisions, preparations would tend towards totality, because no omission could ever be rectified. The sole criterion for preparations which the world of reality could provide would be the measures taken by the adversary, so far as they are known; the rest would once more be reduced to abstract calculations.[20]

This describes nuclear weapons and deterrence theory quite well, and as Howard indicates, the onus falls on the owners of nuclear weapons not to use them. Nuclear weapons are in some sense the final stage of removing the friction that prevented the drive to total war.

The prominence of two revolutionary aspects – destructive power and delivery systems – in the nuclear revolution also needs to be further teased out, as they have contributed in some ways to the paradoxical nature of nuclear weapons.[21] The first revolution, which occurred with the development of atomic weapons, was the increase in destructive capacity. Despite talk of nuclear revolution, nuclear weapons really were the endpoint of an earlier trend: total war and the obsession with destructive capabilities of weapons. For example, the similarities between the bomber-based delivery of nuclear weapons and general theories about air power (especially the debates in the inter-war period) are strikingly similar, viewing strategic airpower as the predominant instrument of war.[22] Total war, in terms of military technology, was primarily focused on the development of greater destructive power. With the development of nuclear bombs, total war reached its endpoint, the ability to inflict almost complete destruction, and in this sense, nuclear weapons were the quintessential weapon of total war.[23]

As missile technology replaced and complemented bomber-delivered weapons, nuclear weapons themselves became part of another revolution, the development of speed and precision found in ballistic missile technology. The development of long-range intercontinental ballistic missiles, effectively reaching anywhere in the globe, also combined with an increasing accuracy of missile technology. All the discussion of the development of a 'missile age' demonstrates the salience of this second revolution: it is no accident Brodie's book was entitled *Strategy in the Missile Age*.[24] If the 'first' revolution had much to do with total war, the 'second' revolution created the possibility for an even larger revolution in strategy, as it enabled the possibility of mutual kill. Both of these aspects combined to bring a real sense of a globalization of security, in terms of the transnationalization of threat.

However, the dramatic augmentation of the precision of nuclear weapons increased the importance of a first-strike, in that just a few missiles could effectively destroy a great deal more targets. The possibility of an effective first-strike capability created problems for deterrence based on a secure second-strike capability (i.e. deterrence by punishment), and began the forthright advocacy of doctrines of war-fighting and denial-based deterrence strategies.[25] Paradoxically, the effect of the second nuclear revolution was to conventionalize nuclear weapons, and bring them into a traditional strategic framework. Though there has been a continuous debate about the revolutionary nature of nuclear weapons, oscillating between a position that conceives of them as just another weapons system, and those who believe that they have radically altered warfare, the logic of the latter position is hard to deny. In fact, many attempts to avoid the logic of Mutually Assured Destruction (MAD) have been primarily on normative grounds: that to concede MAD is morally wrong (as President Reagan argued). However, the conventionalization thesis has always been flawed, in that it not only keeps the logic of the ends of nuclear war out of the realm of politics, it also is rather rosy about the prospects for escalation. Kissinger long ago noted this problem, despite being an advocate for developing limited nuclear war strategies: 'any war will be nuclear, whether or not nuclear weapons are used, in the sense that deployment – even of conventional forces – will have to take place against the backdrop of tactical nuclear weapons, and the risk of escalation, even under conditions of mutual vulnerability, can never be wholly removed'.[26]

The distinction between two revolutions is made in order to tease out the legacies of these revolutions. We should not be surprised that these create paradoxes in the broader impacts of the weapons themselves: such paradoxes have long been noted by commentators on nuclear strategy.[27] However, in terms of the globalization of security, we need not overstate the distinction between the two revolutions. Even if the era of the strategies of total war seem anathema to those of the era of globalization, it must be remembered that total war also created many of the prominent hallmarks of the global age, as argued in Chapter 1. The lack of a clear distinction is also part of the problem of defining total war, which can be understood in two different senses: the Clausewitzian sense, where total war is warfare without regard to limits; and the sense in which total war represents the mobilization of entire societies.[28] Arguments about a nuclear revolution rarely examine these deeper issues of social organization or draw parallels with other military revolutions. Because of such oversights, many of the analyses are rather overstated in the scope of a 'revolution', having more to do with the problems nuclear weapons create for a more narrowly defined military strategy.[29]

The focus on mutual vulnerability, fostered by the scale of destruction and speed and reach of the weapons has important parallels with globalization theory. As much of the emphasis surrounding globalization is on the creation of supraterritorial spaces, interconnections and intensified interdependence (both in terms of vulnerability and sensitivity), often underpinned by technological change, the nuclear revolution can easily be linked with such ideas. The speed of delivery systems and the scale of destructiveness have made nuclear weapons effective on a global scale. Herz's description of the impact of nuclear weapons – 'the decisive change is from "distinctness" and "separateness" to "pervasion", to the absolute permeability of each unit by each of the others, so that the power of everyone is present everywhere simultaneously' – is one that resonates in contemporary descriptions of globalization, and should be taken quite seriously.[30]

However, nuclear weapons are obviously different from much of the rubric of globalization. First, in an obvious but important sense, as tools of violence, they provide a much more negative spin on globalization. More importantly, their globalizing qualities come from a dual sense of potential threat and menace that provides interconnection, as well as the actuality of their potential impact. The abstract nature of nuclear strategy tends to reflect this potentiality of threat (and obviously provides a blueprint for use), something that was never lost on nuclear strategists.

What does this mean for the theses of the early theorists? The lasting contribution is the thesis of mutual vulnerability, which is at the heart of any conception of nuclear weapons as a global threat that has the possibility to transcend the borders of national. The speed and destructive capacity of the weapons themselves defy the space of the nation-state, and therefore are a part of a global risk environment.[31] Although nuclear weapons provide rather severe paradoxes for security, the combination of the scope and scale of destruction, and the speed which this can be brought about is a component of the globalization of security. The very idea of threat has been key in understanding the role and broader impact of nuclear weapons in international relations, which is also behind attempts to alter the provision of security.

The discourse of nuclear interdependence: A global community of fate

As was noted above, the abstract nature of discussions about nuclear weapons led to a rich discourse on nuclear weapons. The discussions of strategy, of the impacts on alliances and the impacts of politics, all took place at a very high level at times: as Kissinger pointed out, 'the novelty of modern weapons systems gives the disputes a metaphysical, almost theological, cast'.[32] The broad discourse was often focused on very specific problems: how to organize the Atlantic alliance, or specific ideas about weapons systems. However, a discourse also existed concerning the nature of changes in contemporary international politics, pointing to increased interdependence. The development of an ideology of globalism surrounding nuclear weapons can therefore be seen at a number of levels. First, in the development of global strategies, that saw the world as a single strategic space: the ability to do so was technologically provided by a number of factors, but the global reach of nuclear weapons was an important part. Second, in the discourse of interdependence surrounding nuclear weapons, that preceded to some extent the idea of economic interdependence made prominent in the 1970s. And finally, the first two aspects were fed by a consciousness of interconnection that 'mutual kill' fed into: a global community of shared fate.

That nuclear weapons provided a shift towards global strategic planning is difficult to dispute, at least in the sense that those states which had arsenals of nuclear weapons that could inflict the mutual kill indicated above had to think about nuclear weapons in a global setting. In the US, the realization of a new strategic reality was seen early on by representatives of the Army and Navy, but also most profoundly, as Gaddis notes, by the Army Air Force, which realized the possible impacts of the confluence between global air power and nuclear weapons.[33] America would be permanently vulnerable, because, as General Henry H. Arnold reported, nuclear weapons could, 'without warning, pass over all formerly visualized barriers or "lines of defense" and ... deliver devastating blows at our population centers and our industrial, economic or governmental heart'.[34] However, such global planning was not just conceived in terms of effects (although these are of paramount importance), but in force structures, in weapons placement and, even more broadly, in the global balance of power that impacted even on seemingly marginal areas to the protagonists in the Cold War. Such global thinking is easily seen in US strategic planning starting with NSC 68, but also in how the nature of MAD, and the need for a secure second strike capability led US military planners towards strategic options that had global implications: the development of the Triad, for example.[35]

The global nature of strategy was further reinforced by the notion of interdependence. Although the nature of interdependence should not be seen as a new phenomenon, especially in the sense that linkages between states can potentially increase vulnerability, the view that nuclear weapons have created new forms of interdependence has much salience in the globalization of security. Such interdependence was noted from the outset by nuclear strategists, and continues to play a role in debates about globalization and nuclear weapons. The sense of interdependence can primarily be seen in the extreme vulnerability which reflects the destructive capacity of nuclear weapons. The impact of vulnerability in broader terms is often reflected implicitly in the writing of many nuclear theorists when they point out the problems of defence for independent national policies.

Writers such as Herz and Kissinger were advocates of such positions.[36] Herz's contention about the domestic influences of nuclear weapons explicitly suggests relationships of interdependence. As he states, in the context of the impact of deterrence and nuclear weapons upon leaders, 'nuclear facts affect domestic affairs; in turn, domestic affairs, so affected, react on the nuclear world situation'.[37] Developing this, Herz quotes Whitehead's description of the new physics behind the atomic bomb, to draw an analogy to the present political situation. As Whitehead states: 'the traditional doctrine of the distinct independence of each bit of matter should be replaced by an emphasis on the pervasive presence of everything everywhere'.[38] These perspectives all point to an important fact about nuclear weapons: that their existence as an abstract global threat does lead to a kind of 'nuclear interdependence', where the political actions of those with nuclear weapons greatly impinge on other national states.

Such views have been revived by contemporary analysts. For example, Harknett's comments about deterrence are suggestive of relationships of increased interdependence: 'continued survival depends not only on one's own actions, but on the continued sanity of one's opponents. The protective structure of the state no longer rests in the set of state strategies and organizations dedicated to protection'.[39] Both of these perspectives acknowledge that nuclear weapons had an effect on the importance of territoriality in international politics, where the bounded territoriality of national states was somewhat compromised by the very existence of such weapons.[40] They also attest to the importance of domestic impacts on international relations as a whole.

However, a distinction needs to be made between two types of interdependence that are played out in the context of nuclear weapons. The first is the relationship of interdependence between the superpowers in the framework of deterrence. In this instance there is a straightforward increased vulnerability on both states through the domestic possession of nuclear weapons, and the defence policies surrounding them. The second sense of interdependence is between the superpowers and nuclear dependants. In this case, there is a threat of global annihilation that is to be mitigated through the dependence on states that utilize nuclear weapons to maintain restraint, or through outright protection.

Furthermore, the importance of interdependence is possibly over-played. It is in many ways a banal truism that domestic events have impacts on international relations. What is more important is if these impacts are in some way novel, or have unforeseen outcomes on the context of international relations. However, mutual deterrence is essentially a doctrine that was intended to maintain current international political stability.[41] Additionally, nuclear weapons have also been used to legitimate existing nation-states as independent. As such, states have primarily used nuclear weapons to maintain the status quo, and as a consequence novel impacts on international relations as a whole are debatable. This overall problem was realized by Herz himself, later arguing that his earlier article not only overstated the amount of change the problem of vulnerability created, but also failed to realize the importance of state adaptation to such problems. The mutual vulnerability created by nuclear weapons was indeed a major problem of the nuclear era, but one that was 'solved' and stabilized through the theory of deterrence. The 'new territoriality' that Herz spoke of described a retrenchment of forms of territoriality, where traditional states adapted to the new environment of permeability created by nuclear weapons.[42]

Despite such shortcomings, a key novelty in the international environment was the sense of a shared community of fate between Western states, that further helped solidify a security interdependence. More generally, the reality of mutual kill ties nuclear weapons into the development of global consciousness, a fact not lost on globalization theorists.[43] For example, Giddens notes that 'nuclear war is plainly the most potentially immediate and catastrophic of all current global dangers ... [I]n such a context, there are no longer "others": the combatants and those uninvolved would all suffer.'[44] Additionally, Held et al. explicitly tie the threat of nuclear destruction into the development of a global consciousness: 'with the arrival of the nuclear age the ever-present possibility that superpower military confrontation could result in the annihilation of the entire planet reinforced the notion of humanity as a single, global community of fate'.[45]

The current recognition of shared fate by globalization theorists attests to the importance of the idea. However, shared fate was not lost on the nuclear strategists either: indeed the main premise of mutual vulnerability relied on a notion of shared fate.[46] Wohlstetter's arguments for the strengthening of the Atlantic alliance were specifically premised on the idea. As he stated, 'the alliance is viable, because neither our allies or the United States in the long run can survive without it. This is the reason for deliberately entangling our forces and their dependents in the lot of Europe. We identify our short-term fate with Europe's because we think our long-term fate cannot be extricated from theirs.'[47] Kenneth Waltz, in a review of a book by Jervis, provides a definitive statement of the shaping of community: 'Although nuclear weapons sharpen conflict, they also promote cooperation. In a nuclear world our fate is the fate of the adversary, and the adversary's fate is ours.'[48]

Overall, a number of shared ideas about nuclear weapons provided a key part of globalism, reinforcing ideas about the need for security cooperation, either in terms of the development of collective defence and a Western community of fate; or sometimes a more broad idea of cooperative security that began to develop at the end of the Cold War.[49] However, this discourse of globalism also provided a cause for the increasing institutionalization of interdependence.

International restraint, nuclear interdependence and extended deterrence: Problems in security provision

The discourse of globalism surrounding nuclear weapons set the context for two key impacts, one concerning the context of international relations, the other about institutionalization. The first was about the impacts of interdependence: the community of fate was seen as leading to an international environment of restraint and caution. The second pointed to the problems of alliance politics, particularly over the role of nuclear weapons in Europe, and especially around extended deterrence.

The early nuclear theorists again provide some important insights into political relationships in the nuclear era. Gray notes that the theorists of the nuclear revolution saw the development of nuclear revolution changing the contexts of the possibility of strategy, which had important implications for politics.[50] If, as Brodie pointed out early on, the only use for nuclear weapons was for the prevention of war, they would seem to have little strategic value in the Clausewitzian sense. As Rapoport comments, 'Clausewitz's view is in almost direct opposition to those who see in perpetual readiness and willingness (but not "eagerness") to wage war a pre-condition for ensuring peace'.[51] The implication for politics at an international level, stressed by Brodie, Mandelbaum and Jervis, is primarily seen in the development of an environment of caution and restraint between the superpowers.[52] Gaddis' argument that the Cold War was essentially an era of a 'long peace' is characteristic of this viewpoint, firmly establishing that nuclear deterrence did much to preserve the international status quo of the post-Second World War period.[53] At the very least, the impact of nuclear weapons on international relations made the stakes much higher between nuclear powers, making security much more desirable; however, it also created major problems between nuclear and non-nuclear powers, from that of the nuclear stalemate providing a direct cause of proxy wars throughout the Third World,[54] through to the issues of alliance politics.

Alliance politics is of course crucial to understanding the element of transatlantic interdependence in the Cold War period. The discourse of globalism surrounding the missile age had a huge impact on the changing organizational environment of alliance politics. While the abstract nature of the debates left much room for manoeuvre in implementation, there was still a basic reality that needed to be dealt with: the provision of deterrence (and security) in the Atlantic community.[55]

All of the arguments above constantly impinged on the implementation of Atlantic strategy, and led, unsurprisingly, to numerous paradoxes, mainly surrounding the problem national sovereignty in the missile age. What was particularly interesting was that despite a continued recognition of the realities of interdependence, independent national strategies played an important role, not just in terms of a symbolic independence, but because of the very leverage that interdependence granted. As Kissinger described it, 'our frequent insistence that in the nuclear age an isolated strategy is no longer possible misses the central point: for this precise reason allies have unprecedented scope for the pursuit of their own objectives'.[56] There was a real tension between the acknowledgement that allies needed each other for protection, and the desire and ability to work autonomously within such strictures.

However, the political context of nuclear weapons in the post-war period does make clear the importance of nuclear interdependence in forming credible threats.[57] The need for credibility is most apparent in the case of extended nuclear deterrence – the extension of the American 'nuclear umbrella' over Western Europe – an important part of a larger strategy of state change. Extended deterrence therefore was the main early manifestation of the globalizing trend associated with nuclear weapons. That the American allies in Western Europe depended on a transnationalization of military force, primarily based on nuclear strategy, attests to the importance of seeing this as a part of a broader trend towards political restructuring. The NATO alliance therefore forms a crucial part of the political restructuring involved with nuclear weapons.[58] However, this is not to say that interdependence was merely American hegemony. As Wohlstetter summarized: 'the need for the American guarantee to deter massive nuclear attack on Europe is a token of the limits of American, as much as European, independence. In fact, the principal implication of my argument is that the much used notion of interdependence has to be taken seriously.'[59] The US needed Europe to be able to defend itself, in order to better provide American security: their fate was inseparable.

Extended deterrence was a doctrine itself fraught with problems, as nuclear interdependence was difficult to maintain in an environment that still maintained the importance of state sovereignty. As Buzan summarizes the problem: 'the logic of MAD led to a convincing paralysis in the use of force by the superpowers directly against each other's homelands, but it left considerable ambiguity as to how far and how effectively this paralysis extended to the protection of secondary security interests'.[60] Therefore the problem of extended deterrence in this context was that deterrence worked theoretically in terms of relations between the US and Soviet Union, but when it came to the US protecting NATO allies through deterrence, the possibilities of conveying credible threats became more problematic.

Despite the vagaries of extended deterrence, nuclear weapons became a major part of American strategy in Europe due to their relative cost-effectiveness compared to building up conventional forces in Europe equivalent to the Soviet Union.[61] The continued commitment of the US to the deployment of nuclear weapons as part of its European strategy locked the US into Europe. As Trachtenberg points out, 'nuclearization ... helped to transform the American presence in Europe from temporary expedient to permanent fact of life'.[62] Furthermore, issues of command and control remained a problematic but important part of the interdependent relationship between the Atlantic alliance. Even though the ultimate authority over nuclear weapons in the alliance remained with the leaders of the United States and Great Britain, as Gregory points out, 'operational nuclear control in NATO was complicated by the multinational nature of the alliance and by the complexity of arrangements for sharing nuclear forces'.[63] NATO effectively changed the way security was provided, by institutionalizing the relationship of interdependence, despite all of the paradoxes and crises that plagued discussions of nuclear weapons in the US and Europe.

Extended deterrence was therefore a hugely important element of political restructuring and the reorganization of military power that came out of the nuclear revolution. It embodied nuclear interdependence in an organizational form: a type of nuclear integration, based on the transnationalization of military force.[64] It was a response to the issue of vulnerability, while also reflecting the political and strategic realities of the period. It effectively tied together nuclear polices for the NATO countries, and as such was part of the post-war American 'empire'.[65] Herz describes how deterrence policies caused a 'dialectic of dependence and counterdependence' within the context of NATO, and the ambiguities involved with extended deterrence.[66] It created dependence in the sense that those powers that did not have nuclear weapons or, later on, an adequate nuclear deterrent, were dependent on the US to supply a credible deterrent; it fostered counter-dependence in that those countries were involved in grave risks and therefore were in a position to sway superpower opinion.[67]

Though moves towards nuclear interdependence paralleled other forms of international integration that were emerging in the post-Second World War period, the desire of many states for independent nuclear forces – for whatever reason – shows a paradox: that interdependence can easily foster countermoves and forms of resistance. Kissinger cites the example of General Gallois, the prominent French nuclear strategist, who argued that 'faced with the risk of total destruction, no nation will jeopardize its survival for another'. Hence, he maintains, 'each country must have its own nuclear arsenal to defend itself against direct attack, while leaving other countries to their fate'.[68] For some, this simply came down to national independence, but can also be seen to reflect a real concern with the nature of nuclear weapons: in a shared community of fate, nuclear monopolies may seem untenable, but an independent deterrent may still be a means to having more control over one's fate.[69]

A further contradiction derives from the fact that nuclear weapons themselves provided both an increased permeability of the state *and* a means of legitimating states in the nuclear era. That is, those that had an independent deterrent were *still* independent, despite the demise of 'hard shell' territoriality. The French and British acquisition of nuclear weapons was a way of maintaining independence, and thereby countering some of the effects of nuclear interdependence.[70] On the other hand, the superiority of American and Soviet nuclear forces meant that independent voices were drowned out not only by strategic superiority in weaponry, but by the political context of the post-war world. Although Britain and France tried to maintain an independent deterrent they were still constrained (less so in the French case) by the American domination of NATO, its overall military superiority, the US technical assistance required to create and preserve the 'independent' deterrent, and by the need for American involvement in the continent.[71]

Moves towards nationalism were also further fostered by the strengthening of state structures, through the increasing cohesion and power of

Western states internally, some of which was a direct response to the nuclear threat. As stated in Chapter 1, the end of the Second World War saw a situation of increased infrastructural power of the state, but an increasing internationalization. The creation of large domestic infrastructures for counter-intelligence programmes, as well as domestic surveillance, could only increase the power of the state.

The situation of the US has been well documented, with domestic intelligence agencies being one part of the creation of a 'national security state'.[72] While the existence of the Cold War is a decisive factor in the increasing power of the state in the US, it was also determined by the impacts of the new military technology. Greater intelligence was needed to avoid a 'nuclear Pearl Harbor'. The broad security apparatus, inaugurated by the 1947 National Security Act, involved an unprecedented intensifying of the institutions of the US state for the purposes of security. As Sherry summarizes:

> It embodied the conviction that in an age of instant and total warfare, the vigilant nation must be constantly prepared by harnessing all its resources and linking its civilian and military institutions – indeed, obliterating the boundary between those institutions, just as the line between war and peace was disappearing.[73]

Such changes were also reflected in smaller powers, such as Britain. Aldrich notes that one of the main reasons of the steady increase of British intelligence services was due to the fear of nuclear threat, referred to in an Air Ministry document as the 'nuclear Pearl Harbor'.[74] Furthermore, the building of a large 'secret' state apparatus, in order to provide a response to the Cold War nuclear threat was also developed, along with the British deterrent.[75]

Overall, the development of nuclear weapons impacted on the core Western states in a number of ways. For those states who acquired nuclear weapons, they helped in some ways to buttress the idea of a security state, through the development of centralized institutions dealing with nuclear strategy, and by using nuclear weapons to independently provide security. Such approaches indicated forms of state retrenchment in the face of the globalization of threat. However, because of their global nature, and because not all states desired nuclear weapons and the minor players who did develop them could not be completely independent of the US, the doctrine of extended deterrence and the role of nuclear weapons in NATO planning led to a much more transnationalized provision of security. Overall, the latter trend is part

of the increased integration which formed part of the transnationalization of military power between Western states in the post-war period,
and as such indicated a degree of scale shift in the provision of security.
However unstable this particular institutionalization was, it was part of
the forces that bound these states together. The connection of nuclear
weapons with technologies of globalization and the development and
implementation of tactical uses of nuclear weapons only increased the
sense of their global threat, underlining the important insights of the
theorists of the nuclear revolution: the 'specialness' of nuclear weapons.
The question remaining is how the continued importance of the aspects
of vulnerability and nuclear interdependence have actually affected the
legitimacy of states in the nuclear era.

Nuclear weapons and state legitimation

The recognition of nuclear weapons as a global threat, and their role in
the transnational organization of military power in the post-war period
contributed to their impact on state–society relations. This was the reason for Herz's initial dramatic pronouncements on the future of the
state in the nuclear era. The contention that nuclear weapons would
lead to the demise of the territorial state was based on the idea that
the existence of such a global threat of permeability endangered the
legitimacy of states. As Herz stated, 'the power of protection, on which
political authority was based in the past, seems to be in jeopardy for
any imaginable entity'.[76] The ability of states to protect themselves from
infringement by other states was a foundation of state security, and the
inability to provide such security was indicative of the end of the state.

Others, such as Mandelbaum, were more cautious regarding the political and social implications of nuclear weapons, noting that they created an environment of political restraint between the superpowers. The
main problem in this is that it ignores the 'domestic' side of the problem, part of the endemic problem of only looking at the 'international'
aspect of such revolutions. Mandelbaum addresses the legitimacy problem obliquely, by interestingly (but rather unconvincingly) engaging in
the psychological effects of the weapons, a common approach of those
dealing with domestic impacts of nuclear weapons. He does believe
they are revolutionary in certain social aspects, particularly in terms of
the way they put familiar moral categories in doubt; and also 'because
cultural mechanisms for coping with death do not work for the scale
of death and destruction that nuclear weapons make possible'.[77] This
existential aspect is echoed in a statement by Jervis, that 'because they

can destroy civilization but may never be used, nuclear weapons cast a shadow that is simultaneously ephemeral and full of menace'.[78]

The Herzian view on the threat to the legitimacy of the state is reflected in a number of recent discussions on the problems of nuclear weapons and the maintenance of security. For example, Tickner comments that with nuclear weapons, 'the state could no longer assure the security of citizens within its own boundaries'. She further adds that 'the military security of the state seemed synonymous with the insecurity of individuals held hostage to nuclear deterrence'.[79] The hostage analogy is also present in Buzan's work, who writes that 'deterrence policy displays the divorce between individual and national security at the highest and most visible level. The apparent end of a long tradition of national defence is a situation in which states seek to preserve themselves by offering up each other their citizens as hostages.'[80] That the relationship between nuclear weapons and security leads to a novel 'hostage' situation not only indicates the changes in the idea of national state territoriality brought about through the nuclear revolution, but a change in how states provide security to their citizens.

The recent revival of Herz by a number of writers has brought legitimacy itself back into focus.[81] Deudney in particular has explicitly addressed the issue of the problem nuclear weapons create for the idea of legitimacy. As he states, 'the basic fact of life in the nuclear world is simple: The state apparatus can no longer relate to civil society as the effective protector of civil society from destruction.'[82] He attempts to demonstrate this through examining the role of the disarmament movement in dealing with the 'legitimacy deficit' which nuclear weapons incurred: 'nuclear weapons deform civil-society relations, and the consequent challenges to legitimacy provide the political energy or impetus to challenge core state principles and institutions'.[83] The potential of powerful social movements seeking to abolish nuclear weapons which have an influence on policy may be an indication that there was a problem with legitimacy on such a level.[84]

It is in the context of legitimacy of states that nuclear weapons are at their most paradoxical. It seems quite obvious that Herz was right in the abstract, in that nuclear weapons should lead to problems in maintaining old notions of territoriality due to the imminent possibility of permeability. The very existence of nuclear weapons seems to undermine the notion of security provision upon which the post-war security state was based. However, this does not seem to have been a major problem for states. Although there is something important in the role of anti-nuclear movements in many nuclear powers expressing a general sense of fear and lack of security, there is also a powerful sense in which nuclear weapons helped maintain the legitimacy of states.

Furthermore, two different types of nuclear interdependence contain the possibilities for differing impacts on the legitimacy of states. In the first instance, the impacts on legitimacy are connected to the ability of the US and USSR to maintain the security of their populations, and are therefore intimately tied up with perceptions that citizens have of the weapons themselves: are nuclear weapons actually seen as providing security? The second type of interdependent relationship includes the perception that states can secure their citizens against nuclear attack, but also contains the additional problem of states providing this protection independently, and their reliance on outside powers makes this problematic. As such, the distinction points to two issues surrounding legitimacy: whether a state can continue to provide security in the nuclear era, and whether or not states who rely on others' nuclear guarantees are effectively independent.

In terms of the latter issue, the possession of nuclear weapons has, throughout the Cold War and beyond, been seen by many states as enhancing sovereignty and independence, acting not only as a status symbol, but as away of avoiding reliance on either superpower. The development of independent nuclear forces by Britain and France provides a telling example.[85] In the French case, the rationale of independence was even more pronounced, as the French withdrawal from the NATO integrated command structure in 1966 demonstrated the reluctance to be dependent on or influenced by the American domination of NATO. The French were responding to the lack of control over nuclear forces in Europe, and saw their own deterrent as a way to regain independence.[86] The British pursued an independent deterrent for similar reasons – the desire to remain a great power – but saw the development of an interdependent relationship with the US as a way of procuring the technology for the deterrent, and as a means to keep the US involved in Europe.[87]

The development of nuclear weapons is also meant to enhance legitimacy on a domestic level, by making the state appear as a provider of security. Indeed, even in the official nuclear powers, despite problems with legitimation that may be implied by the existence of anti-nuclear social movements, there is also a sense that having nuclear weapons is a guarantor of security, despite their nature. The security-enhancing aspect of nuclear weapons is maintained through the policy of deterrence, and, as Deudney points out, 'as long as deterrence does not fail, the gap that exists between security *promise* and *performance* is potential rather than actual'.[88] As such, it is important for states with nuclear weapons to demonstrate ways in which nuclear weapons provide security against threats, and do not lead to greater insecurity as a whole. Demonstrations of security enhancement provide a number of legitimation strategies states can take.

The ways in which nuclear weapons were legitimated domestically can be shown in several examples. One way is seen in how the state goes about developing rhetorical strategies to ease tensions about nuclear weapons. This can be done, for example, through promoting policies of 'declaratory anti-nuclearism'.[89] Such policies show the state's intent to deal with the problems of nuclear weapons; for example, through arms control initiatives, or through rhetorically advocating the abolition of nuclear weapons. Further strategies can be achieved through what Deudney describes as 'reclusion': the attempts by the state to hide away or minimize society's knowledge of the weapons, to keep them out of sight and out of mind.[90] The reclusion strategy can be further demonstrated in Lawrence's contention that 'atomic weapons raised the spectre of global destruction, and were likely to frighten the domestic population. Thus ... reassurance was a vital component of nuclear deterrence.'[91] Lawrence provides numerous examples of how nuclear weapons were legitimated through the development of a nuclear culture (e.g. through the medium of film, especially in the 1950s, and through the larger discourse of security intelligentsia).[92] Another strategy was to minimize the potential impact of deterrence failure thorugh the promotion of a robust civil defence.[93] Deterrence then, comes to provide a rather shaky middle ground between providing security and creating insecurity. The problem of legitimacy can therefore be seen in the context of how states try to re-legitimate themselves in the face of this globalization of security, through both the renegotiation of social compacts regarding security in the nuclear age and through strategies of reclusion.

Legitimation strategies are also seen in attempts by the state to avoid the consequences of the nuclear revolution more broadly. The attempt by US policymakers to escape the 'citizens as hostages' formula of MAD by using approaches that targeted military and state apparatus and avoided collateral damage is a clear example of this strategy.[94] The initial doctrines of nuclear strategy relied on the idea of total destruction of the enemy's society, as envisaged in the doctrine of Massive Retaliation. The first treaty of the Strategic Arms Limitation Talks (SALT I), which put a freeze on offensive weapon force levels and limited the use of anti-ballistic missile (ABM) systems, could even be seen as formalizing this position. As Clark points out, 'the treaty appeared to sanction the hostage relationship whereby the populations of both superpowers would be held in permanent vulnerability as hostages for the good behaviour of their respective governments'.[95]

The development of alternatives to this point of view went along with the desire to create a more flexible nuclear strategy, and specifically the ability to engage in limited nuclear war.[96] An example of this type of approach can be found in arguments that focused on targeting the state apparatus of the Soviet Union instead of the civilian population.[97] The strategy relied on the idea that the Soviets valued state power over civilian lives, and therefore it was better to target the sinews of Soviet power, on both moral and practical levels. Ball notes that in the mid-1970s US policymakers became explicit about not targeting populations, as such strategies contravened treaties which the US was party to.[98] Population avoidance became a key aspect of President Carter's 'countervailing' strategy, which relied on a number of different responses to Soviet aggression, but focused on a nuclear level mainly on counterforce targets – those associated with the enemy's military.[99]

Although these approaches are in many ways flawed, the attempt to move away from the complete destruction approach to strategic thinking shows a genuine concern with the morality of targeting entire populations as part of nuclear strategy.[100] The development of the Strategic Defence Initiative (SDI) by the Reagan administration can be viewed as a prime example of this, an attempt to return to a form of 'hard shell' territoriality.[101] The defensive missile shield would provide protection against 'penetrability', therefore mitigating the effects of the nuclear revolution. Overall, the logic behind SDI stemmed from Reagan's moral critique of the logic of MAD: as he stated, 'to lock down an endless future with both of us sitting here with these horrible missiles aimed at each other, and the only thing preventing a holocaust is just so long as no one pulls the trigger, this is unthinkable'.[102] Such perspectives should be seen as important ways of moving away from the implications of nuclear strategies which have the 'civilian as hostage' at their heart.

Nuclear weapons also played a role in a larger societal shift, a decline in citizen involvement in militarism. As Walter Lipmann argued, nuclear weapons appeared as 'the perfect fulfilment of all wishful thinking on military matters: here is war that requires no national effort, no draft, no training, no discipline, but only money and engineering know-how'.[103] The development of a post-military society, with increasingly professionalized armed forces, as distinct from the large conscript forces of the previous total wars, became of great import.[104] Although this development evolved over the Cold War period, the acceptance of nuclear weapons as part of the defence of the nation certainly played a role in the decline of the mass army.

Mann's notion of the transformation of militarism in this period is also of relevance. The officially sanctioned and private militarism between the superpower elites, that of 'deterrence science', was one that was sanctioned by the public, even if they did not participate in it. Coinciding with this in Western states was the development of 'spectator sport' militarism, where citizens gladly observed the participation of their professional military forces abroad, as long as there were not great losses.[105] The development of nuclear weapons led to the need for limits to be placed on war – with deterrence science, nuclear weapons were placed beyond the pale, and limited wars could be fought in different contexts. All in all, the development of different forms of militarism was another way of shoring up the legitimacy of the state.

The prospects for state legitimacy have not necessarily been adversely affected by the development of nuclear weapons. There is certainly a sense that fears of the destructiveness of nuclear weapons have fuelled some concerns in citizens, but have not threatened the legitimacy of the state as a whole. The example provided by the US has shown that there are a variety of strategies that can be adopted to alleviate fears regarding nuclear weapons, which were implemented with varieties of success. The end of the Cold War has pushed nuclear strategy out of the limelight, and thus the possibly delegitimating effects of the weapons are alleviated even more.[106] Nuclear weapons have impacted on states in terms of their approaches to organized violence, part of the broader societal change in approaches to warfare. This, in the end, may be the lasting legacy of nuclear weapons, especially in the West, with a decline of conscription and societal militarism.

Conclusion

Herz declared the demise of the territorial state prematurely, but his analysis provides a fascinating early recognition of the possibilities of globalization, even if it is not described as such. Ruggie once noted that Herz was one of the few International Relations scholars to actually connect issues of territoriality and security, and in this way we can see him as an early entrant into the debate on globalization.[107] His views of the enormous shift brought by nuclear weapons were not highly influential at the time, but did reflect more specific concerns with how nuclear weapons transformed presumptions about strategy, which left the possibilities of political change in the margins.

In the context of the broader argument of this book, nuclear weapons clearly fit into the framework of a globalization of security. First, nuclear weapons can clearly be seen as part of the transnationalization of threat, in terms of their potential impact if they are used. The destructive capacity and fallout effects of nuclear weapons have potentially global impacts. Additionally, the speed and distance that can be achieved by delivery systems also combines with the destructive power to make these truly global weapons. However, such features are more to do with the potential impacts of the weapons: the actual use is still very much in the hands of states, which somewhat mitigates their transnational nature.

The second facet, the globalism of security, is inherent in many discussions of nuclear weapons during the Cold War, both in terms of the potential impact and the planning of nuclear strategy: the world was clearly seen as a single space, and thinking about security followed; this aspect has also been a common if superficial theme in discussions about globalization and nuclear weapons. Particularly important here was the subjective understanding of nuclear weapons as tying the world into a single 'community of fate', due to the potential for an all-out global nuclear war. Furthermore, the very discursive nature of nuclear strategy also played its part in reinforcing the idea of global community (or at least a Western community) in two ways: first, by constantly reinforcing the interlinked nuclear strategy of the allies in the North Atlantic community; and second, by continually demonstrating the danger of nuclear war. The globalism of nuclear strategy is crucially important in terms of its discourse: as nuclear weapons and nuclear strategy were always dealt with in the realm of discourse and speculation – for obvious reasons – the ideas about nuclear weapons became to some extent more important than their actual military effects.

Finally, the third facet – institutionalization – is represented in terms of how the major holders of such weapons relate to other states, both nuclear and non-nuclear. One reaction to the global threat of nuclear weapons was to deal with it by gaining an independent nuclear capacity. These reactions represented forms of state retrenchment in the face of global threats. However, such attempts were also accompanied by forms of transnationalism, which represented a type of scale shift. The problems of organization and governance had a complementary role to play along with the discourse of nuclear strategy during the Cold War. The nuclear threat, despite any independent provision of a nuclear deterrent, represented a profound form of interdependence – 'nuclear interdependence' – where the impacts of strategic choice went far beyond national defence. There were further impacts of nuclear weapons on security provision, which related both to the revolutionary nature of the weapons, and the profound costs of their acquisition and maintenance: this was the effective structure of a real nuclear interdependence in the Atlantic alliance, found in the abstract in the doctrine of extended deterrence, and more practically in the difficulties of forming NATO command structures to deal with nuclear strategy.

Nuclear weapons therefore existed in a paradoxical relationship to states. They most certainly undermined any thought of the 'impenetrability' of the state, which intimately threatens the security state. The paradox is that in terms of legitimacy, there has not been a huge impact on states with regard to nuclear weapons. There have certainly been direct confrontations with civil society actors concerning nuclear weapons, especially regarding their destructive capability and the idea of keeping citizens as 'hostages'. However, to the extent to which states have been able to legitimate such weapons in terms of providing security, they have been able to marginalize these positions. As much as they were able to do so, and additionally link the possession of nuclear weapons with great power status, nuclear weapons have continued to be important legitimators of states. This, of course, cannot be considered a universal position, as there are many states that have remained nuclear-free or nuclear-dependents, which exist in a complex relationship with the nuclear powers.

Nuclear weapons are part of the globalization of security, representing the first unequivocally global threat. In this sense, nuclear weapons played a part in developing an expanded network of risk, challenging the boundaries of the security state. Their existence made possible speed and levels of destruction never before thought imaginable. Additionally, they played a role in the restructuring of states in the transatlantic region. Although they continue to remain a means of individual states gaining a symbolic legitimacy, it is one that is looked on by many with disdain, part of a continued recognition of the global threat of nuclear weapons.

4
The Security State and the Globalization of the Arms Industry

The previous chapter indicated the importance of the connection between globalization and security, highlighting the growing sense of global threat inherent in the discourse surrounding nuclear weapons. However, it also pointed to the paradoxical impact of global threats, highlighting the ways in which states have sought to mitigate global challenges through forms of state retrenchment. Additionally, this retrenchment demonstrates the continued importance of both globalization and nationalism (or fragmentation), which have both been crucial in understanding the dynamics of the security state. The focus of the present chapter is the contemporary predicament of the globalization of the arms industry, which provides another excellent starting point for an analysis of the relationship between security and globalization.

The arms industry has been under-examined as an important element of international relations.[1] The organization and function of arms industries can be very important for gauging state power in the international system, sitting at the heart of the intersection of states, markets and the organization of military power.[2] The globalization of economic activity has had a delayed impact on the arms industry, which has traditionally stayed under the (at least partial) guidance of national governments for reasons of national security. However, in the 1980s, and more extensively in the post-Cold War environment of the 1990s, there has been a trend in the arms industry to embrace a globalized model of industrial production leading to the development of an industry-led and globalized arms industry.

More and more of what was seen as crucial to the nation state's provision of security has been privatized, globalized and/or civilianized. Such changes can be seen in the development of an increasingly globalized arms industry, and also to some degree in the development of private security firms, and a broader privatization of security.[3] Therefore, to some degree, both the 'inputs' and 'outputs' of national security are being affected by shifting authority.[4] Security, however, sits in an awkward position between states and markets. Markets for military services are not as public as other industries, as states still try to keep some hold of what is seen as vital to national security. In the case of the arms industry, this is particularly pronounced, as even in states most keen on pursuing economic globalization, exemplified by the United Kingdom, provisions are still made for militarily sensitive sectors, or research and design.[5] Despite this caveat, there is a growing sense that globalization trends do have an impact on broader structures of the political economy of defence.

The broad globalization of security must be seen as a larger part of the gradual development of a global arms dynamic and military security system over the latter half of the twentieth century. Although not necessarily unprecedented, this development does challenge the notion of a traditional nation-state that is a discrete 'bordered power container',[6] or has a Weberian monopoly on legitimate violence. Leading states in the eighteenth and nineteenth centuries stressed the importance of maintaining indigenous defence industries to keep ahead technologically and to survive wars of attrition: 'in short, defence industries became an element of national sovereignty'.[7] There is a crucial link between modern statehood and independent military means, and it is this ideal of the modern nation-state that is undergoing transformation through globalization. As such, the 'security state' described in Chapter 1 may be seen as undergoing a transformation. However, such a transformation should not be prejudged. As seen in the previous chapter, globalization is often unevenly developed, and its impacts are varied and contradictory. Additionally, to the extent to which Northern states are forgoing defence production autonomy to further their individual security may rather point to the continued salience of the security state. The contemporary developments in the security industries reflect broader changes in international political economy and in the shifting structure of states and their relationship to the politics and production of armed force. The main benefactors of globalization activities have been in Northern states themselves, seen in an increasing integration of security policies, the gradual development of a transnational (and transatlantic) defence-industrial base, and the continued dominance of transatlantic-based firms that participate in the arms production system. The consequences of this for the rest of the world has been an increasing reliance on Western technology, and, with the end of the

Cold War, an increased commercialization and corporate influence dictating arms procurement.

The present chapter will pursue these arguments through a more thorough analysis of the globalization and privatization of security industries, through the framework of the three facets of globalization outlined in Chapter 2. First, the chapter analyses the contemporary transnationalization of the arms industry, with a focus on how this has been interpreted as a threat. Mainly the threat has been conceived of in two ways: threats that arise from the diffusion of military technology globally; and threats that arise from increased interdependence. The second section will focus on the development of a discourse of globalism surrounding arms industries. The discourse is strongly evident in arguments and justifications for the need to pursue globalization strategies to provide better defence, rather than as direct responses to global threats. The third section provides an examination of the institutionalization of a global arms industry, mainly in terms of a transatlantic security community. Finally, impacts on legitimacy will be examined, by looking into the impact of globalization and privatization activities on the security state.

The transnationalization of the arms industry

The modern state has long had as its goal an overall self-sufficiency in terms of its security and survival. From the origins in policies of mercantilism pursued by early-modern European states, to the more complicated arrangements that developed with the rise of liberal economics, there has long been a focus on states pursuing military autonomy. Although the primary way this has manifested itself is in terms of the monopoly of violence within states through a process of internal pacification,[8] there has also been a continued interest in being able to provide military technology autonomously as well. The arms industry has long been a protected sector that has had a different relationship with the state than with civil industry due to its obvious importance to national security. The dominance of a mercantilist doctrine in early-modern Europe also contributed to this, emphasizing the importance of having a self-sufficient industrial base, which tended towards the pursuit of autonomous arms industries.[9] However, even Adam Smith promoted the idea that states should have indigenous arms production, in order to maintain national security.[10] Trends towards autarkic defence-industrial policy also combined with the decline of the use of mercenary armies, and the emphasis on national armies.[11]

However, despite the reasoning that arms production should be domestically based, and ideally autarkic, an international arms trade has existed since the development of states in Europe in the early-modern period, in order to bypass many of the efficiency problems with home production.[12] The industrial revolution caused a shift in how arms were produced, and how technological innovation proceeded, as the private sector drove change in the military, and even led technological change in civilian industry.[13] There was also an underlying change in the ideology of economics, as free trade displaced the dominance of mercantilism, and capitalism became a driving force of armaments production.[14] While private industry continued the international trade in armaments, there was still emphasis on leading states to have indigenous arms industries, even if they were not state controlled, or completely autarkic. Free trade did not necessarily put an end to the idea of domestic industries as an element of national sovereignty. The importance of having indigenous defence industries (if not complete autarky) was also emphasized in terms of gaining access to the technological leading edge.[15] Overall, nineteenth-century arms industries played an important role in statehood, but also sat on the edge between the state and market, between their economic role and security role.

During the early part of the nineteenth century, there was a focus on how the development of extensive national armouries placed attention on domestic production. Here states tended to take the lead in dictating production, in addition to organizing production itself. The system was breaking down by the late nineteenth century due to the acceleration in technological development, much coming from the more dynamic private enterprise.[16] The dynamism of nineteenth-century private industry in developing arms technology led to a gradual shift towards its integration into a state-led arms industry, where the state would identify research priorities that it was interested in. Such an arrangement reflected the character of much of the twentieth-century arms production system.[17]

In the post-Cold War world, the ideals and reality of an independent defence-industrial base and a 'public' military have become more and more challenged. Arms industries pursue globalization strategies, in terms of both production and marketing, and a plethora of private firms providing a broad range of military services have been created and are flourishing. As such, there has been a broad change in the provision of both the inputs and outputs of national military security, impacted by the globalization and transnationalization of firms, and overall trends towards 'civilianization' in these 'security' industries.

These trends can be described very broadly as the *privatization of security*, in the sense that some aspects of the provision of security seem to be more and more connected to the private sphere of commerce, and less to a broader public good. As such, they are connected to broader trends in the globalization of economic power, and clearly provide some threat to the security state.

With the increasing power of economic globalization, the possibility of maintaining or pursuing autonomy or autarky in arms production has become increasingly difficult. The trends of economic globalization have had a belated impact on the arms industry, which during the Cold War period had not been open to market forces to the same extent as civilian industries. As noted above, there has long been thinking that autarkic arms production is crucial to national security, as not to succumb to the problems of foreign dependence, or give important technologies to potential enemies. As Bitzinger states, 'arms production was usually placed outside the bounds of free-market economics, and the typical free-market standards of open competition, efficiency, and even profitability were secondary to guaranteeing that a nation could internally mobilize the resources it needed for national defense'.[18] In the past three decades, there has been a gradual rethinking of the strategies of arms manufacturers, as they seek to remain competitive and improve the efficiency of the industry. The end of the Cold War shrank most defence budgets, and arms industries faced a downturn in business and a severe problem with overcapacity. Globalization became a solution, much as it had in the civilian sector.[19] Such trends have seen a sharp decline in the number of states that are truly, or even largely, independent in their provision of defence equipment.

The internationalization and globalization of the arms industry in the transatlantic region has followed along two main paths: the consolidation of firms on a national level (e.g. the development of 'national champions' in Europe, national level mergers in the US), and the increase in internationalization activities.[20] A shift towards a more globalized model of production in the defence industry can be identified in developments such as the consolidation of many of the major arms manufacturers through mergers and acquisitions, and the increasing number of collaboratory projects, such as licensed production, strategic alliances and joint venture companies.[21] Other types of globalization can be seen in armaments collaboration in the areas of subcontracting, offsets, dual-use technologies, data transfers and basic research. Due to a number of factors, perhaps most importantly the geographic context of the US firms' consolidation (i.e. within a national context), the strategies of European companies has been much more geared towards strategic alliances.[22] The aerospace industry provides a solid example, as there has been much cross-border collaboration, though few outright mergers or acquisitions.

While the socio-spatial changes in the organization of arms industries is the most visible aspect of globalization, shifts in production strategies are also impacting on the relationships between states and industry. Whereas previously the arms industries were much more state-led in terms of the kinds of products being provided, there is a definite switch towards an increased civilianization and 'privatization' of the industry overall. This is not to say that arms industries are going to sell to non-state groups, but that the production and distribution of arms is becoming further entangled with the globalization of economic power, leading states to become mere buyers of products, rather than having the industry as something special, and necessarily protected.[23]

The arms industry is becoming increasingly led by firms instead of governments, reversing the major change of the early twentieth century. As Bitzinger states, 'the contraction of defense markets and the collapse of many government-sponsored codevelopment projects during the 1980s has pressured defense firms to take the lead in consolidating and rationalizing armaments production, including globalizing operations'.[24]

The increased civilianization has been exacerbated by the pace of technological change, and the fact that civilian industry is outstripping the defence industry in cutting-edge technology. There has always been interaction between the two, but the defence industry had generally been at the technological forefront, as developments in the armaments sector 'spun-off' into the civilian. The present switch to a civilian-led industry is exemplified by the increasing importance of 'spin-on' technology; that is, military technologies that emerge directly from the civilian sectors. Because dual-use technologies and spin-ons are heavily traded on the world market, it is easy for these technologies to become diffused in the international system.[25] Hayward further points out that globalization is much more apparent below the 'surface' of the industry – that is outside of the sphere of prime contractors – because leading-edge commercial technology is a necessary part of advanced military technology, and plays a large role in the development of globalization activities.[26]

Civilianization is also reflected in the continued blurring of the civilian and military sectors through the development of dual-use technologies. The two sectors have become less and less distinct in the contemporary system as the current revolution in technologies affects the process of innovation in armaments technologies. An excellent example of this can be seen in the way Boeing restructured itself in its 1997 merger with McDonnell Douglas, which saw a mainly civilian company merge with a defence firm. Although the merged firm was eventually restructured around servicing its different clients, at the heart is a shared R&D centre that serves to integrate the group as well as act as a technology generator.[27] The bringing in of production techniques to the armaments sector that had been part of the civilian sector for some twenty years is another consequence of this technological shift. For example, the use of 'agile manufacturing' has been pursued in the US for a number a years as a means to overcome the problems of the costs of producing advanced military technology, where it is difficult to achieve the large production runs needed to achieve economies of scale.[28]

A number of commentators have compared the current round of internationalization and globalization to the past. Lovering, for example, makes the point that the future is looking more like the past, especially to the late nineteenth century, where firms such as Vickers and Krupp did almost whatever they wished, without regard to their home state.[29] Moravcsik hints at the problem with the US example in this pronouncement on its future: 'US attitudes towards autarky in the procurements to military products have been shaped by attributes that could have described some European countries a century ago: its relative size, its technological and financial preeminence, and its capacity for political leadership.'[30] Although this is most certainly partially true, there is a major difference. Companies in Europe a century ago were essentially dealing in an unregulated international market, but they were still producing nationally. The main element of qualitative change can be seen in the gradual development of transnational production, and the move away from the export of nationally produced finished weapons, to a variety of new ways of producing and distributing arms. The contemporary scene is therefore somewhat different from the free trade in arms in that it involves an internationalized and globalized *production* system.[31] The change in production further obscures what truly 'national' industry is, therefore, in one sense, connecting arms industries more clearly with the private sector more generally. The distinctive nature of the industry – that is, the sale of arms – is of course still a crucial dimension, as the spread of arms and arms technology is a vital part of the globalization of the industry.

Although by no means amounting to complete integration, all of these developments point towards the development of an increasingly globalized and transnationalized arms industry. As Lovering summarizes, 'the result is a complex and rapidly developing juxtaposition of nation[al], international, and global circuits of arms-related production'.[32] Overall, a rethink needs to be made concerning defence as a 'national' industry. As Taylor states, 'to think of defence corporations as national entities under the dominant influence of their home governments is less and less appropriate. The development and production of defence equipment is increasingly being organised on an international basis.'[33] Although the US may provide an exception to this development, US firms themselves can also be seen at the heart of globalization process, whatever restraints are placed on them in the national context.

While much of this has been accepted as a necessity (this will be returned to in the next section), the transnationalization moves have not gone without comment on their impact on security. The most often-cited security concern with globalization trends in the arms industries concerns the problems of dependence and interdependence. An important security problem has been identified in the reliance on foreign technologies and companies, which is thrown up by the possibilities of the globalization of arms production. The touch point here is Keohane and Nye's work on interdependence. In essence, the debate is concerned with how dependence on foreign industry – especially the penetration of multinational corporations – could pose problems to state sovereignty. Under conditions of interdependence, the authors maintain, states do not always benefit from increased ties with other states, as interdependence will always involve costs, 'since interdependence restricts autonomy'.[34] The connection between arms industry restructuring and interdependence is quite clear; as Held et al. point out, 'since they make the acquisition and crucially the use of arms and weapons systems (not to mention defence-industrial policy) potentially subject to the decisions and actions of other authorities or corporations beyond the scope of national jurisdiction'.[35]

The consequences for security here are perhaps greater than those initially indicated in the case of the standard interdependence model, as they pose a threat to the very foundation of the modern nation-state, its ability to effectively provide independent military security, through the dismantling (or transformation) of the national military-industrial base. The argument is that the globalization of the arms industry leads to a threat of foreign dependence in key sectors, which could lead to security threats if suppliers decided to suspend trade, and additionally, creates problems for the diffusion of military technology, which would have been previously controlled through state-based industry.[36]

In this literature, this position has largely been discussed in terms of the American example, seen as facing a crucial challenge to its autonomy in defence-industrial maters. As Moran pointed out in 1990,

> the Defense Science Board, the undersecretary of defense for acquisition, the Office of Technology Assessment, and a variety of congressional committees join in warning that U.S. defense increasingly relies on foreign technologies, foreign-sourced products, or domestic-sourced products purchased from local subsidiaries of foreign corporations.[37]

Borrus and Zysman also point to this change in American security problems, noting that resources no longer need to be controlled through armed force, they can be controlled through markets, and therefore, 'market structure and functioning must become a matter of direct security concern'.[38] For Borrus and Zysman, the security problem for America is not primarily the lack of autonomy in terms of arms production, but also a general decline in the industrial base, which will create problems in the future.[39] America has begun to slide from this position of dominance, 'risking dependence in industry, finance, and critical segments of technology'.[40]

Crawford describes the problem as the new 'economic security dilemma'.[41] The dilemma is quite simply the choice between the desire to maintain state control over the defence industry, thus moving away from problems of vulnerability (such as foreign dependence on crucial defence technologies, and the diffusion of defence technologies to possible enemies), or to take advantage of the fruits of globalization. As Crawford states, 'autarky and a narrow focus on military R&D in the face of globalization of commercial high technology production and exchange severs the state from the fruits of technological innovation'.[42] To stay ahead of, or even in line with, other states seems to require an acquiescence to globalizing tendencies in the defence industries so as to remain competitive. The problem is that this may leave the state open to problems of foreign influence and control.[43]

There will always be some reluctance to pursue transnationalization, especially in first-tier arms-producing states that have near autarky in production. In this light the US has had some of the greatest reluctance in promoting transnational links, especially in the area of prime contractors, but also in restrictions on technology transfers.[44] This is one reason why the future may be more in the strategic alliance concept, as outlined above. However, with the promotion of a radical privatization of all things defence, even the recent Bush Administration promoted transnational links up to a point.[45] Such linkages seem to make sense both in terms of making the industry more productive and efficient and also in producing the cutting-edge technology desired by US defence planners. Additionally, politics can also play an important role in promoting transnational ties. For example, despite huge differences in other areas, Boeing and European Aeronautic, Defence and Space Company (EADS) agreed to promote alliances to produce missiles for the US missile defence program: surely a political move.[46]

A final issue surrounding interdependence and civilianization concerns the impact of globalization on the loss of national firms and the overall 'loyalty' they engender. As Bitzinger argues, 'as Western defence firms become more transnational, their domestic identities and loyalties could begin to blur, making it more difficult to expect them to regulate their potential proliferation activities'.[47] This was a common complaint about the use of mercenaries, one that Machiavelli honed in on in the *Art of War*: the unreliability of hired warriors with no sense of political loyalty to the state they are working for.[48]

While the problems with interdependence are often seen as the most pressing, especially from the US perspective, a final problem is often cited as a potential security issue. The globalization of the arms industry is seen as facilitating a wide spread of technology transfer and proliferation, as industries straddle national boundaries and the flow and diffusion of technology becomes increasingly unhindered.[49] Part of the problem with proliferation is the lack of transparency and accountability in the trade in international armaments, which is compounded by the globalization process, adding unseen technological transfers to this process.[50] As spin-ons become more important, and innovations from civilian sectors become crucial to military technology, the potential transfer of military technology becomes more and more likely, and less and less controllable. Such transfers and proliferation have the obvious consequences of creating security issues for leading states, though likely to spread commonly used technology, it would still not be possible for anything but leading states to produce capital-intensive military technology.

Overall, transnational economic power has had a late but important impact on the organization of arms industries in the transatlantic region, increasingly delinking them from the state. The civilianization process has led to the situation where firms now lead production and marketing, and are increasingly separating themselves from the national context. There have been indications of concern about the threatening

nature of such activities, mainly in terms of the problems of dependence and of technological diffusion. However, the former concern especially has mainly been the concern of the US, who really has the most
to lose, as the majority of other states have never been independent in
arms production. As such, much of the discourse framing arms industry globalization has been in terms of support for various strands of
globalism, as we shall see in the next section.

Globalism and the arms industry

The existence of an ideology of globalism has rarely been couched in
terms of an answer to the threats from diffusion and interdependence,
but more in terms of the necessity of globalization strategies to make
Western states *more* secure. The ideology of globalism here latches on
to broader perspectives that extol the virtues of economic liberalism.
To the extent to which such an ideology is in place, it has significantly
impacted on the ways in which governments approach defence industries, and additionally in terms of how defence industries act within
the broader global political economy.[51] To the extent to which the logic
of integration is accepted in these broader terms, it tends to influence
the entire political economy of security, especially as seen in the organization of the production system, but also in terms of the enmeshment
of all states into a transatlantic security community (to be discussed
further in the next section). The ideology comprises both perspectives
within industry promoting the virtues of globalization, and those of
governments who concede such claims.

The main factor that has kept the arms industry from following the
lead of civilian industries has been government involvement, through
legislative activities that prohibit internationalization, and through economic factors, such as government contracts, procurement policies and
degrees of state ownership.[52] Political influence is still quite obviously
in the hands of states, as both the European and American examples demonstrate, but this does not mean that there is not a significant move
towards globalization and civilianization of such industries. Some governments do worry about guarding technology, but it is clear that 'if
the industry's bosses were left to themselves, they would be stitching
together transatlantic alliances at an accelerating pace'.[53]

Within the US, the 1990s saw a spate of mergers and acquisitions,
resulting in the domination of three major producers: Boeing, Lockheed
Martin, and Raytheon.[54] The end of the Cold War and the consequent
downturn in defence spending led many companies to shed their

defence components, and smaller firms sold their businesses out-right.[55] These measures have also gained much acceptance in Europe, as national governments have slowly conceded that in order for European industries to remain competitive with the US, they will need to pursue similar strategies to US companies, increasingly on a transnational level. Europe's arms industry has a severe overcapacity problem, and eventually its firms are going to have to work more with US companies, and transatlantic links are likely going to become commonplace.[56] As Pierre Chao of Credit Suisse First Boston states, 'economic realities will grind away, and over time a transatlantic defence industry will become inevitable'.[57]

Moves towards globalization activities can be seen in the realization of the French government, traditionally the most protective of its state-run arms industry, that it can no longer attempt to be autonomous in defence procurement.[58] The October 1999 merger of the German firm DaimlerChrysler Aerospace (DASA) with the French firm Lagardere Matra to form the EADS is also an important example, creating Europe's largest aerospace group.[59] The British-based BAE Systems can also be seen as a leader in this regard, both in its sizeable US assets and in current collaborative projects with US companies, epitomized by the Joint Strike Fighter (JSF) project with Lockheed Martin.[60]

Although European states have moved towards a common aerospace firm in EADS, it negotiates in a complex web of still existent national firms, with partial stakes in many other companies.[61] There is some recognition that this may be the future direction of US firms as well. Both academic analysts and the US Department of Defense have noted problems with the massive consolidation of the industry in the 1990s, especially pointing to the lack of competition and the continued problems of overcapacity.[62] The DoD especially has promoted greater initiative in the private sector, focusing on technological innovation in secondary industry, in the form of spin-ons from the private sector.[63]

Overcapacity is not just a transatlantic problem. States which form the 'second' tier[64] of the arms industry, that aspire towards autarky for a variety of reasons, have also run into major problems with the end of the Cold War. Mainly developing or newly industrialized, many of these countries are failing to keep up with technological advances in the first tier, while continuing to overproduce indigenous products that are more expensive to make and less sound than products that could be imported. Though there are a number of options for restructuring the arms industries in these countries, many have chosen the route of globalization, mainly in terms of no longer aiming towards autarky, and focusing on a combination of importing equipment and technological transfer, and allowing transnational takeovers of indigenous defence firms.[65]

Consequently, it has been defence firms themselves that have been taking the initiative to create such arrangements, where previously it involved coordination between member countries and their defence industries. Lovering provides an example: 'as a director in one leading European defence company put it, "industry isn't waiting for these things ... the restructuring of the defence industry will be determined by/led by the industry itself rather than the politicians"'.[66] Though defence planning through NATO has had much support from national governments, they have had little impact on corporate planning: 'They are said to be dominated by "military kinds of people" who don't understand business.'[67]

However, it is interesting that states are often encouraging the increased civilianization of such industries, though aware of some of the problems that they may be creating.[68] Civilianization is also connected with the ideological trends towards privatization and liberalization (economic globalization), and the defence industries are often put into this overall context. For example, Jacques Gansler had recommended such a shift to the Clinton Administration in his capacity as Undersecretary for Defense for Acquisition and Technology, promoting both the development of a transatlantic defence-industrial base, and the integration of the defence industry into the civilian.[69] As Gansler stated in the late-1990s, 'because of the continuation of outmoded export control policies and practices, defense industries in both the United States and allied European and Asian countries have attempted to remain autarkic – a self sufficiency that is counter to the needs and realities in a world of coalition warfare and industrial globalization'.[70] The promotion of a transnationalized defence-industrial base seems to have cooled off somewhat in the Bush Administration, but there is still a significant push towards increased civilianization and privatization.[71]

Britain provides a remarkable example for the extent to which its defence industries became civilianized in the 1980s, as the Thatcher government did away with any lingering state involvement in the arms industry.[72] In the 1990s, under the Blair government, Britain has taken the lead in both the privatization of industry and the promotion of transnational linkages.[73] Globalization activities in the defence sector are to be promoted, in as much as technologies with direct impacts on national security are not affected.[74] The overall national security picture is similar, with the British government having done much to reshape the Ministry of Defence (MoD) towards a more commercial model: almost everything outside a core of direct combat functions are run by a variety of private commercial companies. The MoD outsources much of its logistics and service support: the Defence Procurement Agency is a quasi-governmental organization, outside the MoD itself; there is much work done by the Territorial Army (such as medical, etc.); and the Defence Evaluation and Research Agency (DERA), the main research agency, has become a private commercial firm QinetiQ (while dstl remained part of the MoD, to handle the most sensitive research).[75]

Such trends are also gaining salience in the US more broadly. The 2001 Quadrennial Defense Review called for a stripping down of the Department of Defense: 'any function that can be provided by the private sector is not a core government function'.[76] The report identifies three broad categories of functions: functions directly related to warfighting and best served by federal government; functions indirectly related to warfighting, and best served by Private Public Partnerships; and functions not linked to warfighting, best provided by the private sector.[77]

In many ways it is not entirely surprising that the globalizing ideology has become broadly supported, as the states in the transatlantic region have all been accepting the globalizing logic for decades, albeit with varying degrees of enthusiasm.[78] Though states such as France with a long tradition of nationalized defence industries have been reluctant to join the trend, the evidence above has shown that like other elements of economic globalization, arms industry globalization is increasingly seen in terms of 'there is no alternative'. State leaders tend to put this into both a commercial logic (for their own companies to remain competitive) and a best-practice military logic (that civilianization is better for military power, and transnationalization for coalition warfare and collective defence). All in all, these trends are reflected in an increasing institutionalization of arms production and procurement on a transnational level.

Globalization and the transatlantic security community

The existence of a strong globalism reflects (and obviously impacts upon) an increasingly institutionalized transnational defence-industrial base across the transatlantic area. The meshing of the ideology of globalization in a broad sense with security integration is clearly part of the globalization of the arms industry, as the need for further globalization is often predicated on the needs of defence cooperation, particularly through security organizations like NATO. However, the development of transatlantic linkages, and a potential transatlantic defence-industrial base is predicated on the broader development of a transatlantic security community, involving the close relationship between Western states and how they have evolved into a 'zone of peace'.[79]

There have been several important attempts to deal with this evolution, for example through the notion of a 'democratic peace', but also through the description of a development of a 'security community'. This notion, derived from Karl Deutsch's study of the Atlantic community, describes a situation where states no longer see each other as a threat, and have commonalities in their security thinking.[80] This is crucial for the development of arms industry globalization, where the industry is no longer seen as a special case. As Buzan and Herring have pointed out, 'as long as the leading powers continue to form a security community, and to perceive a low risk of world war, they are likely to follow the logic of economic efficiency to continue eroding their national capacities for independent arms production'.[81]

The security community is backed up institutionally by the development of the increasing integration of Western state structures, through a number of overlapping institutions, the core of which is NATO, but also including the WEU, the EU (through the Common Foreign and Security Policy) and the Organization for Security and Co-operation in Europe (OSCE). These institutions developed from the internationalizing and globalizing aspects of total war and Cold War, and the development of internationalized bloc states in the Cold War period had a large impact on the structure of these states involved. The Western bloc, led by the US, moved towards a security community not only to avoid the possibility of another World War, but to oppose the Soviet Union. Undoubtedly this slowly evolved into a greater recognition of a security community cognitively, but it was also reflected in the increasing institutionalization of the relationship, through a variety of overlapping intergovernmental organizations.[82] This has increasingly formed a series of interlocking, integrated and reinforcing institutions and relationships.[83]

The development of a transnational defence-industrial base in Europe, and increasingly transatlantically, is the institutionalization of transnational economic power that is also intertwined with military power. The need for transnational defence planning in NATO, the pursuit of Common Foreign and Security Policy (CFSP) in the EU and other transatlantic projects have made the possibilities for globalization of defence industries within the transatlantic region much easier, especially within the EU.[84] As these security states find it necessary (and plausible) to allow defence industries to become competitive and integrated into global markets, states are also pursuing security goals in an increasingly internationalized and globalized level.

It would be simplistic to say that this relationship was entirely cooperative, or that there is no possibility of its reversal. For example the development of European arms cooperation has been primarily to counter the dominance of US producers.[85] However, the fact that this competition is almost exclusively on an economic level says something important about its relevance to security in the region. There is still a large degree of national autonomy, and different perspectives on the ways to accomplish security goals – however, the ends of security are fairly consistent, and primarily concern actors outside of the transatlantic area. As was shown in the previous chapter, globalizing tendencies are often fraught with contradictions: the increased globalization may be, paradoxically, a means to promoting national autonomy; or possibly a comprise position between the financial and political costs of autarky and the security costs of free trade.[86] In the case of arms industries, the nature of contemporary advanced military technology necessitates internationalization; but internationalization and globalization can be seen as a *means* to maintain national autonomy.[87] A good example can be found in the JSF project. Here the US government has allowed unprecedented international collaboration at all stages of the creation of the aircraft. Though much of the argument behind the collaboration is economic – that is, sharing the financial burdens of production, allowing allies in so they will also purchase the final product, in order to secure unique technology – but a key argument was also the desire for interoperability with NATO and other allies.[88]

The question that remains concerns the impact on the security state of the institutionalization of both transatlantic economic power and military power. Where the traditional nation-state would see the autonomous provision of defence and security as an essential ideal, the increasing integration of the transatlantic states has permitted a progressive and steady unbundling of this aspect, to the point where the economics of the defence industry have taken precedence within the community. As Taylor has pointed out 'developments on the defence-industrial front seem to undermine the contribution of Power Politics thinking to our understanding of defence policy, a broad area where such thinking has traditionally been dominant'.[89]

While interdependence certainly does not herald the end of states themselves, it does perhaps mean the beginning of the unravelling of the security state. There needs to be some questioning of how the globalization of the arms industry affects the traditional relationship between organized violence and the security state. The tension between inter-nationalization and nationalization was inherent in the development of the security state, so as such, economic transnationalization does not necessitate the end of the security state. However, if there is some recognition of a decline in security competitiveness and increasing integration of many formerly national factors within the transatlantic area, the traditional motive forces that have shaped the production and transfer system can be seen to be declining, allowing for a redefinition of the state's role in the provision of arms, and more broadly, in defence autonomy itself. While it would be too early to outline precise changes, one can already see growing concerns about how the shift in govern-ment industry relations has affected the power of arms producers. As Markusen points out, 'a global defence industry will mean a few, large transnational contractors facing a wider array of buyers. Market power will shift from governments to the private sector'.[90]

If there exists a significant security community, reflected in the continued integration of even defence industries within the core, how do these relate to those outside the transatlantic region? The increas-ing integration of defence production and security provision in the Western core points to the region as a whole constituting a first-tier pro-ducer, and it sets the lead for the rest of the world. It is notable that the internationalization and transnationalization of production has been most prevalent in the US and Western Europe. Many countries outside the core have tried to develop degrees of autarky for both security and domestic economic reasons, but there has been little real success, as many of the firms are already heavily indebted to those in the core for technological diffusion and sales. Some can be considered reasonably major manufacturers (e.g. Israel, China, Russia), but for the most part, investment is concentrated in the US and Europe.[91]

At the level of prime contractors – epitomized by Boeing, Lockheed Martin, Raytheon, and BAE Systems – there is not a great deal of collab-oration outside of the West. However, at the level of semi-primes and sub-contracting, there is a great deal more, much of which goes unnoticed. The increasing importance of embedded technology in weaponry means that much subcontracting goes towards high-technology components that are not necessarily just weapons technology. This 'dual-use' technol-ogy is therefore often subcontracted to civilian industries.[92] The trans-mission of notions of 'appropriate' military technology (i.e. Western military technology) has also had a major influence on the emergence of the new defence and industrial capabilities of the Asia-Pacific. In some cases, governments have specifically chosen Western technologies in order to influence the supplier country to become more deeply involved in that country's national defence.[93]

However, taken as a whole, the international production of weaponry has also been transformed into a more thoroughly integrated system. Buzan and Herring have noted that the traditional descriptions of the arms production hierarchy have been increasingly complicated. It is no longer the case that there is a simple dichotomy between producer/suppliers and non-producer/recipients. Indeed everywhere this has become more complex, as there are an increasing number of part-producers globally.[94] Indeed many producers outside the transatlantic region are attempting to cope with globalization through a number of strategies, but mainly by recognizing the autarky is no longer possible.[95] However, the category of non-producers is little changed, as those states remain consumers of weaponry, and often account for the weakest states in the international system.

All of the above points to the development of an increasingly undifferentiated (in terms of types of technology) global military order among contemporary states, amounting to an increasingly globalized and internationalized system for providing the means of violence. The broader ideological trends of economic globalization, combined with the development of a substantial Western 'security community' have very much facilitated the integration of the defence industry in the West, and cannot be separated from these broader trends. Overall, this integration, while possibly serving the needs of the Western core of states that strongly profit from it, both financially and in terms of their own perceived security needs, could be something that over time impacts on the structure of states as they become more institutionally integrated into a global security system.

The key to all of this is in understanding the decisive change in the nature of threat, and the development of a more integrated security community. The main areas of threat discussed in the first section have not diminished the promotion of globalism as an ideology, which is increasingly not transcendent, but imminent in terms of reproducing existing institutional arrangements. The shifts towards arms industry globalization need to be seen in a broader context of changing dimensions of military power, and the development of a transatlantic security community overall necessitates a change from the more 'autonomous' ideal of the security state. The security state was intended as a means of protecting national autonomy through internationalization. Economic transnationalism in the military sphere does not seem any more to be just a means to protect national autonomy, but is a means to protecting the transatlantic region as a whole. While it is far too early to say that there is a new security compact developing, this case fairly clearly demonstrates the salience of the globalization of security, and a clear sense of scale shift in terms of the circuits of defence production and (to a lesser degree) military power itself in the transatlantic region. State retrenchment has barely figured as a response, except possibly in the US, which seemingly has the most to lose in terms of allowing further denationalization of its own firms.[96] However, the US is also the heart of globalization, in terms of promoting globalism and through the transnational power of its own arms industry, so complete retrenchment, outside of debates over foreign ownership, is improbable in the near future. So here, unlike in the case of nuclear weapons, there is some degree of scale shift away from the security state, and towards more diffused modes of global authority in the circuits of arms production.

Arms industry globalization, security and state legitimacy

The development of transnationalism in defence production and the strength of the transatlantic security community, like other forms of emergent globalization, do raise issues concerning the legitimacy of nation-states. To the extent that transnationalism is becoming more prevalent, and more diffused forms of authority over the inputs (and possibly outputs) of security exist, then the traditional roles of national governments in the security sector are transformed. As argued above, while a fully developed transnational defence-industrial base does not exist, transnationalism has been accepted and implemented in varying degrees: through attempts to streamline defence structures, to provide economies of scale in defence production, and to provide interoperability between national military establishments. However, as with other forms of private authority, questions of accountability and overall legitimacy begin to come to the forefront. There is a serious issue between the pursuit of profit and the pursuit of public good, and also between transnational authority and power in the provision of armaments.

The globalization and privatization of the arms industries are therefore complex but important in terms of the impacts on state legitimacy seen in the globalization of security. As stated at the outset, arms industries have always sat on the edge of the public–private divide because of their relationship with the economy and civil society, but have also been seen by states as necessary for security. As such, the issue of state legitimacy is robustly connected to the impacts that globalization and privatization have for the provision of security: do globalizing trends make providing security more difficult for nation-states? The concern with globalization leads directly to a problem with state–society relations. This arises from the fact that leaving arms provision to transnational networks deprives the state, to a certain degree, of its absolute monopoly over security in its territory. If security states have traditionally had a monopoly over security, the privatization and globalization of such means indicates a shift in this dimension of state power.

While security privatization has had major impacts on states in the developing world (particularly through the use of Private Military Companies (PMCs)), legitimacy problems in the transatlantic region are perhaps more subtle and sometimes more technical than in other regions. The main concerns of policymakers were outlined above, in terms of the problems of autonomy that transnationalization can provide for states. The issue of autonomy creates potential legitimacy problems only in terms of the ability of states to provide security to their citizens. However, as mentioned in the previous section, the concerns with security are also in the broader background of globalization that has facilitated the changes in the industry, which mitigates security concerns. Additionally, the pursuit of integration has always been to pursue *greater security* in a changed environment, and (as with nuclear weapons) to the extent to which states succeed in providing security, the impact of globalization on legitimacy will in fact be positive.

While it is clear that the nation-states in the transatlantic region have pursued globalization strategies in the arms industries in order to provide better security (i.e. internationalism for national autonomy), potential changes are inherent in the new arrangements, which could pose legitimacy problems in the future. These legitimacy problems come in two varieties.

First, to the extent to which a transatlantic security community remains robust, and transnationalism in the arms industry continues, multiple centres of authority will exist in the realm of security provision for the region. As such, the diffusion of authority potentially undermines the security compact on which the security state is based, by having a monopoly on the security provision to society. The more intensely that security becomes governed transnationally, there is a sense that the provision of the inputs of security is being outsourced, and not easily brought back into the security state.[97] If the security state maintained legitimacy by promoting internationalism for national autonomy, the breakdown in the compromise will be seen in a system where internationalism and globalization will take priority over national autonomy, or impinge on autonomy in a significant manner. As such, a real shift in legitimacy will be facilitated in the unintended consequences of such changes, as they often are. The potential scale shift borne out through security privatization may best be seen in the development of modes of private authority, similarly to other areas of global governance in the global political economy.[98]

A second scenario would involve a retrenchment of national power over security, which would reflect a variety of potential failures of the transatlantic security community. While this has not yet happened, the senses in which arms industry globalization becomes seen as threatening can provide states with incentives to retrench power in this area, however difficult it might be. The most obvious area of importance concerns the global diffusion of weapons technology. The spread of technology that globalization allows for could be seen to threaten openness, even potentially through the transatlantic security community itself (to the extent to which shared technology spreads outside of the community). Threats to states that occur through such diffusion may come to be seen as so threatening to overall legitimacy that the best solution is to retrench power, and 'de-globalize' arms industries to some extent. While such an approach looks unlikely at present, and poses huge opportunity costs for most states in the transatlantic region, it certainly is one solution to a potential legitimacy problem.

An additional issue is more attached to privatization trends within the industry, which are fairly robustly connected to globalization, but analytically separate. The mediation of an arms industry through networks of private authority may not seem as serious as an outsourcing of actual combat forces seen in the use of private military companies (PMCs).[99] However, in the long run, it could lead to some of the legitimacy problems already seen in that sector. With PMCs, the largest sector in economic terms is not from firms providing direct combat functions, but from those providing logistics and training, and the similarities between these kinds of firms and those in the arms industry is more apparent. Here a number of issues have impacted on legitimacy and accountability,[100] but the main problem is in term of the relationship between consumers and providers. Singer has described this in terms of 'contractual dilemmas', being the problem of the goals of the 'principal' versus those of the 'agent' – or, substantively, the difference between the public good of security and the private profit motives.[101] To the extent to which these principal–agent problems become an issue, this could have further legitimacy problems for national states, especially as many of these firms become more interlinked to global circuits of arms production and industry.

The implications of privatization also go much deeper than just the relationship between arms industries and states. Shaw has noted the rise of 'post-military' societies, where the link between democratic rights obtained in a trade-off for universal military service have been eroded. As changes in the way wars are fought are combined with a changing perception of armed conflict, there is a move away from conscription, therefore raising a problem in the foundations of liberal democratic states.[102] There is an important connection between this and the trend towards the privatization of security, even that found in the arms industry, in that privatization goes along with the increasing professionalization and commercialization of the armed forces – a move away from citizen armies.[103] The demilitarization of citizenship goes along with the decline of the nation-state as a sole provider of many kinds of security, as security functions are privatized and outsourced. These broader changes may just indicate a changing nation-state, but the long-term consequences are hard to predict, and much depends on the robustness of the national project, as well as the robustness of a transnational security community.

The privatization of security provision, of which the defence industry is a part, can be seen as a consequence, at least on some level, as one of the problems globalization creates for maintaining traditional relationships between the state and organized violence. Although the arms industry provides a difficult example to fit into this context, as it is about the production of weapons and not their use, the need for states to allow industry to take the lead over state concerns indicates some disconnection from the process of security provision. The main problem is that it at least partially erodes one of the foundations of the security state, its monopoly over the provision of security. When combined with Shaw's argument about the disconnection between citizenship and the professionalization of the armed forces, it is apparent that the privatization and marketization of security may impact more crucially on this fundamental institution of state legitimacy.

Placing the arms industries in the broader context of international social change certainly helps to more clearly analyse the larger trends, and possibilities for the future of the legitimacy of the security state. In this light, the increased marketization and globalization of the arms industry does not necessitate a wholesale erosion of the security state, but it does lead to a rethinking of the state's ability to provide security when such provision is mediated globally and transnationally.

Conclusion

The globalization of the arms industry within the transatlantic region can be seen as part of the rise of the security state as a particular form of state–society relations. Arms industry globalization occurred in a context where states began to pursue internationalization activities in a usually protected industry, as a means of maintaining national autonomy. While certainly done at a time where the security environment was favourable for transnationalism in the region (both during the Cold War and after), the beginnings of internationalism were certainly not premised on a desire to form a transnational industrial base, much less a globalization of security provision, but as a means of providing better national defence. That such changes have unpredictable futures is not entirely surprising.

The evidence above demonstrated that while globalization activities in the arms industry have had some security implications, they have mainly been seen in the context of a broader globalism in economy: that national autonomy is fostered through economic openness, despite some risks. The discourse of globalism has been most clear at the level of industry, which sees globalization and transnationalism as both desirable and inevitable. At the level of government, such trends have been slowly embraced, though with differing levels of enthusiasm. Those governments most keen to privatize industries have also been reasonably keen to promote forms of transnationalism in industry more broadly. Such drives are not only seen as part of a broader strategy of improving military effectiveness; they are also wrapped up in debates about the relationship between national economic power and military power. The UK and US support of globalization has certainly been partially due to their own leading role in the international arms trade, and Europe's slow embrace of globalization activities has been partially a response to the domination of American firms.

However, the development of a globalized arms industry in the region is also played out against the backdrop of a fairly well-developed transatlantic security community, which has been a prime reason why globalization has been possible at all. The development of forms of transnational security governance within the region has made arms industry globalization plausible by taking away many of the security issues usually involved with the sector. That the competition above is couched almost entirely in economic terms (about jobs and marketshare) attests to the significance of the security community itself. The combination of these elements has made a significant potential for the development of a transnational industrial base, a diffused transnational circuit of arms production and provision, within the transatlantic region.

We therefore see the beginnings of a globalization of security in the region, to the extent to which the development of the transnationaliza-tion of defence production is considered a means of providing security to the region as a whole. Consequently, there is a possibility that the future of the security state, and its attendant monopoly on the provi-sion of security, is potentially at risk, to be replaced by a more transna-tionalized arrangement of state (and regional) power.

It is important not to overestimate changes to the contemporary state system, but it is also crucial to recognize the possibility of trends toward the restructuring of security. The restructuring of the arms industry itself is indicative of a shift to a more privatized and globalized pro-vision of the means of violence. This is part of a larger trend towards political restructuring that has been accelerating since the end of the Cold War, and is likely to continue. What is apparent is that the trends of post-war restructuring of the international system have continued to be entrenched through processes of globalization. It needs to be recog-nized that there is an important political side to globalization, which affects the structure of states in the international system, which can be described as a globalization of security. This is not in terms of homo-geneity of security relationships worldwide, but the entrenchment of a global system of security relations with the Western core at its centre. The larger social and political transformation that is a part of global-ization, regardless of its cause, should be seen as a part of the chan-ging nature of the relationship between state and industry, indicating a deeper change in social organization than is implied by those who discuss security primarily in terms of interdependence.

Although the changes in the political structure of the security state have had a positive impact on the security relations between the states in the transatlantic region, the motive forces that drive the arms indus-try are still present in the global military system, in various forms of militarism that have driven Western armaments policy for decades. It must be stressed that this is part of a restructuring of the state's ability to control the means of violence, and should not be seen necessarily as a shift towards demilitarization. As Lovering has pointed out, 'the half decade since the end of the Cold War has seen not a purging of organ-ized violence from the international state system, but a restructuring of the ways in which it is organized and supplied. Not demilitarisation but remilitarisation.'[104] However, this is not to say that this development is necessarily entirely problematic. It is another demonstration of how the globalization of security is changing the relationship between states and organized violence, and what is of most importance is how power is reorganized.

5
Global Migration, Security and Citizenship

The migration of peoples to different areas of the world has been important in the development of civilizations throughout history. Movements of people were not only crucial to survival, but also led to the development of new societies, and the dispersion of technologies and cultures.[1] Since the development of the nation-states system, migration has taken on new significance. From the forced labour migration of slavery and colonialism to non-coercive labour migrations, the movement of populations as a result of war, and so on, migration has gone hand in hand with the development of contemporary nation-states. As Weiner describes it, the most distinctive feature of the various waves of migration of previous centuries 'is that they changed the social structures, and especially the ethnic compositions, of both sending and receiving countries'.[2] The movement of new peoples and cultures not only added to the productivity of states, it also led to new cultural dynamics, and resulting social structures; 'in short, migrants create states, and states create migrants'.[3]

Contemporary patterns of migration have become globalized, in a number of ways. First, migration itself has become a global phenomenon. All states are now involved in the system of international migration, though they are affected in different, uneven ways.[4] Second, much of contemporary migration patterns have been affected by the globalization of economic relations, and the development of faster and cheaper forms of communication and transport. This has profoundly affected the shape of migration. There has been a major reversal in flows of migration from the North–South movement of the previous boom of migration in the nineteenth century, and changes in the types of migrants. As such, the states of the transatlantic core have been subject to much migration in the contemporary period, and have begun to see a number of ways such migration may impact on their security.

Accompanying the change in direction of flows and the shift in the kinds of migrants, there is an increased tension in contemporary states over the status of migrants. Much of the tension is seen in the increased politicization of migration, in the sense that there is a struggle over the status and future of migration. Such tensions can be characterized as the pressure which comes out of the patterns of inclusivity and exclusivity provided by the modern nation-states system. As Held et al. point out, 'the integrity of territorial borders and the distinction between citizens and foreigners is constitutive of the modern nation-state'.[5] The ability of 'foreigners' to integrate and adapt has been crucial to the maintenance of states. Migration has always been a political issue, in that the state has always been involved in challenges over what types of migrants to allow in, and what types to exclude. Changes in the structures shaping migration and resulting shifts in the composition of migrant flows have also challenged states in terms of their abilities to deal with migrants. The migration boom in the nineteenth century was a welcome one – there were explicitly racist forms of exclusion, but on the whole there was a need for migrants and they were not necessarily seen as unsettling. Migration was seen as beneficial, as it could bring people into states to fill labour shortages, and generally help the maintenance of the economy and polity, as long as states retained control over entry. It has only been in the past few decades that the debate over migration has intensified. The contemporary reversal of flows sees a bigger threat to established social orders. This can be seen especially in terms of migrants' integration into new states and societies, and the consequent strains this puts on the security state. These issues are at the centre of problems concerning migration and security.

The increased politicization of migration is reflected by the recent 'securitizing' of migration.[6] The recognition of migration as a security issue is a rather recent one, perhaps first gaining prominence in the discussion within the United States of Mexican economic migrants in the 1970s, and now has a place in the literature on security within International Relations. The numerous ways in which migrants are seen as a security issue will be surveyed later in the chapter. What are consistent with all of the ideas about threat are the challenges that are posed against the security state. There has been a clear conflict or contest between the state and transnational networks of migration. As Hollifield notes, this is in many ways is a 'liberal paradox', the consequence of promoting economic openness within a states system based on territorial exclusivity.[7] In this context, the politics of migration is what makes it an important social process, and the meeting of the global and state levels is where this contest is played out. While this recognition has been articulated in a number of recent analyses of security and migration, much of the emphasis has been on state responses rather than the overall potential challenge of state transformation.[8] The globalization of migration also represents a challenge to the security state in terms of how it renegotiates its powers and roles with its constituent society in a globalized environment.

Therefore the globalization of migration may have a profound effect on state–society relations, particularly in terms of citizenship.[9] The extent to which the problem of integration is further tested by processes of globalization will impact on the possibilities and prospects of national citizenship. Security is primarily based on particular relationships between state and society – states provide security to citizens – so if the conception of citizenship is being changed by the globalization of migration, then it stands to reason that there is the possibility of a change in state–society relations concerning security. Changes in migration have always impacted upon the social structures of states, and this is also the case under conditions of globalization, where new compacts between state and societies are being developed through the renegotiation of citizenship and security provision. To the extent to which we see an unbundling of the security state in terms of migration, it would be mainly in terms of the provision of core rights of citizenship occurring at other spatial levels.

The chapter, as with the previous two, develops in four stages. First, transnational aspects of migration are analysed in order to see the global dimensions of migration. Such transnational migration networks tie in with the first facet of the globalization of security, the development of transnational threat. Second, moves to discuss the issue of migration in global terms are apparent, though mainly seen in terms of the protection of migrants from the capriciousness of states. The existence of global norms regarding the treatment of migrants also mitigates against their securitization to a certain degree, especially to the extent that certain rights entail a global provision of security for migrants. Third, despite such attempts at global thinking, and also despite the difficulties of policing migration in a global system, states have fairly effectively put a block on the global institutionalization of migration, through politicization and securitization moves. As such, states have tried to maintain traditional hard borders in this area, despite globalizing trends. All in all, there is a tension between the idea of migration as a security problem, states' attempts retrench their power and the existence of global human rights norms. As such, migration and security is a continued problem for the security state, where the provision of rights to citizens is complicated by the need for migrants, and the rights of migrants that go beyond the provision of rights nationally.

Transnational migration networks and security

Migration has been in some senses always 'global', in that the networks propelling it have always existed 'beyond' the national level in some manner. As Cohen has pointed out, 'international migrants are the very embodiment of an extended sense of space, penetrating beyond, between, and underneath such conventional categories of international history as the nation-state, kingdoms, regions, and empires'.[10] Flows of people should be considered a transnational phenomenon, and the networks and structures which cause such flows, such as the movement and sites of the accumulation of capital, are part of global networks associated with capitalism. In the contemporary world, however, there is a qualitative and quantitative change in these networks. There are a number of social processes that have been transformed in the context of globalization, particularly in terms of the structure of labour markets associated with the development of a global economy, and the development of new cheaper means of transportation and communication. These aspects of globalization have changed profoundly the structures of migration networks, in terms of push–pull factors, and in terms of their composition.

Contemporary migration theory breaks down the networks of migration into two categories: macro and micro.[11] Macro-networks refer to large-scale institutional factors, which would include the structure of the world economy, interstate relationships and the laws, structures and practices that sending and receiving states have developed to deal with migration.[12] Micro-networks refer to networks of the migrants themselves, informal social networks which help migrants to deal with the problems of migration and settlement.[13] As Gurak and Caces state, 'networks link populations in sending and receiving countries in a dynamic manner. They serve as mechanisms for interpreting data and feeding information and other resources in both directions. They are simple structures with the potential to evolve into more complex mechanisms as migration systems evolve.'[14]

The importance of such networks is how they have changed under conditions of globalization. Both sets of networks are important for the

globalization of migration, in that they structure and reinforce migration patterns on different levels. Macro-networks are often seen as the
most important aspect (especially in the discussion of globalization),
but micro-networks play an important role in the maintenance and
reproduction of established patterns of migration, and as such are a crucial part of the migration process. Both types of structures have existed
at the global scale for some time, and there is a need to demonstrate
how they qualitatively change under conditions of globalization.

The prime motivation of early modern migrations was through
(forced or otherwise) labour migration, starting with the slave trade,
through the 'coolie' system, and ending, during the industrial revolution, with labour recruitment.[15] The twentieth century has continued
this trend of labour migration, primarily through the advent of bilateral agreements between states for the purpose of providing temporary
contract migration. This can be seen particularly clearly in the post-
Second World War economic boom, where bilateral agreements, such
as the *Bracero* program initiated between the United States and Mexico,
and the German–Turkish guest-worker program in the 1950s, were the
norm in advanced capitalist countries.[16] During this period, migrations
were primarily economically motivated, and were characterized by an
increasing diversity of countries of origin, and also the major reversal of migrant flows from North–South to South–North.[17] Figure 5.1

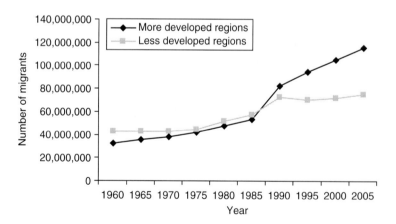

Figure 5.1 Estimated Number of Migrants at Mid-year in MDRs and LDRs,
1960–2005.[18]

Data Source: Population Division of the Department of Economic and Social Affairs of the
United Nations Secretariat, *Trends in Total Migrant Stock: The 2005 Revision*, Monday, 25
August 2008, accessed from http://esa.un.org/migration

shows the change in numbers of migrants from the developed and less developed world from 1960 to 2005, demonstrating a significant rise in migration to the developed world. Additionally, when examined in terms of the percentage of migrants living within each region, shown in Figure 5.2, the numbers become even greater, due to demographic shifts within the developed states.

With the expansion of the global economy and the processes of industry restructuring that have accompanied it, especially in the early 1970s, there have been major changes in the development of these global networks. The first major shift can be seen in the development of global labour markets. Labour markets have increasingly moved beyond the confines of the nation-state, with employers and governments looking abroad to find skilled workers.[19] The change in labour markets has developed due to the restructuring of industry that began in the 1970s. This is well documented by a report from the US Department of Labor, published in 1989:

> Just as a firm expands from production for a local market to sell overseas in an international market, local labor markets are transformed through economic development into regional and international labor exchanges ... Flows of labor occur within an international division of labor with increasingly integrated production, exchange and consumption processes that extend beyond national boundaries.[20]

While such global labour markets differ from the rather freer flow of other factors of production (e.g. capital and goods) due to continued state control of migration, the movement of economic migrants has increased in the post-war period, and especially since the early 1970s. Table 5.1 shows a steady increase in foreign workers in a number of industrial economies over a twelve-year period, illustrating the trend towards the development of global labour markets; Figure 5.3 shows the aggregate and mean of the data, again illustrating the upward trend.[21]

Economic globalization has profoundly affected the structure of international labour markets, signalling a change in this particular macro-network.[22]

The prime qualitative effect this has had is not in terms of the number of migrants, which have been on the increase throughout the latter part of the twentieth century (for a variety of reasons), but in shifts in the types of migrants and their employment prospects. Increasing numbers of migrants now go into service industries and domestic services, whereas

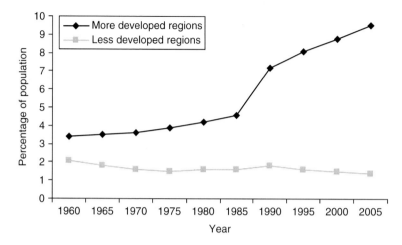

Figure 5.2   International Migrants as a Percentage of the Population in MDRs and LDRs, 1960–2005.

Data Source: Population Division of the Department of Economic and Social Affairs of the United Nations Secretariat, *Trends in Total Migrant Stock: The 2005 Revision*, Monday, 25 August 2008, accessed from http://esa.un.org/migration

Table 5.1   Entries of Temporary Workers in Selected OECD Countries (in Thousands)

	1992	2002	2004
France	18.1	23.4	25.7
Italy	1.7	68.0	77.0
Korea	8.3	137.7	
US	47.8	280.3	321.0
UK	27.6	62.3	106.4
New Zealand	64.5	67.0	75.2
Germany	332.6	348.4	358.2
Aggregate	500.6	987.1	963.5
Average	71.5	141.0	160.6

Data Source: OECD, *International Migration Outlook* (Paris: Organisation for Economic Co-operation and Development, 2006).

formerly the prime employment opportunities were in the public service sector, or 'dirty' jobs in the manufacturing sector, reflecting a shift in advanced capitalist democracies to forms of 'post-industrialization'.[23]

There has also been a rise in skilled labour migration, described as 'executive nomads' by King, which provides a good expression of the

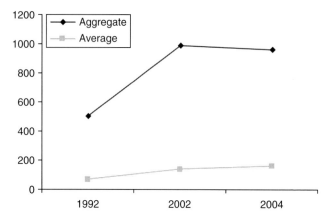

Figure 5.3   Entries of Temporary Workers in Selected OECD Countries (in Thousands).

Source: OECD, International Migration Outlook 2006.

globalization of economic life.[24] These 'skilled transients' (as they are also described in the literature) are quantitatively less important than past labour migrations, but have enormous influence over the functioning of the global economy. One of the interesting things about the development of skilled transients is that they are often referred to as a form of 'invisible' migration, because it is not noticed by the population at large, as it does not pose a perceived social and economic threat to the countries involved.[25] As Findlay describes them, 'these invisible migration streams are made up of highly skilled persons moving internationally on relatively short-term assignments before returning to their place of origin or transferring to another international location'.[26] The movement of skilled transients has been further facilitated through recruitment policies in industrialized states. Often special visas, or fast-tracking through immigration services are used. Some countries, such as Finland, are waiving work permit regulations for some categories of highly skilled migrants.[27] The increasing salience of such workers is illustrated through the rise of intra-company transfers within the Organisation for Economic Co-operation and Development (OECD).[28]

Another effect of the new structure of labour markets can be found in a more visible form of migration, which Castles and Miller refer to as the 'feminisation of migration'.[29] This includes the large increase of female migration as a part of the global labour market, particularly in the secondary services market (but also in some types of industry), and also the newer phenomenon of increased family reunion migration, replacing single-male migration as the primary form after the Second World War. As Campani points out, 'new migratory flows are no longer male dominated; there is a growing demand for female labour and new social needs have created a demand for services in which only migrant women are prepared to work'.[30]

Modern transport is also an important network facilitating contemporary migration. The increasing ease of mobility through transportation networks, and especially through air transport, has helped to revolutionize the ways in which migrants get around. These networks have always been important in migration, and have had an obvious influence on the development of certain places which were nodes in these networks.[31] Airports are the hubs of immigration in the contemporary world, creating new kinds of links between states; for example, between the airports of increasingly global cities. Though these revolutions in transport, reflecting the increasing speed and shrinking cost of transport, make the movement of people easier, they also have the effect of concentrating the arrival points of people, thus increasing the ability of states to police migration. As Held et al. point out, 'as a consequence, migratory flows to the West now encounter a more formidable and institutionalized set of border and entry controls than was ever possible on long, unpoliced land borders in an era when citizenship documents were rare and thinly spread'.[32]

Though macro-networks have accounted for important, and perhaps the most visible changes, micro-networks have also played an important role in the globalization process, by creating conditions that maintain and sustain migration. Micro-networks include such things as kinship networks, personal relationships, family ties and community ties. These networks link migrants to communities in their countries of origin, which helps to solidify particular patterns of migration. They are of great importance in both starting and maintaining particular migration flows. As Boyd states,

> Once begun, migration flows often become self-sustaining, reflecting the establishment of networks of information, assistance and obligations which develop between migrants in the host society and friends and relatives in the sending area. These networks link populations in origin and receiving countries and ensure that movements are not necessarily limited in time, unidirectional or permanent.[33]

Such networks are often transnational and deterritorialized in nature, thus again pointing to the global nature of migration.

Pellerin has described this aspect of migration as 'socialisation', noting how it reflects a form of resistance to being treated as a disposable factor of production.[34] As Pellerin states, 'the existence of social networks reduces both migrants' potential mobility and the extent to which they are affected by the economic and political processes in receiving countries'.[35] The adjustment in settler countries is often assisted by the establishment of or integration into networks of kinship ties, often provided by membership in ethnic associations or communities.[36] These networks do not only provide support in this social manner, they also form the basis of remittances which flow back into countries of origin.[37]

The communications revolution has made the establishment and maintenance of personal networks much easier. Media such as telephone and email have made communication cost-effective and quick, thus enabling the easy transmission of information through kinship networks. They reinforce such micro-networks, by increasing the ease of communicating vital information about life in host countries, and also by providing a support network for ethnic minority communities. The developments in both the communications and transportation fields have helped to deterritorialize certain aspects of migration structures, in the sense that they have shrunk the distances between the points of contact in such networks through the improved speed and reduced cost of such technologies.

Micro-networks, once established, help to continue migration patterns even after changes in the structural conditions which prompted them in the first place.[38] Kritz and Zlotnik have pointed out that democracies, by giving close attention to personal and family ties, have created a situation where chain migration is the dominant pattern; migrants themselves have much influence on maintaining and increasing migration flows, and developing micro-networks.[39] Micro-networks are important in the globalization of migration in this sense; they assist in maintaining migration, and also are characterized by deterritorialization themselves.

Migration, though ostensibly always a transnational phenomenon, has become substantially more so due to changes in the networks of migration, which have become highly globalized. With macro-networks, this can be primarily seen in terms of the change in types of migrants, and how networks have shifted to accommodate them. There has also been a move to a more globalized environment of policymaking for states, indicating an important qualitative shift in the area of interstate relations. With regard to micro-networks, their main importance is in the maintenance of migration patterns, and that they are characterized by degrees of deterritorialization, pointing to globalized structures of migration.

Overall, it is clear that contemporary migration is part of the transnationalizing of economic power in the contemporary world. Like other areas where there has been an increased transnationalization, migration has also been come to perceived as a security issue, in a variety of ways. First, there is the straightforward category of migrants as direct military-security problems. An example is the existence of immigrant and refugee communities who use their host nation as a base for opposition to their home regime, which could become a security problem for both home and host state, especially if the host state politically supports the immigrant or refugee community.[40] Additional problems could manifest in host countries, especially if armed migrant communities feel somehow slighted by the host state.[41] This category of security problem covers a broad range from the creation of difficulties in relations between states, to actual military support for immigrant communities (as, for example, in the case of US–Cuba relations), to problems with migrants living in the host state. More recently, concerns with terrorism have placed an increasing emphasis on the connections between migration and terrorism, and the broader issues of integration.[42]

A second category envisages the possibility of migrants being a threat to the capacity of states to control entry, primarily in terms of illegal entry. Illegal immigration is seen to be on the rise, despite increasing state control over migration.[43] Such perceptions also fuel the politicization of migration, as the control of illegal entry becomes part of everyday debate. This is seen as a challenge to states' control over their borders, an obvious threat to the security of states, as traditionally conceived.[44] Such concerns pose an obvious challenge to the ability of security states to maintain autonomy, if they are perceived as unable to keep out unwanted movements of people.

A third category includes the broad range of problems associated with migrants being perceived as burden both economically and socially. This obviously reflects a broadening of the security agenda to include economic factors, and mainly involves the ability of states to cope economically with large number of migrants who will be using its social programmes, and will also be involved in national labour markets.[45] As security states are meant to provide quite a broad array of security functions including the provision of economic security, the impact of migrants on economic security is an important aspect of the future of the security state. However, such impacts are difficult to calculate, and can also not be entirely divorced from broader problems in the decline of economic welfare provision.

A final category, often intertwined with the third, involves the integration of ethnic minorities into national communities. This is essentially about the identity of national communities, which can seem to be under threat from influxes of ethnically distinct immigrants with obviously different systems of values.[46] Waever, Buzan and their colleagues have specifically singled this out as a problem for 'societal security', or the integrity of the identity of particular societies.[47] This is also the most common way that a security analysis can be interpreted in the majority of research done on international migration from scholars outside the field of International Relations. The concern in the literature with the problems of ethnic minorities in host countries, and problems with multicultural citizenship fit into this category.[48]

Overall, migration has been profoundly impacted by transnational economic power to the extent that we can talk of a globalization of migration. The networks that facilitate and push and pull migration are substantially transnationalized, if still utilized by core states to draw migrants in for economic reasons. All of the perceived security implications of globalized migration, outlined above, demonstrate a real tension between globalizing and nationalizing dynamics. The ways in which the security state manages migration as a fundamental social process are therefore very important for understanding the relationship between globalization and security. At its most fundamental, the problem is seen in terms of the management of citizenship rights. To the extent to which transatlantic states unbundle citizenship rights, as facilitated by global thinking and institutionalization, we should see a globalization of security provision in this area. However, as will be argued below, in this area, states have been the most adept, despite increasing difficulty at retrenching state power.

Migrants and the changing nature of citizenship

The perceived threats from migration have been subject to a highly powerful (and emotional) discourse concerning the desirability of 'foreigners' within national contexts, and a powerful politics has developed in all of the transatlantic states (and the developed world as a whole) around issues of immigration.[49] All of this discourse is premised around issues of the security state: direct military threats from terrorism, threats to the integrity of national communities, threats to the provision of economic welfare. As such, the main conception of threat is one that demands not a global response, but a more heavily national one. However, despite the strength of this discourse, there has been the development of a reasonably strong globalism that does not so much outsource the provision of security, rather than reshape the discourse of threat itself. A broad discourse of globalism, which is directly related to the economic globalism of the previous chapter, focuses on the free movement of labour. Related to this is the focus on transnational rights of migrants as citizens have become the most important aspect of this globalism, and the state response to such trends is of crucial importance to understanding the response to the globalization of migration.

The politicization of migration has been on the increase in the past few decades, primarily due to the influx and character of many new migrants, and this has led to much of the 'security talk' surrounding migration. Migration has always been politicized in the sense that states and societies contest who should be allowed in. The reason one speaks of 'international' migration at all is because of the existence and importance of states and borders. Migrations contain an irreducible political element, entailing a change not just in physical location, but in membership and jurisdiction. As Zolberg states, 'one important theoretical development over the past quarter of a century is recognition that it is precisely the control which states exercise over borders that defines international migration as a distinctive social process'.[50] As such, international migration has become debated more heatedly as both the environment of migration has become increasingly globalized, and greater numbers of more diverse categories of peoples migrate.

Much of the debate concerning migration and nation-states is essentially about the role of citizenship in a globalized world. The focus of the debate can be better seen in the way that citizenship has changed in nature over the past two centuries, in terms of what being a citizen means, and how this conception is being scrutinized under conditions of globalization. The politicization and securitization of migration comes through the renegotiation of bonds between state and society, a contestation over the provision of security, in this case demonstrated by the changing capacity of states to distribute social goods in the global era.

T. H. Marshall described three facets of citizenship that have developed with the rise of nation-states: the first is the civil rights of citizenship, rights which guarantee individual freedom, and are exemplified by such things as the rights to property and justice; second is the group of political rights, developed in the nineteenth century, comprising rights to participate in the political process; third are social rights to citizenship, which have been cultivated mainly in the twentieth century, concerning elements of social welfare and security.[51]

The gradual development of different bundles of rights associated with citizenship has also been accompanied by varying notions of what it means to be a citizen, or how one actually becomes a member of a particular political community. These conceptions generally fall into two broad categories. The first is the citizen as member of the political community, where, essentially, one must only meet the condition of being a full participant in the political community. This contrasts with notions of citizenship which are based on 'natural' ties, where the sufficient condition for membership relies on cultural particularities. These two models can respectively be referred to as the political and national approaches to membership.[52]

Many of the problems with citizenship come from this very idea of inclusion and exclusion, which concerns the coming together of citizenship and statehood. The tension is essentially between the idea of group solidarity and the claims of sovereign power, which is part of the modern nation-state.[53] This problem has regained significance, as van Steenbergen notes, 'with the emergence of a new underclass, the emancipation of minority groups, the attacks on the welfare state and the questions surrounding participation and marginalization'.[54] The debate should also include the debates over citizenship that have been securitized in the case of migration.

The issue of citizenship primarily leads to the problem of integration, the resistance by newcomers to becoming incorporated into the national and political culture of their host state, creating a variety of tensions.[55] Migration breaks cultural criteria for belonging in the state, and therefore fosters some problems. For example, most post-Second World War immigrants were not considered to be a part of their new societies, as they were seen as not being a part of the building of such societies, or descended from its inhabitants.[56]

The problems of integration have been fruitfully analysed by Waever, Buzan and their colleagues, who, using Europe as an example, have looked at how migration can cause threats to 'societal security', causing existential problems concerning identities.[57] Though this is of interest, it does not say much about how this provides a challenge to the state, only about how migration may be seen as a specific security problem. There is some indication of what it may mean to states in the long term; as Heisler and Layton-Henry suggest, migration may affect 'the stability of society and therefore the ability of receiving states to govern. Over time, it may affect the legitimacy of their regimes and the self-conception of the nation.'[58] Part of the problem is that this approach tends to assume that there is not a dynamic relationship between contemporary trends such as the globalization of migration and the contemporary state, which allows for the possibility of change in ideas concerning legitimacy and citizenship.

What is interesting about contemporary problems with citizenship is not only how the tensions in its relationship to statehood are put under increased pressure under conditions of globalization, but additionally how new forms of citizenship are possibly emerging. Citizenship, as an ideal, involves group solidarity around the deliberation of rights, and not necessarily belonging to a nation, or obedience to sovereign power. This points to the possibility of moving ideas about citizenship beyond the linkage with the nation-state. Citizenship is not necessarily moving beyond territorial boundaries, but can in some ways seem to be transforming into a hybrid form.

Urry has noted that since the transformations in the international system of 1989, claims to citizenship have become ubiquitous. However, these claims have come in an environment that is making citizenship itself problematic. As Urry states, 'just as everyone is seeking to be a citizen of society, so global processes appear to undermine what it is to be a national citizen'.[59] Similar developments have been noted by Held, who claims that conditions of globalization have made most of the traditional conceptions of citizenship, and the rights that go with it, problematic. As Held states,

> the implications of this are profound, not only for the categories of consent and legitimacy but for all the key ideas of democratic thought: the nature of a constituency, the meaning of accountability, the proper form and scope of political participation, and the relevance of the nation-state, faced with unsettling patterns of national and international relations and processes, as the guarantor of the rights and duties of subjects.[60]

The sociology of citizenship had taken the idea of a bounded society as central, and when the most important types of social transactions and 'flows' are seen as occurring within a bounded territory, this has profound implications for how citizenship is conceived.

Commentators have noted that citizenship is becoming a more universal notion of membership, leading to an increasingly deterritorialized notion, which can be linked with the rise of global rules and conceptions of universal human rights. For example, Soysal describes this as the development of 'postnational' citizenship, where 'what were previously defined as national rights become entitlements legitimized on the basis of personhood'.[61] Some of these new types of citizenship are outlined by Urry: cultural citizenship, right to full cultural participation within a society; minority citizenship; ecological citizenship; cosmopolitan citizenship; consumer citizenship; mobility citizenship.[62] These alternatives to Marshall's civil-political-social conception of citizenship are in opposition to the citizenship of stasis: they are 'citizenships of flow': 'citizenship of flow de-differentiates civil, political and social rights and responsibilities'.[63]

Refugees and immigrants have gained considerable rights which devalue national citizenship as a means of accessing rights. As Sassen states, 'human rights are not dependent on nationality, unlike political, social, and civil rights, which are predicated on the distinction between national and alien. Human rights override such distinctions and hence can be seen as potentially contesting state sovereignty and devaluing citizenship.'[64] Human rights conventions, while not legally binding, have taken on more and more significance as greater numbers of people utilize them to make claims on governments. States have recognized this, and human rights conventions, especially the Universal Declaration of Human Rights (1948), are now considered to be customary international law. Soysal has described the ways in which this has complicated policymaking, by developing pressures on states to act in accordance with such norms.[65]

For example, one of the largest new categories of migrants is that of refugees, which have increased from approximately 9 million in 1980 (9.1 per cent of all migrants) to 13.5 million in 2005 (7.1 per cent of all migrants), with a peak of almost 12 million from 1985 to 1990.[66] The Universal Declaration makes specific reference to rights for migrants in Articles 13 and 14.[67] These rights deal with freedom of movement, and the right to asylum, though not conflicting with the principle of state sovereignty. The status of refugees and their right to not be forcibly returned are established in international law, but there is no corresponding right to asylum, which is up to the discretion of the receiving state. These provisions are a starting point for the development of global notions of rights that are akin to some of the rights of citizenship. The allowing of refugees into developed states is one of many political processes that are now governed by international human rights regimes and therefore points to the importance of globalized or transnational norms concerning migration, which has certainly contributed to the possibility of refugee migration to Western industrialized states.

Other important institutionalizations can be found in the International Labour Organization decisions on the rights of migrant workers (especially in the 1949 Migration for Employment Convention and the 1974 Migrant Workers Convention), and the considerably more comprehensive UN Convention for the Protection of The Rights of All Migrant Workers and Their Families (1990). The latter was adopted the General Assembly of the United Nations on 18 December 1990. The purpose of the UN convention was to codify a number of rights for migrant workers and their families. Rights which the treaty protects include: due process of law in criminal proceedings; free expression and religious tolerance; domestic privacy; equality with nationals before the courts; emergency medical care; education for children; respect for cultural identity; and process rights in the detention and deportation context.[68] All of these conventions have sought to give labour migrants the same rights in their host country as given to all other workers, and as such have helped not only to give rights to migrant workers, but when combined with other general human rights treaties, also to allow for the potentiality of other kinds of migration to accompany it, such as family reunification.[69]

The European Convention for the Protection of Human Rights and Freedoms (1950) has proved important in this regard as well, as it took steps to collectively enforce certain rights of the UN charter. For example, European citizens can now directly petition against their own governments to the European Commission of Human Rights.[70] This example has gone much farther than anything that the UN has been able to establish, as it has codified certain aspects of human rights into a supranational legal framework of human rights, which has had an important impact on states. For example, Sassen notes that several states have codified decisions made by the European Court into their domestic law (for example, Germany, the Netherlands, France, Spain, Switzerland and Turkey), thus showing the extent of its impact.[71]

The discussion of the development of global human rights regimes has yielded two important insights. First, they are leading to the mediation of certain aspects of citizenship at the global level, thus conflicting with some of the claims of national citizens. Second, the process of the creation of such regimes indicates an important role for the state, where conditions of globalization do not necessitate the 'diminishing' of sovereignty as such, but a situation where compromises and trade-offs are made between the state and global levels. Therefore, the globalization of migration has led to, at the very least, the beginnings of changes in security states, in terms of the rights provided by citizenship. This has also been compounded by the restructuring of states themselves, in that the states of the Western core are being internationalized in ways in which enable them to pursue non-national forms of citizenship.

Global citizenship and its attendant institutionalization therefore demonstrates a form of globalism that moves away from nation-state exclusivity which would effectively remove one of the prime sources of security threat. However, the main issue with the globalization of migration is whether states are making policies that effectively attempt to retrench state power, despite such a discourse. States have always tried to control immigration on some level, whether this was in terms of encouraging certain types of migrants, or allowing a 'laissez-faire' entry policy on migrants. Despite such attempts, states have often had difficulties controlling the consequences of their immigration polices. As Sassen notes, 'immigration can be seen as a strategic research site for the examination of the relation – the distance, the tension – between the idea of sovereignty as control over who enters and the constraints states encounter in making actual policy on the matter'.[72] In fact, it is more a case that migration serves an example of the tension between the realities of state power (in terms of the globalization of economic power) and its interaction with various international legal regimes dealing with migrants. As we shall see, while states have certainly internationalized aspects of universalized human rights, they have been very reluctant to give up the prerogatives of state power over the entry of people.

State strategies in a global context

The importance of the development of globalism for global migration is in terms of how deeply it institutionalizes new types of citizenship which challenge traditional notions of 'national' citizenship. Are we seeing a real 'scale shift' in terms of the governance of migration, especially in terms of the rights and duties migrants are able to claim? If so, such a change would find a true challenge to the security state, as if the rights of citizenship are effectively unpackaged to different scales, the security state would lose its exclusivity as a security provider. An analysis of the development of global human rights regimes surrounding migrants suggests that there is a potential scale shift, but in this case, more so than any other, states have repeatedly tried to mitigate the effects of such institutions through retrenching patterns of exclusivity. There are three main ways in which this is demonstrated. First, the international legal conventions discussed above have all been resolutely negotiated as *international means* of maintaining state power. As such they are resolutely in line with the idea of the security state. Second, much of the context of entry and exit policy are determined by *international* dynamics, and not transnational. Finally, the politicization of migration has been a paramount part of the strategy of state retrenchment, and the state control over economic migrants has been a prime demonstration of this. However, there are still issues with what states actually have the capacity to do.

Although the development of international institutions dealing with the rights of migrants has been a strong aspect of globalism concerning migration and citizenship, this development has not been in a zero-sum relationship with the security state. The role of the state in this process is crucial, in that it demonstrates a real tension between global networks of migration, and the renegotiation of state power. As Sassen states, 'the tension between state sovereignty and international human rights should not be seen as involving an internal and an outside base: the international human rights regime operates partly inside the national state'.[73] The space of the state in providing a base for globalization is crucial.

The two migration conventions discussed in the previous section provide important examples of this. For example, the UN convention is not without some ambiguity as it is repeatedly stressed that the provisions to be granted to migrants (with greater emphasis on documented migrants) are by no means an infringement on sovereignty, and particularly with regard to the state's power to regulate entry.[74] This should be seen as an example of how the state plays an important role in the negotiation of the process of globalization of human rights. As Bosniak notes, 'the ultimate result is a hybrid instrument, at once a ringing declaration of individual rights and a staunch manifesto in support of state territorial sovereignty'.[75] The conflict between the global and the state arises in two domains: the control of admissions and expulsions, and the treatment of aliens within states' territories. The former has been, for the most part, resolved in favour of the state. However, the second is where the interplay between the two principles is more complicated, and the Convention should be seen as an effort to come to terms with this.[76] The ways in which states (and especially the security state) have used such treaties as ways of maintaining autonomy while maintaining the importance citizenship rights should be seen not as a giving up of power, but a means of shoring up power.

Additionally, international processes are still of crucial importance for migration patterns: they are not merely a result of economic transnationalization and its attendant support networks. International contexts therefore become important in understanding the ability of states to control and politicize migration. The restructuring of the macro-networks of interstate relationships has also been quite important in terms of a changing context of international migration, as a number of commentators have pointed out.[77] This is primarily because international relations and foreign policy decisions help to shape the flows of international migration (which can be seen clearly in the example of US–Cuba relations).[78] International migration policies affect a state's international relations, in that the particular policies a state pursues can possibly affect the way it is perceived and treated internationally. Political links between states may allow for some lenience over migration (e.g. France admitting African migrants compared to the risk of losing African markets, or Germany allowing for the continued presence of Turkish migrants for strategic reasons).[79] It could also be argued that there are structural economic reasons for the continuation of illegal migration, as illegal labour is still of vital importance to certain sectors of the economy (e.g. farming in the US); as Zolberg points out, with the cancellation of the *Bracero* program, the loss in legal migrant labour was made up by substantial illegal labour migration, which posed no risk at all to employers.[80]

Furthermore, the context in which laws of entry and exit are created indicates the importance of interstate relations. As Weiner has pointed out, 'states increasingly recognize that under some circumstances (both when rules are incompatible and when they are compatible), it is in their interests to negotiate migration policies with other states, for they can no longer regard their own exit and entry rules as strictly internal matters'.[81] As such emigration and immigration policies are not solely a domestic issue, and are increasingly influenced by the decisions of other countries.[82] This can be seen, for example, in the importance of imperial connections and obligations, which helped to structure a major portion of post-1945 migration.[83] Colonial ties have been especially important in influencing the source of migration to various countries, and such links have continued into the post-colonial era. This can be seen, for example, in the continued links between France and Algeria, Britain and the West Indies, and the Netherlands and Surinam, among others.[84] While this certainly suggests an increased interdependence in terms of setting policy, it also demonstrates that interstate or international relations are still quite important for determining flows of migration, and while 'keeping the gates closed' is increasingly difficult (and subject to high opportunity costs), states have managed to maintain powers over migration.

Finally, the politicization of migration is a primary way that the security state attempts to maintain its power, through the continued legitimation of its powers to create immigration policies.[85] There is a two-fold process about how boundary maintenance (in a broad sense) helps to secure the state as a holder of particular identity, and it can be implemented through the development of legal codes concerning migration and organizations that implement them.[86] International boundaries are relatively new, a phenomenon which accompanied the development of the nation-state; the caging of national societies into distinct states through the strengthening of central infrastructural power went hand in hand with the development (and possibility) of stronger controls over migration.

The forms of border control associated with the modern state were pioneered in the US in the nineteenth century to deal with the period's huge waves of immigration. The concentration of migration through key centres (e.g. Ellis Island in New York), made control cost-effective. The development of reception centres, passport control and immigration criteria were, ironically, part of an era of relative openness of migration.[87] The US has always controlled immigration in some manner, despite its reliance on migration in its creation. The manner of control usually concerned identifying various types of migrants that were allowed entry. The 1880s saw the beginning of the development of an ever lengthening list of 'undesirables', which included 'prostitutes, convicts, Chinese, lunatics, idiots, and contract labourers' (1885). These were followed by quantitative (1907) and national origins (1921) restrictions.[88]

One important example of early attempts to control migration was the development of contract labour migration, movements which have been significant since the nineteenth century, and related to other forms of coercive labour mobilization.[89] Contract labour migration became prevalent in the late twentieth century, increasing in volume after the Second World War. This kind of migration was meant to sort out temporary labour shortages and not entitle migrants to the possibility of citizenship or other rights accorded to permanent migrants. Such schemes were originally used in Europe and the US, but have expanded to newly developed countries and oil-producing countries in the past three decades.

In the US, the best example of contract labour migration was the *Bracero* (Spanish for 'day-labourer') program developed after the Second World War. The US and Mexico had initiated bilateral agreements over temporary labourers at the end of the First World War, until 1921, when the recruitment of legal Mexican workers was stopped.[90] The *Bracero* program was an extension of such bilateral agreements, created during the Second World War, renewed during the Korean war, and continued under pressure from farmers until it was abolished in 1964. The program gave Mexican workers extensive rights and protections, such as regulations for transportation, wage protection, medical care and other benefits, but these were laxly regulated.[91] The terms of the agreement were difficult to enforce, however, and employers tended to turn towards illegal immigrants for labour purposes.[92]

Though the program was ended in 1964, it created migration patterns to the region (primarily the south-west), which continued through illegal migration.[93] Concern over this illegal immigration became quite important during Nixon's presidency. General Chapman (head of INS) and Charles Colby (CIA) 'regarded the US–Mexican border as "the greatest threat posed to national security"'.[94] President Carter developed a number of proposals to deal with this problem, including the increased surveillance of the border, limited amnesty for undocumented aliens, and aid programmes. These were overturned by a combination of agribusiness interests and minority communities (who were against the second-class citizenship implied by the amnesty proposals).[95]

The example of the US was repeated throughout the transatlantic region: for example, the German–Turkish guest-worker programme of the 1950s–70s; and the agreement between France and Algeria.[96] In the European example, as with the American, guest workers were initially just seen as an external labour force, necessitated by internal labour shortages. However, as in the US, the 1970s and 80s saw an increasing societal concern with migration. The linkage between illegal immigration and asylum was one way that such concerns were reinforced, despite the two things being entirely different.[97] As Huysmans has demonstrated, the development of differential policies concerning the movement of EU nationals and those from outside the EU not only helped develop the concept of 'fortress Europe', but went some way towards presenting external migration as a security threat, through emphasizing concerns about social order and cultural composition, and additionally connecting immigration and asylum to border control security issues such as terrorism and crime.[98] The move from seeing contract labourers as economically useful to a security threat provides a way in which states have tried to maintain control over migration, and in fact retrench state power.

Overall, these three strategies have all been ways of shoring up state power. Regardless of the pervasiveness of transnational networks pushing and pulling migration, states have shored up power by increasingly rigorously defining who is a citizen and who is not, and who has right of entry and who does not: as Huysmans states, 'security policy is a specific policy of mediating belonging'.[99] While many critics focus on the actual power of states to keep people out in terms of the effectiveness of border control in a global system, in some ways this misses the point.[100] As Rudolph has effectively argued, states merely need to assuage the fear that control is being lost as a means to providing societal stability (or reproducing national identity).[101] As has been demonstrated, state power in the transatlantic area has long been internationalized in the security state model, and the interaction between states and international law seems robustly part of this kind of arrangement: global integration for maintenance of national power.

Additionally, the rhetorical anti-immigration policies are not primarily about actually keeping people in or out, but are part of broader securitization strategies. The playing up of 'illegal immigrants', for example, needs to be seen as a broader discursive strategy to shore up state power in terms of defining who belongs and who does not.[102] The start of the regulation of migration in the mid-nineteenth century created the possibility for unauthorized entry, employment and residence by aliens; before this time, there was really no such thing as an 'illegal'.[103] Kritz and Zlotnik point out that with the enormous increase in migration in the past two decades, combined with the increase of 'grand strategies' initiated by states aiming at further restrictions on migration, it is easy to see that there would be an increase of non-traditional forms of migration.[104] As a politicized issue, it is often overlooked that there are a large number of illegal migrants between *developed* states; as a 1993 survey in New York demonstrated, the largest number of illegals living in New York were Italian in origin.[105] In addition to this, there are increasing numbers of illegals who are students and tourists who have overstayed their visas, in addition to other categories of migrants who have entered countries legally, but have remained illegally.

In some respects, these types of illegals are 'invisible', in that they rarely play a role in the politicization of migration. They are akin in some ways to the 'skilled transients', described above, in that their presence is not noted in the way other types of migrants, illegal or legal are. As Findlay states, 'the fact that most states welcome skilled transients in an era when other forms of migration engender such hostility is in itself interesting, and attests the economic benefits if not necessity perceived to be attached to this form of highly skilled migration'.[106] Though this is not in itself surprising, since migrants who fit in well with the established social order are not as readily pointed to by critics of immigration, it does highlight some of the problems with the politicization of migration.

Overall, states have managed to retrench power through various strategies. However, there still exists the potentiality for scale shift that is inherent in the global dynamics of migration. Here the critics are on firmer ground. A two-fold problem can be seen in contemporary migration policy that may well lead over time to further scale shift. First, the politicization of migration still goes hand in hand with economic liberalization, and to the extent to which security states require labour migration, the politicization will be challenged.[107] The 'liberal paradox' that Hollifield has rightly noted is the paramount issue in the transatlantic security states. A firm example of this is the way in which there is uneasy tension in approaches migration policy in the United States. On the one hand, it is politically difficult for politicians to argue for amnesty for illegal economic migrants, both for reasons of security (especially after 9/11) and the usual reasons of social stability. On the other, the desire of economic interests in maintaining flows of labour from abroad, and the increasing significance of ethnic minorities (both legal citizens and illegal migrants) politically and socially has meant that politicians can no longer easily put illegal migration in politicized or securitized terms. Core examples of this tension can be seen in the following examples: New York governor Eliot Spitzer's aim to grant illegal migrants driving licences; 2008 Republican Presidential primary candidate Mike Huckabee's proposal for granting the children of illegal immigrants tuition breaks; and the huge Congressional debate over President Bush's 'amnesty' proposal for resident illegal immigrants.[108]

Second, to the extent to which security states of the transatlantic region still promote economic liberalism, the key sources of migration will remain transnational, giving further potential backing for scale shift in the future. The problems for state control are further complicated with the enmeshment of global migration and the global political economy, where the globalized economic structures and networks influence the flow of migration. As Papademetriou states, 'the flow of labour is neither temporary nor limited to a specific region. Rather it is a structural component of the contemporary world economy and signifies the sending country's penetration by, and incorporation into, the world economy.'[109] The late twentieth century has certainly witnessed an unprecedented attempt by Western states to control their borders in terms of migration. Although the security state may maintain powerful legal capacities over immigration, its actual ability to maintain control is becoming rather diminished. The question of control should not be seen in terms of the ability to regulate the borders, but in terms of control over the networks that actually influence migration, both in causing and maintaining it. As Sassen states, 'a national state may have the power to write the text of an immigration policy, but it is likely to be dealing with complex, transnational processes that it can only partly address or regulate through immigration policy as conventionally understood'.[110]

To the extent to which states in the transatlantic core begin to accept this logic, what Hollifield describes as the 'migration state' may become more pronounced, where the solution to the liberal paradox is found in states that promote migration for the purpose of 'global competitiveness', and forgo problems concerning exclusivity.[111] Moves in this direction are already seen within the European Union, where labour migration is unregulated for European Union nationals.[112] Transatlantic links are not as developed, especially when it comes to more general economic migration, but there are few barriers to 'skilled' labour migration, which is even promoted in cases where there are key shortages.[113] Furthermore, the potential of NAFTA becoming an area of free migration is not entirely implausible.[114]

As such, there are difficulties and complexities in looking at the future of the security state in terms of the globalization of migration. While it is clear that a global discourse of human rights and rights of migrant workers does exist, the discourse and legal regimes work in a complex relationship with national state power. Though the EU provides one clear example of scale shift in terms of the provision of basic rights and free movement, such rights are still limited to EU citizens, and state power over the provision of broader benefits of citizenship still dominates. However, in the end, the need for temporary migrant workers, the international politics of migration and the development of international and global norms for migrants all impact on the ability of states to control migration, and therefore may in the future impact further on the ability of the security state to effectively deal with migration itself. Overall, the globalization of migration networks has changed the policymaking environment of the state, leading to a situation where the state still retains control over the ability of migrants to enter, but the structural causes for these movements is mediated globally. Despite this, whatever the complexities of present arrangements, except for privileged transnational elites, citizenship remains fairly resolutely national, and state control, despite the difficulties of making policy under globalizing conditions, is still dominated by the security state model: internationalization to protect domestic autonomy.

Conclusion: Migration, security and legitimacy

The contemporary globalization of migration provides a challenge for analysing changes in the security state. While migration does provide some obvious military-security threats (seen especially in contemporary concerns about the movement of terrorists), the threats to the security state are more elusive, and tend to go beyond the mere issue of migration. The nature of migration has meant that it has always had global dimension, and what is of primary interest here is not in terms of its direct military threat, but how the enmeshment of migration with global economic integration conflicts with the exclusivity of national power. The security state has historically allowed international migration in order to benefit economically from the international movement of labour. With the clear transnationalization of economic power within the transatlantic region, migration networks have begun to reflect the free movement of goods and capital.

However, such movements not only challenge the capacity of states to control movements over their borders, but also their capacity to be the exclusive regulators of belonging within national communities. The focus on citizenship is therefore justified by showing not only a tangible marker of belonging, but also in the way in which citizenship confers rights that are clearly part of the security relationship in security states. To the extent to which there is a scale shift of both the control of migration and the provision of social goods facilitated by citizenship, there would be a fundamental challenge to the security state compact.

The argument above showed there to be some ambiguity in the extent to which the provision of security in this instance can be said to be globalized. On the one hand, the development of a global human rights regime, and the development of international treaties concerning the rights of migrant workers and human rights more broadly clearly points to the beginnings of a globalized citizenship that does not focus on the exclusivity of particular national domains in providing fundamental rights. On the other hand, states have resolutely attempted to retrench power over borders, a clear means of increasing and maintaining this fundamental aspect of state power. Additionally, such border controls also have the effect of states reinforcing the exclusivity of citizenship, both in terms of states themselves being the ones who determine who belongs to a specific national context, but also in terms of mediating international agreements about rights by reinforcing state power to control entry and exit.

The prime arena of contestation has been over citizenship. The development of global universal human rights regimes conflicts with the provision of such rights as a condition of national citizenship. This can be better understood through Marshall's 'bundles of rights' that make up modern citizenship, especially through the development of social rights, which have an important connection to security. As Rose states, 'codifiers such as Bevridge and Marshall constructed a vision in which security against hardship, like hardship itself, was social and to be provided by measures of benefit and insurance that, in name at least, were to be termed "universal", including all within a unified "social citizenship"'.[115] Such rights are a crucial part of the contemporary security state, a part of the security provision providing legitimation between state and society. If migrants are able to claim such rights without citizenship, traditional relationships between state and society are put in to question on some level.[116] To the extent that non-national citizens do acquire rights that are part of traditional compacts of security provision, the state may eventually become one 'agency' providing security among others.

The idea of the state representing one agency in security provision also provides the ground for the intersection of other trends associated with globalization, particularly the connection of the global economy with issues surrounding social security. The development of more extensive forms of security after the Second World War was part of the post-war consensus of embedded liberalism, the compact giving citizens more security for the trade-off of the state being more integrated into the world economy.[117] As the state has become increasingly integrated into the global economy, the compact between state and society has become frayed as problems with the tension between national states and economic globalization have increased. Rodrik points out that international trade creates the possibility for arbitrage in the markets for goods, services, labour and capital, and, as he states, 'this form of arbitrage results, indirectly, as the costs of maintaining divergent social arrangements go up. As a consequence, open trade can conflict with long-standing social contracts that protect certain activities from the relentlessness of the free market. This is a key tension generated by globalization.'[118] As a consequence, the state and its independent social arrangements are becoming more and more problematic with the increasing globalization of the economy.

The deepening of the security state in a globalized environment is a major reason why migration has become a security issue in the past two decades, as Western states see themselves as being threatened by increasing social costs related to large influxes of migrants. There is a growing sense that states can no longer continue to expand their security functions, as they become more costly, and as citizens become increasingly resistant to taxation. There is also a sense among policy-makers that social aspects of security are a part of the problem, in that they have become disincentives.[119] This issue is tangled up with the conceptions of citizenship discussed above, as it shows the intersection between the problems the state faces with the globalization of the economic networks within which migration is located, and the consequent compromise of mediating certain rights at the global level. The main problem to be addressed is how the liberal post-war consensus can be maintained under conditions of increased globalization. The renegotiation of citizenship at a global level is one form of compromise.

However, migration as a globalized security problem is challenging the state–society compact. It contains a tension between the way that it has led to new notions of global citizenship and globally mediated rights, and the way in which global networks have also made some of the social security functions of the state more problematic. The globalization of migration has pushed the concept of citizenship towards a transformation that may lead to its debasement, as the state becomes a more 'minimalist' security provider. As nation-states move towards more expansive notions of citizenship, their role as a provider of security may actually diminish. One solution to this is found in the actual restructuring of states themselves that is part of the globalization process. The restructuring of states in the Western core has demonstrated to some extent that there needs to be specific global aspects of political power to make the rights of citizenship enforceable. Another response is in the increased resistance to global migration, though border controls, nationalism and other localized responses to globalization. Such tensions between the global and national should not be surprising, as they have been seen in the previous two cases, and do point to the central paradoxes of recent international and global history.

6
Conclusion: The Globalization of Security and the Future of the Security State

The goal of this book has been to chart the relationship between globalization and security, in order to assess the potential impacts on the 'security state'. Globalization has had an important impact on security in terms of shifting the organization of state power beyond the national level. However, the argument and evidence consistently showed that such shifts were the product of a tension between state power and the transnationalization of power, and as such, a constant strand throughout has been to emphasize the continuing political power of the state: not necessarily the continuation of the *nation*-state, but in terms of the transformation of the spatial reach of state power. If the development of nation-states was largely about the bounding of social power within the territorial borders of the state, globalization has primarily concerned the expansion of social power beyond and through the borders of the state. The study has indicated that such changes do not necessitate an end to the state as the institutional source of political power, but does have important impacts on the organization of states, pointing to the development of an increasingly integrated transatlantic region, and a potential scale shift of the governance of security functions. A *restructuring* of state power rather than the *end* of the state.

The key to the examination has been the recognition that multiple strands of power play a crucial role in globalization. Although those who emphasize the economic aspects of globalization have been quick to recognize the impacts of economic power, there has been insufficient examination of other arguably equally important features, especially that of ideological, political and military power. These power networks are sometimes recognized as being the effects of the globalization of economic power, but need instead to be examined as aspects of global-ization in their own right. The emphasis on security was a part of this attempt to change the focus of the study of globalization. Security has been examined in a broad manner, incorporating a number of features, including military, political, economic and societal. The stress has been on the security provision of states for their citizens. While it is clear that this may not be the only way that people obtain security, highlighting the role of the state as a security provider is important for the insights it draws for globalization. The state has been the target of many analyses of globalization, and it is clear that any globalization of security must impact on the ability of states to provide security. The issue of provision is especially important in the context of the transatlantic region, as it was argued in Chapter 1 that states in the post-Second World War period came to possess a monopoly of security provision, beyond just the narrow realm of military security and military power. The remainder of the conclusion will explain how this argument impacts on the three main concepts utilized in this study: security, globalization and the future of state legitimacy.

Security and the security state

It was argued that security can be seen to be globalizing in three dif-ferent, but connected, ways. First, there is the development of security issues that transcend the national borders of the state and become global problems. These affect the ability of the security state to provide secur-ity against contingency, as the environment of security encompasses threats that are not easily located inside or outside the state. Second, the development of a global ideology of security that goes against the 'go it alone' mentality of national security measures reflects an increasing recognition of the development of global security challenges. Finally, the reaction of nation-states towards the globalization of security can be seen in terms of two options: attempts to retrench current state power; or 'scale shift', where power begins to be organized on different levels. The potential development of institutionalized security provision at other spatial levels impacts upon the security state's monopoly of secur-ity provision, potentially making it only one provider among others, or at the very least, a non-exclusive provider of security. The three facets and their impacts in the cases are summarized in Table 6.1.

The first aspect has been described in Chapter 2 as the expansion of conditions of risk and insecurity. This was best demonstrated in the case of the development of nuclear weapons, which has led to an increased sense of global risk and insecurity, one that expands beyond

Table 6.1 Summary of Cases

Example	Facet 1	Facet 2	Facet 3	Overall impact
Nuclear weapons	Expanded notion of threat: challenges discrete boundaries of state	Global strategy; community of danger	Nuclear interdependence	Mixed: nuclear interdependence, but limited emphasis on nuclear independence as well
Security privatization	International and increasingly transnational production and provision of armaments and military security	Market ideology; global business environment; security communities	Tied up in politics of alliances; development of transatlantic defence industrial base	Scale shift: diffused modes of global authority in the circuits of arms production
Migration	Transnational networks of migration: dual source of 'threat'	Global citizenship	Legal networks; international norms	State retrenchment over migrants, but with real potential for scale shift

the boundaries of nation-states. In arms industry restructuring we saw the development of transnational armament firms which created a global market for armaments. The possibility of a more market-driven system of armament production causes some concern for the proliferation of weapons, especially when an accompanying shift in technology has made the difference between weapons technology and that of the civilian sector less clear. The possible threats to state autonomy due to the globalization of production have also been seen as highly problematic for security (but often outweighed by the economics of globalization, which are seen as providing better security than autarky). In the globalization of migration there has been a clear problem with the ability of nation-states to impact on the structures pushing migration itself, as they exist more and more outside the boundaries of the state. However, this has been somewhat mitigated by the continued power of states to set policy over the entry of migrants, particularly as states continue to see many threats emanating from migration, from the direct military threat of terrorism to more diffuse but important threats to national identity.

In these examples, there is scope for a negative impact on the ability of the security state to provide security in a traditional manner. Despite the continued importance of nation-state power in all of these examples, they demonstrate that certain security concerns are being entwined with a transnational level. As nuclear weapons can effectively destroy states at a distance, as networks for the provision of weaponry are organized globally instead of nationally, as networks of migration continue to be driven by global networks of economic power, the scope for nation-state control over these issues is increasingly at risk.

The second aspect concerns the development of globalism in security matters. The ideology of global security has manifested itself in a number of ways in the cases. The discourse of strategy and thinking surrounding nuclear weapons demonstrated not only an increased thinking of security in a global space as part of the grand strategy of the Cold War, but also a firm recognition of nuclear weapons as a global danger that created a global community of fate. Responses to both of these articulations of course varied, but they played a large role in expressing security as a manifestly global concern. In the case of the arms industry, globalism is expressed in two ways: first as part of a broader ideology of liberalism or market liberalization that went along with the globalization of the industry; and second in terms of the increasing development of a transatlantic security community that gave space for such liberalization to occur. In this case, the changes in the arms industry were more linked to broader changes in the transatlantic community. Finally, migration demonstrated the development of global norms concerning rights of migrants that were linked to a possible and potential global citizenship.

The third aspect of the globalization of security has been examined at a very basic level – the nation-state's monopoly over the provision of security. Traditionally modern nation-states have held this as an important principle and practice of security provision, that the state was the sole legitimate holder of the means of violence. This was seen as a major part of the security state's ability to provide security. However, this aspect has been challenged by the expansion of risk and insecurity, and with the restructuring of state power, especially in the development of the international state of the core.

This is most clearly demonstrated in the development of NATO as a transnational organization of military power. NATO has gone beyond the structure of a typical military alliance, as it has effectively integrated military planning within the alliance.[1] As argued in Chapter 3, nuclear planning within the NATO alliance provided a powerful example of this tendency. Although the overall technological dominance was American, there was still a need for the other alliance partners to share responsibilities in training and planning. This effectively put the provision of security, in terms of the control over the means of violence, at a different spatial scale. Although nation-states were still a crucial part of this arrangement, as the dominant role of the US, and the desire for independence by the French and British demonstrates, there was a definite move towards transnational defence planning and nuclear interdependence.

The case of arms industry restructuring also illustrates the trend towards a renegotiation of the monopoly of security provision. Autarky in arms provision was a hallmark of the nation-state, and the development of transnational defence firms muddies this relationship between states and armaments. While not indicating a complete break in the control over legitimate violence, it does reduce the state's role in the provision of arms. The trend towards the marketization of arms provision makes this point clearer. It is in this respect, whereby arms provision becomes part of a global marketplace, that nation-states have lost a complete monopoly over the provision of the means of legitimate violence and monopoly of security. This is also indicative of another strand of the renegotiation of security provision: the privatization and marketization of security.

Under conditions of globalization, the traditional focus of security and the nation-state begins to become problematic: the security state is no longer at the centre of security concerns, as it loses the ability to exclusively provide insurance against contingency, as both the scope of security issues change (from the strictly national level to include the global and local), and the functions of the state are integrated into institutions at other levels. The consequences of this for the structure of international or world order are important, as functional aspects of states are further integrated on the international and global scale. The transatlantic states form an ever-closer integrated region, which is potentially becoming a kind of 'state conglomerate' in its own right. Globalization has therefore potentially undercut the security state configuration through a process of restructuring, where power networks are constituted on multiple scales.

Security provision has by no means been abandoned by the nation-state completely, and in fact it is still nation-states that provide the bulk of what can broadly be referred to as security. But as a result of state renegotiation of the security they provide, combined with an increasing marketization and privatization of security, stability of the security state has been challenged. Nation-states remain important centres of power and security providers, but increasingly their role becomes tied up with other institutionalized levels of security provision. The case of global migration presents a clear example of this, where the development of global norms for social security is diminishing the state's role as a provider of security for its citizens. As the connection between citizenship and nationalism is eroded, the security relationship between states and societies is potentially called into question.

Globalization and the security state

At the outset of the book, it was indicated that the study of globalization has been made increasingly difficult due to a plurality of competing definitions and conceptualizations. The approach taken here has been towards a more sociological definition of globalization, where there is a transnationalization of power in a variety of spheres: ideological, economic, military and political. Chapter 1 argued that a more historical approach to the state is necessary, in order to view it as an institution that has developed over time, and has been adaptable and malleable. Seeing the state as a manifestation of political power that has the potential for change helps to clarify its possible roles in globalization. In this sense, the discussion should not be about the state *against* globalization, but the state's role *in* globalization. The two state responses to globalization outlined in Chapter 2 have been utilized throughout the study in order to get a better overall sense of whether global security challenges have truly transformed the provision of security. While all three cases showed a tension between the national and international level, and some degree of state retrenchment, there were also very strong indications of the development of (at the very least) a potential scale shift, best conceptualized as a developing 'international state' (detailed in Chapter 2) across the transatlantic region.

The potential existence and development of an internationalized state has been borne out in the case studies in several ways. In Chapter 3, the case of nuclear weapons provided mixed evidence at best in terms of the effect of nuclear weapons on states. It demonstrated that although there was certainly a sense of a globalization of risk caused by the existence and possession of nuclear weapons, it was less clear that this had much of an impact on political change within states. Nuclear weapons have tended to reinforce the territoriality of states, as they increased the legitimacy of states as security providers, and as great powers. However, it was certainly evident that nuclear weapons impacted on the structure of military power transatlantically. This was primarily seen in the guarantees of extended deterrence provided by the US, and how the integration of nuclear strategy into the NATO command structure saw the beginnings of a transnationalization of military power. This contributed to the military reorganization of power that advanced the development of an international state.

As discussed in Chapter 4, the restructuring of the arms industry in the Western core has also demonstrated the importance of the international state concept. The increasing numbers of transnational projects within the core itself have reflected the transformation of state structures through globalization. The development of a robust transatlantic security community, the need for transnationalized defence planning in NATO, the desire for a common European Union defence policy, and other defence-related matters that have existed above national defence policies have contributed to the possibilities and need for a transformation of the arms industry. This has contributed to a broader conception of a defence industrial base, which increasingly exists transnationally instead of exclusively at a national level. The armament firms of the transatlantic region also have a global reach in terms of supply networks, outsourcing and direct sales.

As detailed in Chapter 5, the globalization of migration reflected not only the global scope of migration, but also the increased importance of global structures that influence migration patterns. While state retrenchment in the transatlantic region has been the main response to globalization, the efforts of states to shore up autonomy may not last, as the pressures of security provision and the economic need for migrants increase. The potential for scale shift is therefore already a reality in the case of migration. The rights of migrants, increasingly divorced from notions of national citizenship, have led to a reformulation of the importance of citizenship. The increased recognition of citizenship rights that are not tied in with nation-states has been much reliant on changing forms of political power. Such changes have been most obviously effective in the case of the EU, where common citizenship for members of the EU is already a reality.

The international state represents a scale shift towards a more centralized international system, with overlapping networks of state power. These networks are in tension with the nation-state, but as has been demonstrated, such tensions are crucial for understanding the dynamics of globalization. It should be understood that the development of transformation in the organization of power are not entirely novel, or without precedent. Such transformations can be compared historically to the organization of imperial states, which had similar sets of relations, and did in fact represent an earlier form of globalization.[2] The political restructuring that is a major part of the globalization of security involves the development of forms of centralized or imperial political rule. This does not mean that states are vanishing, but that they are being restructured by their involvement in the global level. The post-war international order was founded on principles of sovereignty, but these principles were tied up with the recognition that internationalization was also crucial to protect state autonomy. The suggestion that this order in some ways is analogous to previous imperial orders is useful to a point: it certainly helps to recognize the hierarchical relationships of rule, but the negative associations with 'empire' probably decrease the utility of the term. However, the relationship political restructuring has with older forms of rule is of relevance, in that it can help to shed some light on future possibilities. It also highlights that international relations are no longer (and never were) exclusively anarchical: informal and formal structures of hierarchy coexist with anarchical relations.[3]

The international state also has an increasingly global role, as its power structures have also been constitutive of those at the global level. The end of the Cold War has made these arrangements much more obvious, as the domination of inter-bloc rivalries has ended, the pre-dominance of the North in directing global institutions has become clear. This dominance is also mitigated by the consensual nature of the Western power, which therefore makes problematic simple claims of dominance of other non-Western states.[4] However, it has led to the near impossibility of opting out of the liberal system, as much as some states have tried. The continuing importance of institutions such as the United Nations, the World Bank, the International Monetary Fund and the World Trade Organization, all of which are backed considerably by Western power, attest to this point. This can also be seen in the ways in which all nation-states have given up some degree of autonomy to intergovernmental organizations.

There is nonetheless a danger in overstating the cohesiveness of the international state. This is especially apparent in the relationship between the United States and the other states involved, especially with the European Union as an increasingly cohesive political power in its own right. Although many institutional links exist between the nation-states that make up the international state, there are also tendencies towards scepticism and withdrawal from policies that would integrate states further. The tensions in the transatlantic relationship seen over the 2003 invasion of Iraq provide a prime example.[5] The varying ways in which US allies have reacted to the 'war on terror' also exemplify the problem. A final tension can be seen in the increasing tendency of the US to attempt to withdraw from defence matters in Europe as a whole, particularly with arguments about the free-rider aspects of European security provision. While this often amounts to disagreements concerning policy matters, it also displays the ability for globalization that is part of the international state project to be contested by powerful nation-states. Further changes to grand strategy by the US may mean a change in dynamic for an international state, an increasing challenge over centres of power within the international state, or even the development of competing integrated regional blocs.[6] The tension between national state power and further integration should be no surprise, as it was seen in all of the cases, from the way in which nuclear interdependence fostered moves for independence to the paradoxes of defence industry integration, and how the politicization of migration is used to rearticulate borders in an age where borders are supposedly becoming more porous. Finally, there is a tension between the ideology of the international state, and that of those outside, which becomes more problematic in situations where the international state either fails in its own provision of security, or its provision is threatening to those outside.

Despite the tensions within the international state as a form of scale shift, it is still a crucial addition to the analysis of globalization. The importance of the idea of political restructuring that is represented in the international state for a theory of globalization is that it brings political power back into globalization, while not denying the capacity for state change. It sees an interaction between a tendency towards globalization and a reconfiguration of state power: states are not victims of globalization as they are complicit in the process. However, states are also increasingly prey to change due to their actions in pursuing globalization.

The future of state legitimacy

Security as provided by states has been at the centre of this study. Security has not only been an insufficiently developed aspect of the globalization debate, but also has intimate connections with political legitimacy. The development of the 'security state' model in Chapter 1 contributed to the understanding of how the connections between globalization, states and legitimacy have developed and have been represented in modern nation-states. The security state represented a particular moment in the development of security compacts between state and society, where the state provided external and internal protection against threat, as a means to furthering its own autonomy. The security state was at the heart of a post-Second World War compromise between state and society, providing insurance against contingency. Citizenship is the key connection in this relationship, as membership in the nation-state provides the basis for the guarantee of security. This connection is crucial, as the legitimacy of the state has often been at the heart of the debates about the impacts of globalization.

The political restructuring of the transatlantic region seen in the scale shift described above, combined with an expansion of the scope of security issues, has led to tensions in the provision of security in nation-states. As functional aspects of states are institutionalized at other levels, the ability of states to *exclusively* provide security to their citizens is made problematic. It has led to a situation where the previously stable border between external and internal security upon which the security state was based has been breached. In this sense we can discuss a globalization of risk and insecurity, and an outsourcing of security provision.

What is of great importance is how restructuring possibly affects a 'give and take' between state and society, and if a key part of the security state compromise is threatened, is legitimacy put at risk? As security functions that were once key to the legitimation of the security state are outsourced, does this point to a reconfiguration of security compacts within the state? The answers to these questions depend upon how security is possibly being renegotiated, or its provision becoming globalized. The post-war compromise found in the security state has been jeopardized through globalization, as the expansion of security issues beyond the scope of the nation-state and the restructuring of core states into an international state has affected the ability of nation-states to provide security. The crumbling of the post-war compromise therefore has important consequences for the legitimacy of nation-states.

There are two related challenges to the legitimacy of the idea(l) of the nation-state: the impact on state autonomy, and the corresponding impact on accountability. The question of state autonomy revolves around how much the state relinquishes control of security matters to other sources and how this impacts on state control. The degree of state autonomy (in terms of its ability to provide security to its citizenry) impacts on legitimacy by affecting how states can actually perform domestically. This can be seen as a basic problem of interdependence.[7] If the ideal of the sovereign nation-state has been effective control of national security matters, the degree to which these are circumscribed by the actions of others has important impacts on the idea of legitimacy, be it through the expansion of threats or through changes in the practices of security. The consequences of this have primarily been to affect the *de facto* autonomy of the state in many areas, challenging its role as sole security provider.

The most important impact of the challenge to state autonomy over security concerns accountability. The development of transnational networks of security provision raises questions concerning accountability in common with other questions about globalization and governance. It is related to autonomy in terms of how states can be accountable to citizens when security functions are effectively out of their hands, to various degrees. There are two facets to this aspect. The first is when security functions are broadly 'outsourced'. There is in this circumstance a question of responsibility for the provision of security. The second is what Leander refers to as 'un-governance', where functions that are essentially part of governance are simply left ungoverned, and the government is pushed out.[8] While the latter is more extreme, both facets push the state out of its responsibility for the provision of security, and raise questions about 'state complicity' for its previously maintained functions.[9]

Despite the more obvious nature of the legitimacy problematic in 'weak' or developing states, I would suggest that there is a subtle issue involved in such practices in Western core more broadly, and the transatlantic region specifically.[10] Legitimacy and authority are intricately linked, and instead of seeing a *crisis* of legitimacy in the core states, it is probably better to see a possible reconfiguring of legitimate authority.[11] This goes against much conventional thinking about the international system, in terms of legitimate authority existing at a global level. Where legitimate authority exists at a non-state level, 'compliance is no longer motivated by the simple fear of retribution, or by a calculation of self-interest, but instead by an internal sense of moral obligation: control is legitimate to the extent that it is approved or regarded as "right".'[12]

The location of authority here is crucial. Though strong states may outsource some of their legitimate coercive power (and this is mainly to do with national military security), all states are also increasingly scrutinized in terms of the use of their internal and external use of coercive power. As Leander points out, the state 'has to consider the legitimacy of its monopoly on violence in international terms and count on the fact that the recognition of its legitimacy might very well be conditional upon following specific rules'.[13] The location of state legitimacy

is therefore also impacted. It is no longer that the monopoly of legitimate violence and security is the means for international legitimacy
(or recognition), but the uses to which this is put are also judged from
'internal' and 'external' viewpoints. The very legitimacy of violence
itself is thus questioned.

Overall, the impacts on legitimacy need to be seen as a part of a
reconfiguring of state power, instead of a collapse of state power. This is
important to emphasize, as it does not necessitate a demise of the state.
As Mandel notes, in the context of security privatization, 'the emergence of private subnational and transnational organizations seeming
to usurp the role of the state may instead simply transform the expectations and the reality of what the state performs for the society, altering in the process the social contract between ruling regimes and their
citizenry'.[14] The effects on legitimacy in strong states are therefore still
'up for grabs': the outsourcing and relocation of sources of legitimate
authority may be ways of strengthening the state, and part of reconfiguring of the state's relationship with military power and security more
generally.

With these caveats in mind, what is the future of state legitimacy
when the security state is being transformed and social compacts being
renegotiated? Again, there are two key dimensions to this question. The
first concerns the ability of nation-states to retain legitimacy with their
citizenship as security is globalized, both in the scope of the security
environment and the establishment of globalized networks of security
provision. The legitimacy of the security state was premised on the connection between citizenship and security provision, and as that connection becomes more tenuous, legitimacy becomes unstable. This is
in some senses the most common response to globalization's impacts
on states, and therefore needs to be supplemented by a second aspect of
legitimacy, namely, the solution to the problem of decreased national
legitimacy, that of the restructuring of the terms of legitimacy itself.

As regards the first issue, the results of the study have been somewhat mixed. Although there is indeed a perception that legitimacy has
been threatened to some degree by the globalization of security, nation-
states still retain a powerful hold on legitimacy. In the case of nuclear
weapons, there was a real disjuncture between the state as a provider
of security and the provision of security through nuclear deterrence.
Although this creates a paradoxical relationship, it tended not to have
much effect on the legitimacy of holders of nuclear weapons, as the
mere possession of the weapons was itself seen as a symbol of legitimacy. This is particularly clear in the continuing importance of nuclear

weapons, as represented by nuclear holders such as India and Pakistan, and the problems with proliferation in states pursuing nuclear technology, such as North Korea and Iran. This represents a continuation of the equation of nuclear weapons as a symbol of great power status, one reason for the French and British acquisition during the Cold War. Beyond the symbolic level of legitimacy, it was also seen by these states as an essential aspect of providing security, that nuclear weapons were required to maintain their status as nation-states, not dependent on others for providing security.

Arms industry restructuring provides a difficult example to demonstrate impacts on legitimacy. There is the suggestion of a changing role of the state in an area that used to be a main aspect of its credentials as a security provider, as the provision of weaponry is mediated at levels other than that of the state, and the provision of armaments is increasingly subject to commercial and market pressures. The argument concerning legitimacy emerges more clearly when placed in the context of other trends towards the commercialization of security, such as the increased privatization of internal security forces (i.e. policing), the professionalization of armed forces, and the increasing use of commercial force (e.g. private military companies). The question this creates for legitimacy is how states can remain legitimate when security provision is outsourced, and subject to market pressures. Although not entirely debilitating on state legitimacy, it certainly demands a rethink about the state being directly responsible for security provision.

The impacts of migration on citizenship have most clearly changed the relationship between states and security provision, at least in its social aspect. However, as the rights of citizenship are delinked from national political participation, nation-states still have strong powers over migration, and still remain important centres of political power. In this instance, a bigger worry is that as states get out of the business of the social provision of security, there may be no stronger replacement for security provision.

In terms of the second issue, the potential and partial restructuring of the core states into an international state conglomerate provides an answer to the problem of legitimacy. The international state represents a renegotiation of centres of power, where the centres of nation-state legitimacy are increasingly combined with those that impact on the international state more generally. New centres of power which set policy transnationally represent possible new centres of political legitimacy. As these new centres become more powerful, the question of where legitimacy resides becomes evermore important. With political access still mainly remaining in nation-states, the importance of access to these new centres becomes a crucial issue surrounding the legitimacy of the international state conglomerate. In fact it has become one of the crucial questions of globalization: as political power is restructured in new ways, how does the state remain accountable to its citizenry?

This issue represents a significant challenge to nation-states and the continued development of an international state. Accountability is built into the security compact between state and society as part of the demands and responsibilities of citizenship. As nation-states out-source their security, in terms of an increased privatization of security itself or as part of a process of the transnationalization of state power, the question of where legitimacy and accountability reside becomes crucial. This study has recognized that it would be premature to say that state restructuring has affected nation-states to a degree where the post-war compromise has become completely untenable, but as security issues and provision become mediated on levels other than that of the national, a replacement for the post-war compromise becomes neces-sary. Any such action would be essential not only for the question of the continued existence of nation-states, but also for those that rely on them for security.

Conclusion

Examining the globalization of security through a historical sociological understanding of state power has brought many benefits. It primarily gets away from an all or nothing and ahistoric notion of state power, where states either have total autonomy or are moribund. Instead, we find the development and transformation of state power in time, with state power a dynamic variable in understanding the location and reach of political power in given historical contexts. A second benefit has been to better conceptualize the development of transnational sources of power, and the kinds of challenges they pose to extant forms of power. Instead of seeing globalized power networks as fundamentally against states, we get a better sense of the historical existence of transnational power that has always been in tension with the national level.

The development of what can be described as a 'historical sociology of security' enabled a better understanding overall of both globaliza-tion and security, as well as the crucial role of state power in under-standing contemporary changes in the security environment, and more crucially, the provision of security. The advent of a nascent and poten-tial international state, a scale shift from national spatial networks of security provision attests to the potential for change in international relations. However, as the conclusion has indicated, such changes can be quite fragile, and the international state seems to be in tension with a number of competing forces: the needs of its own states to retain levels of autonomy; an increasing tension with actors outside of the international state; and finally an overall tension with what further transformation could mean for the future of state legitimacy.

Notes

Introduction: The Globalization of Security?

1. It therefore belongs properly to the growing tradition of 'international historical sociology' in International Relations scholarship. See the following for overviews: Roland Dannreuther and James Kennedy, 'Historical Sociology in Sociology: British Decline and US Hegemony with Lessons for International Relations', *International Politics* Vol. 44, No. 4 (2007): 369–89; Stephen Hobden and John M. Hobson (eds), *The Historical Sociology of International Relations* (Cambridge: Cambridge University Press, 2002); John M. Hobson, 'The "Second Wave" of Weberian Historical Sociology – The Historical Sociology of the State and the State of Historical Sociology in International Relations', *Review of International Political Economy* Vol. 5, No. 2 (1998): 284–320; George Lawson, 'The Promise of Historical Sociology in International Relations', *International Studies Review* Vol. 8, No. 3 (2006): 397–423; and Justin Rosenberg, 'Why Is There No International Historical Sociology?', *European Journal of International Relations* Vol. 12, No. 3 (2006): 307–40.
2. Mann's core analytic and historical work is found in his two volume *Sources of Social Power* (eventually to be four volumes): Michael Mann, *Sources of Social Power, Vols. I and II* (Cambridge: Cambridge University Press, 1986 and 1993). Mann has yet to draw up his own detailed account of globalization, but has left some fragmentary evidence that has been useful in my own account: Michael Mann, 'Has Globalization Ended the Rise and Rise of the Nation-State?', *Review of International Political Economy* Vol. 4, No. 3 (1997): 472–96; and Michael Mann, 'Globalization and September 11', *New Left Review* (Second Series), No. 12 (2001): 51–72. His recent work on ethnic cleansing and Fascism also give some detail on his views on the twentieth century state: Michael Mann, *The Dark Side of Democracy* (Cambridge: Cambridge University Press, 2005); and Michael Mann, *Fascists* (Cambridge: Cambridge University Press, 2004).
3. William J. Clinton, 'Speech to Meeting on Progressive Governance in Twenty-first Century, Florence, Italy, 20 November 1999', *Public Papers of the President of the United States, 1999, Vol. II: William J. Clinton* (Washington, DC: GPO, 2001), 2127, 2130.
4. Compare the diversity found in ideas about security in the following: Paul Rogers, *Losing Control: Global Security in the Twenty-first Century* (London: Pluto, 2000); Caroline Thomas, *Global Governance, Development and Human Security: The Challenge of Poverty and Inequality* (London: Pluto, 2000); United Nations Development Programme, *Human Development Report 1994* (Oxford: Oxford University Press, 1994); and the 2002 US National Security Strategy.
5. See, for example, Daniel Benjamin and Steven Simon, *The Age of Sacred Terror* (New York: Random House, 2003); Ken Booth and Tim Dunne (eds), *World in Collision: Terror and the Future of Global Order* (London: Palgrave, 2002); Audrey Kurth Cronin, 'Behind the Curve: Globalization and International Terrorism',

International Security Vol. 27, No. 3 (2002/03): 30–58; Barry Posen, 'The Struggle Against Terrorism: Grand Strategy, Strategy and Tactics', *International Security* Vol. 26, No. 3 (2001/02): 39–55; and Mikkel Vedby Rasmussen, 'A Parallel Globalization of Terror: 9–11, Security and Globalization', *Cooperation and Conflict* Vol. 37, No. 3 (2002): 323–49.

6. For example, Martin Albrow, *The Global Age: State and Society Beyond Modernity* (Cambridge: Polity, 1996).

7. Some important examples include: Ersel Aydinli and James N. Rosenau (eds), *Globalization, Security, and the Nation State: Paradigms in Transition* (New York: State University of New York Press, 2005); Victor D. Cha, 'Globalization and the Study of International Security', *Journal of Peace Research* Vol. 37, No. 3 (2000): 391–403; Robert W. Cox, 'Production and Security', in Timothy J. Sinclair (ed.), *Approaches to World Order* (Cambridge: Cambridge University Press, 1996), 276–95; Lynn E. Davis, 'Globalization's Security Implications', *Rand Issue Paper* (Santa Monica, CA: RAND, 2003); Jean-Marie Guéhenno, 'The Impact of Globalization on Strategy', *Survival* Vol. 40, No. 4 (Winter, 1998–9): 5–19; Ali E. Hillal Dessouki, 'Globalization and the Two Spheres of Security', *Washington Quarterly* Vol. 16, No. 4 (Autumn 1993): 109–20; Sean Kay, 'Globalization, Power, Security', *Security Dialogue* Vol. 35, No. 1 (2004): 9–25; Jonathan Kirshner (ed.), *Globalization and National Security* (London: Routledge, 2006); John D. Steinbrunner, *Principles of Global Security* (Washington, DC: Brookings, 2000); T. V. Paul, 'States, Security Function, and the New Global Forces', in T. V. Paul, G. John Ikenberry and John A. Hall (eds), *The Nation-State in Question* (Princeton, NJ: Princeton University Press, 2003); and Norrin M. Ripsman and T. V. Paul, 'Globalization and the National Security State: A Framework for Analysis', *International Studies Review* Vol. 7, No. 2 (2005): 199–227.

    More recently, and mainly reflecting on the situation post-9/11: Christopher W. Hughes, 'Reflections on Globalisation, Security and 9/11', *Cambridge Review of International Affairs* Vol. 15, No. 9 (2002): 421–33; and Rasmussen, 'Parallel Globalization of Terror'. There has also been an increasing recognition that globalization provides new opportunities for the spatial reach of organized violence: for example, Richard Devetak and Christopher W. Hughes (eds), *The Globalization of Political Violence: Globalization's Shadow* (London: Routledge, 2008); and Avery Bernamzohn, Mark Ungar and Kenton Worcestor (eds), *Violence and Politics: Globalization's Paradox* (London: Routledge, 2002).

8. For good examples of this line of thinking, see Cha, 'Globalization and the Study of Security'; and Guéhenno, 'Impact of Globalization on Strategy'.

9. For good examples, see Paul Collier and Nicholas Sambanis (eds), *Understanding Civil Wars: Evidence and Analysis vols 1 and 2* (Washington, DC: World Bank, 2005); Mary Kaldor, *New and Old Wars* (Cambridge: Polity Press, 1999); Frances Stewart and Valpy Fitzgerald (eds), *War and Underdevelopment, vols 1 and 2* (Oxford: Oxford University Press, 2000); Susan Woodard, *Balkan Tragedy* (Washington, DC: Brookings, 1994); and Devetak and Hughes, *Globalization of Political Violence*.

10. For example, see Charlotte Bretherton, 'Security after the Cold War: Towards a Global Paradigm?', in Charlotte Bretherton and Geoffrey Ponton (eds), *Global Politics: An Introduction* (Oxford: Blackwell, 1996), 126–51. Cf. Aydinli

and Rosenau, *Globalization, Security, and the Nation State*; and Robert G. Patman (ed.), *Globalization and Conflict* (London: Routledge, 2006).

11. However, see Tarak Barkawi, *Globalization and War* (Lanham, MD: Rowman and Littlefield, 2006). The following works also attempt to put security (or military power) in the broader discussion of globalization: Ian Clark, *Globalization and International Relations Theory* (Oxford: Oxford University Press, 1999), ch. 6; and David Held et al., *Global Transformations: Politics, Economics and Culture* (Cambridge: Polity, 1999), ch. 2.

12. A notable exception has been the recent work of T. V. Paul and Norman Ripsman, who have systematically examined the impacts of globalization on the 'national security state'. While the analysis here certainly chimes with some of their sceptical arguments and conclusions, the approach to security and the conceptualization of globalization itself is somewhat broader than their more traditional realist approach. See T. V. Paul and Norrin Ripsman, 'Under Pressure?: Globalisation and the National Security State', *Millennium* Vol. 33, No. 2 (2004): 355–80; Ripsman and Paul, 'Globalization and the National Security State'. Cf. Aydinli and Rosenau, *Globalization, Security, and the Nation State*; and Paul, Ikenberry and Hall, *The Nation-State in Question*.

13. See for example, in Hughes, 'Reflections'; Paul and Ripsman, 'Under Pressure?' Cf. Barkawi, *Globalization and War*.

14. A longer version of this critique is developed by Shaw; see Martin Shaw, 'The Contemporary Mode of Warfare? Mary Kaldor's Theory of New Wars', *Review of International Political Economy* Vol. 7, No. 1 (2000): 171–92; and Martin Shaw, *The New Western Way of War: Risk-Transfer War and Its Crisis in Iraq* (Cambridge: Polity, 2005).

15. Tarak Barkawi and Mark Laffey, 'The Postcolonial Moment in Security Studies', *Review of International Studies* Vol. 32, No. 4 (2006): 329–52.

16. For globalization in history, see A. G. Hopkins (ed.), *Globalization in World History* (London: Pimlico, 2002); Roland Robertson, *Globalization: Social Theory and Global Culture* (London: Sage, 1992); and Randall Germain, 'Globalisation in Historical Perspective', in Randall Germain (ed.), *Globalisation and Its Critics: Perspectives from Political Economy* (New York: St Martin's Press, 1999), 67–90.

17. Justin Rosenberg, 'Globalization Theory: A Post Mortem', *International Politics* Vol. 42, No. 1 (2005): 12.

18. For example, Kenichi Ohmae, *The Borderless World: Power and Strategy in the Interlinked Economy* (London: HarperCollins, 1994).

19. Compare Susan Strange, *The Retreat of the State: The Diffusion of Power in the World Economy* (Cambridge: Cambridge University Press, 1996); and Paul Hirst and Grahame Thompson, *Globalization in Question*, 2nd ed. (Cambridge: Polity Press, 1999).

20. Ripsman and Paul, 'Globalization and the National Security State', 224. Ripsman and Paul would likely disagree with much of the analysis here, but the sceptical conclusions they draw out about state power are actually rather consistent with the findings of this study.

21. Kaldor, *New and Old Wars*.

22. Mats Berdal, 'How "New" Are "New Wars"? Global Economic Changes and the Study of Civil War', *Global Governance* Vol. 9, No. 4 (2003): 477–502; Stathias Kalyvas, ' "New" and "Old" Civil Wars: A Valid Distinction?', *World*

Politics Vol. 54, No. 1 (2001): 99–118; and Edward Newman, 'The "New Wars" Debate: A Historical Perspective is Needed', *Security Dialogue* Vol. 35, No. 2 (2004): 173–89.

23. The literature is quite large, and will be fully discussed in the next chapter. The main source of inspiration in the study is from the broadly neo-Weberian school, especially Mann, but also Charles Tilly and Anthony Giddens. This is not to denigrate the Marxist tradition, but this tradition has had much less to say about the nature of security in state power. A recent exception is the work of Gopal Balakrishnan; see, for example, Gopal Balakrishnan, 'States of War', *New Left Review* (2nd Series) No. 36 (2005): 5–32; and Gopal Balakrishnan, 'Algorithms of War', *New Left Review* (2nd series) No. 23 (2003): 5–33.

24. Randall Collins, 'Mann's Transformations of the Classical Sociological Traditions', in John A. Hall and Ralph Schroeder (eds), *An Anatomy of Power: The Social Theory of Michael Mann* (Cambridge: Cambridge University Press, 2006), 26.

1 The 'Security State' and the Evolution of Security Provision

1. Ian Clark uses 'globalization and fragmentation' as one way of organizing the international history of the twentieth century. Ian Clark, *Globalization and Fragmentation: International Relations in the Twentieth Century* (Oxford: Oxford University Press, 1997).

2. See especially the discussions in Barry Buzan and Richard Little, *International Systems in World History* (Oxford: Oxford University Press, 2000); and Robert Keohane (ed.), *Neorealism and its Critics* (New York: Columbia University Press, 1986). Constructivists have also added much to the debate about long-term change in international systems; see Rodney Bruce Hall, *National Collective Identity* (New York: Columbia University Press, 1999); Christian Reus-Smit, *The Moral Purpose of the State* (Princeton, NJ: Princeton University Press, 1999); and also see the overview in Daniel H. Nexon, 'Zeigeist?: The New Idealism in the Study of International Change', *Review of International Political Economy* Vol. 12, No. 4 (2005): 700–19.

3. However, see Barry Buzan, '"Change and Insecurity" Reconsidered', in Stuart Croft and Terry Terriff (eds), *Critical Reflections on Security and Change* (London: Frank Cass, 2000).

4. For a good overview, see Stuart Croft and Terry Terriff (eds), *Critical Reflections on Security and Change* (London: Frank Cass, 2000).

5. This was noted over a decade ago by Halliday, and has continued to be an important point of contention, especially seen in the current interest in the historical sociology of international relations. Fred Halliday, 'State and Society in International Relations: A Second Agenda', *Millennium* Vol. 16, No. 2 (1987): 215–29; and John M. Hobson, *The State and International Relations* (Cambridge: Cambridge University Press, 2000).

6. See Held et al., *Global Transformations*, Introduction.

7. Horsman and Marshall, *After the Nation State*; and Ohmae, *The Borderless World*.

8. On some of the problems with the literature on sovereignty and the origins of the state in the Peace of Westphalia, see Stephen Krasner, 'Westphalia and All That', in Judith Goldstein and Robert Keohane (eds), *Ideas and Foreign Policy* (London: Cornell University Press, 1993); and Andreas Osiander, 'Sovereignty, International Relations and the Westphalian Myth', *International Organization* Vol. 55, No. 2 (2001): 251–87.

    For further challenges to this convention, see particularly the work of Justin Rosenberg and Benno Teschke, who both argue that the most important transformation was the development of capitalist social relations (mainly in the eighteenth and nineteenth centuries) which not only impacted on international relations, but essentially created the modern state and international relations as we know it today: Justin Rosenberg, *The Empire of Civil Society* (London: Verso, 1994); and Benno Teschke, 'Theorizing the Westphalian System of State: International Relations from Absolutism to Capitalism', *European Journal of International Relations* Vol. 8, No. 1 (2002): 5–48. Anthony Giddens also argues for a more recent development of modern international relations: Anthony Giddens, *The Nation-State and Violence* (Berkley, CA: University of California Press, 1987).

9. Michael Mann, 'Nation-States in Europe and Other Continents: Diversifying, Developing, Not Dying', *Daedalus* Vol. 122 (Summer 1993): 115–40.

10. Halliday, 'State and Society', 217.

11. John M. Hobson, 'What's at Stake in "Bringing Historical Sociological back into International Relations"? Transcending "Chronofetishism" and "Tempocentrisim" in International Relations', in Hobden and Hobson, *Historical Sociology*.

12. Representative examples of traditional realist and neo-realist approaches can be found in Barry Buzan, *People, States and Fear*, 2nd ed. (Boulder, CO: Lynne Rienner, 1991); Hans J. Morgenthau, *Politics Among Nations*, 5th ed. (New York: Knopf, 1978); Stephen Walt, 'The Renaissance of Security Studies', *International Studies Quarterly* Vol. 35 (1991): 211–39; Kenneth Waltz, *Theory of International Politics* (Boston, MA: Addison-Wesley, 1979); Kenneth Waltz, *Man, the State, and War* (New York: Columbia University Press, 1959); and Arnold Wolfers, *Discord and Collaboration* (Baltimore, MD: Johns Hopkins University Press, 1962).

13. John Herz, 'The Rise and Demise of Territorial State', *World Politics* Vol. 9, No. 4 (1957): 473–93.

14. For example, Bretherton, 'Security After the Cold War'; Roger Carey and Trevor C. Salmon (eds), *International Security in the Modern World*, rev. ed. (London: Macmillan, 1996); and Caroline Kennedy-Pipe (ed.), *International Security in a Global Age: Securing the Twenty-first Century* (London: Frank Cass, 2000).

15. See especially Ken Booth, 'Security and Emancipation', *Review of International Studies* Vol. 17, No. 4 (1991): 313–27; Keith Krause and Michael Williams, 'From Strategy to Security: Foundations of Critical Security Studies', in Keith Krause and Michael C. Williams (eds), *Critical Security Studies: Concepts and Cases* (London: UCL Press, 1997), 33–59; Steve Smith 'Mature Anarchy, Strong States, and Security', *Arms Control* Vol. 12 (1991): 325–39; and Richard Wyn Jones, *Security, Strategy, and Critical Theory* (Boulder, CO: Lynne Rienner, 1999).

16. This is perhaps less true of recent constructivist works on security, which have examined the constructed and contingent nature of the development of various facets of security. This is clear in a variety of works, but comes in three main forms: securitization approaches, those that focus on the impact of national cultural norms, and those that follow a more general 'culturalist' logic. Exemplars of each can be seen in, respectively Barry Buzan, Ole Waever and Jaap de Wilde, *Security: A New Framework for Analysis* (London: Lynne Rienner, 1998); Peter Katzenstein, *Cultural Norms and National Security: Police and Military in Postwar Japan* (Ithaca, NY: Cornell University Press, 1998); and Jutta Weldes, Mark Laffey and Hugh Gusterson (eds), *Cultures of Insecurity: States, Communities, and the Production of Danger* (Minneapolis, MN: University of Minnesota Press, 1999). For a good overview, see Theo Farrell, 'Constructivist Security Studies: Portrait of a Research Program', *International Studies Review* Vol. 4, No. 1 (2002): 49–72. More broadly, constructivists have looked at the constitution of particular ideas of the state through their interactions with particular international orders; see Reus-Smit, *Moral Purpose of the State*; and Hall, *National Collective Identity*. Post-structuralist accounts of security have been more attentive to the purpose of security and interaction of states through constructions of security, in that ideas about threats actually constitute the state itself. For the best example of this line of thinking, see David Campbell, *Writing Security*, 2nd ed. (Manchester: Manchester University Press, 1998). The view here is that all of these approaches still provide a highly partial account of state power, that only looks at the ideological sources of state power, and theoretically unwilling to engage with other power resources.

17. For some exceptions, see the discussions in Buzan, *People, States and Fear*, especially chs 1 and 2; and Martin Shaw, *Global Society and International Relations* (Cambridge: Polity, 1994), ch. 4.

18. This is mainly a debate between traditional or realist scholars and critical security studies scholars. The former prioritize national security, or the security of the state, while the latter (in the main) focus on the relevance of individuals and other social groupings. For an overview, see Krause and Williams, 'From Strategy to Security', 44–5.

19. Bill McSweeney, *Security, Identity and Interests* (Cambridge: Cambridge University Press, 1999), ch. 3.

20. The focus on 'societal security' through the concept of identity is one way Buzan, Waever and their colleagues have attempted to get past some of the problems with a state centred analysis. However, this work replicates some of the problems – societal security is about cohesive identities, and does not really have much to say about the relationship between state and society. This is outlined in the following collaborative works: Ole Waever et al., *Identity, Migration and the New Security Agenda in Europe* (London: Pinter, 1993); and Buzan, Waever and de Wilde, *Security*.

21. For the maximal state, see Buzan, *People, States and Fear*. This aspect comes out quite clearly in the joint authored work on identity. See Waever et al., *Identity, Migration and the New Security Agenda in Europe*, especially ch. 2; and Buzan, Waever and de Wilde, *Security*.

22. Shaw, *Global Society*, 94.

23. See Teschke, 'Westphalian System'; and also Robert Brenner, 'From Theory to History: "The European Dynamic" or Feudalism to Capitalism?', in John A. Hall and Ralph Schroeder (eds), *An Anatomy of Power: The Social Theory of Michael Mann* (Cambridge: Cambridge University Press, 2006); and Geoffrey Symcox (ed.), *War, Diplomacy, and Imperialism: 1618–1763* (London: Harper & Row, 1973).

24. Halliday, 'State and Society'; John M. Hobson, *The Wealth of States: A Comparative Sociology of International Economic and Political Change (Cambridge: Cambridge University Press, 1997)*; cf. Theda Skocpol, *States and Social Revolutions: A Comparative Analysis of France, Russia and China* (Cambridge: Cambridge University Press, 1979).

25. Representative examples of the neo-Weberian position can be found in the following works: Giddens, *Nation-State and Violence*; John A. Hall and G. John Ikenberry, *The State* (Milton Keynes: Open University Press, 1989); Michael Mann, *The Sources of Social Power, Vols I and II* (Cambridge: Cambridge University Press, 1986 and 1993); Gianfranco Poggi, *The State: Its Nature, Development, and Prospects* (Cambridge: Polity, 1990); Charles Tilly, 'War Making and State Making as Organized Crime', in P. B. Evans, D. Rueschemeyer, and T. Skocpol (eds), *Bringing the State Back In* (Cambridge: Cambridge University Press, 1985), 169–91; and Charles Tilly, *Coercion, Capital, and European States: AD 990–1990* (Oxford: Basil Blackwell, 1990). For a succinct statement of Weber's position on the state, see Max Weber, 'The Profession and Vocation of Politics', in Peter Lassman and Ronald Speirs (eds), *Weber: Political Writings* (Cambridge: Cambridge University Press, 1994), 309–69. This essay is more commonly known as 'Politics as a Vocation'.

    Marxist theorists, especially since the 'relative autonomy' debates of the 1970s have also begun to see the state in similar terms, though still debating the primacy of the mode of production or the social relations of historical formations of political economy. For useful examples, see Perry Anderson, *Lineages of the Absolutist State* (London: Verso, 1979); Bob Jessop, *State Theory* (Cambridge: Polity, 1990); Bob Jessop, *State Power* (Cambridge: Polity, 2008); and Colin Hay, *Re-Stating Social and Political Change* (Buckingham: Open University Press, 1996).

26. Randall Collins, *Four Sociological Traditions* (New York: Oxford University Press, 1999).

27. The recent debates on 'empire' and 'imperialism' have been illuminating in this regard, with many Marxists relying on a theorization of imperialism where geopolitics (and military power generally) is an extension of the power of capital. For example, Alex Callinicos, *The New Mandarins of American Power: The Bush Administration's Plans for the World* (Cambridge: Polity, 2003); and David Harvey, *The New Imperialism* (Oxford: Oxford University Press, 2003). However, see Balakrishnan and Kiely for different points of view; Balakrishnan, 'States of War'; and Ray Kiely, 'United States Hegemony and Globalisation: What Role for Theories of Imperialism?', *Cambridge Review of International Affairs* Vol. 19, No. 2 (2006): 205–21.

28. See Giddens, *Nation-State and Violence*; Tilly, Coercion; Mann, *Sources Vols I and II*; Skocpol, *States and Social Revolutions* . Though Justin Rosenberg has been explicitly trying to overcome this issue from the historical materialist tradition with the theory of 'combined and uneven development'; see Rosenberg, 'Historical Sociology?'. However, the role of the international

in neo-Weberian analyses has been criticized by some international relations scholars for being crudely realist. On this point, see Stephen Hobden, 'Theorising the International System', *Review of International Studies* Vol. 25 (1999): 257–71; and John M. Hobson, 'Mann, the State and War', in John A. Hall and Ralph Schroeder (eds), *An Anatomy of Power: The Social Theory of Michael Mann* (Cambridge: Cambridge University Press, 2006).

29. Weber, 'Profession and Vocation of Politics', 310–11.
30. See John M. Hobson and Leonard Seabrooke, 'Reimagining Weber: Constructing International Society and the Social Balance of Power', *European Journal of International Relations* Vol. 7, No. 2 (2001): 239–74.
31. Mann, *Sources Vol. II*, 55.
32. Poggi, *The State*, 98.
33. It should be noted that this is not solely a Weberian innovation, as the 1970s Marxist debates over the 'relative autonomy' of the state demonstrated. For further discussion, see Clyde W. Barrow, 'The Miliband-Poulantzas Debate: An Intellectual History', in Stanley Aronowitz and Peter Bratsis (eds), *Paradigm Lost: State Theory Reconsidered* (Minneapolis, MN: University of Minnesota Press, 2002). For more on the relative autonomy argument, see Jessop, *State Theory*.
34. Social power and change will be discussed in more detail in the next chapter in the context of globalization.
35. See Michael Mann, 'The Autonomous Power of the State: Its Origins, Mechanisms and Results', in *States, War and Capitalism* (Oxford: Basil Blackwell, 1988). Also see Clark, *Globalization and International Relations Theory*.
36. Mann, *Sources Vol. II*, 59.
37. For the link between surveillance and citizenship, see Giddens, *Nation-State and Violence*, 202–9. For a more general discussion of surveillance and its links with administrative power, see Giddens, *Nation-State and Violence*, ch. 7. Giddens' notion of surveillance overlaps suggestively with the one developed by Foucault, but Giddens is keen to disentangle them. See Giddens, *Nation-State and Violence*, 185–6; and Michel Foucault, *Discipline and Punish: The Birth of the Prison*, trans. Alan Sheridan (New York: Vintage, 1979).
38. Tilly, 'War Making', 172.
39. Giddens, *Nation-State and Violence*, 18–19.
40. Max Weber, *Economy and Society*, ed. Guenther Roth and Claus Wittich (Berkeley: University of California Press, 1978), 904–5.
41. Mann does not include the monopoly of organized violence in his definition of the state, as many historic states did not monopolize the means of violence, and in many contemporary states, the means of physical force have been autonomous from the state itself. Mann, *Sources Vol. II*, 55; also see Giddens, *Nation-State and Violence*, 18–19. Janice Thomson's work on the history of non-state violence, and its de-legitimation in the nineteenth century, also draws attention to the historical nature of the state's claim to a monopoly of legitimate violence. Janice Thompson, *Mercenaries, Pirates, and Sovereigns: State-Building and Extraterritorial Violence in Early Modern Europe* (Princeton, NJ: Princeton University Press, 1994).
42. See for example, Hedley Bull, *The Anarchical Society*, 2nd ed. (New York: Columbia University Press, 1995); Robert Jackson, *Quasi-States: Sovereignty, International Relations and the Third World* (Cambridge: Cambridge University

Press, 1990); and Daniel Philpott, 'Westphalia, Authority and International Society', *Political Studies* Vol. 47, No. 3 (1999): 566–89.

43. See Bruce W. Jentleson, 'Preventative Statecraft: A Realist Strategy for the Post-Cold War Era', in Chester A. Crocker, Fen Osler Hampson and Pamela Aall (eds), *Turbulent Peace: The Challenges of Managing International Conflict* (Washington: United States Institute of Peace, 2001); and Nicholas J. Wheeler, *Saving Strangers: Humanitarian Intervention in International Society* (Oxford: Oxford University Press, 2000).

44. For a reconstruction of the English school which relies on this problematic, see Barry Buzan, *From International to World Society?: English School Theory and the Social Structure of Globalisation* (Cambridge: Cambridge University Press, 2004).

45. Giddens, *Nation-State and Violence*.

46. Rosenberg, 'Historical Sociology?'.

47. There has been a slowly increasing interface between these perspectives. See, for example, the analysis of American political development in terms of international relations, found in the following volumes: Ira Katznelson and Martin Shefter (eds), *Shaped by War and Trade: International Influences on American Political Development* (Princeton, NJ: Princeton University Press, 2002); and Michael S. Sherry, *In the Shadow of War: America since the 1930s* (New Haven, CT: Yale University Press, 1997).

48. A good sampling of these perspectives can be found, though sometimes tangentially, in the following works: Martin van Creveld, *The Rise and Decline of the State* (Cambridge: Cambridge University Press, 1999); Paul Kennedy, *The Rise and Fall of the Great Powers* (London: Fontana, 1989); Michael Howard, *War in European History* (Oxford: Oxford University Press, 1977); Tilly, 'War Making'; William H. McNeill, *The Pursuit of Power: Technology, Armed Force and Society since A.D. 1000* (Chicago, IL: University of Chicago Press, 1982); Mann, *Sources Vols I and II*. Spruyt has challenged this story in terms of its inevitability, postulating that states were part of a system that included other actors, and were better equipped to face contemporary challenges. Hendrik Spruyt, *The Sovereign State and its Competitors* (Princeton, NJ: Princeton University Press, 1996).

49. This is pointed out by van Creveld, *Rise and Decline of the State*, ch. 3. There is some contention in this matter over the role of ideational factors in historical sociological analysis, which has primarily (though not exclusively) looked at material motivations for the development of states and the states system. See the critique from a sympathetic theorist in Christian Reus-Smit, 'The Idea of History and History of Ideas', in Hobden and Hobson, *Historical Sociology*, 120–40.

50. See, for example, Mlada Bukovansky, 'The Altered State and the State of Nature – the French Revolution and International Politics', *Review of International Studies* Vol. 25, No. 2 (1999): 197–216. Teschke's analysis of changes in social-property relations come to similar conclusions about changes in international relations, but derived from the advent of capitalist social property relations in Britain in the eighteenth century (i.e. the development of the public-private split helped provide the foundations of geopolitics and the abstract national interest, divorced as it was from the state as the ruler's personal property as found in Absolutism). See Teschke, 'Westphalian System'; cf. Anderson, *Lineages*.

51. In addition to resisting telling the story of the state in developmental terms – that is, as a history of increased freedoms – it is also crucial to resist the idea of the 'onward and upward' progression of the state, where the state is seen as progressively growing over time. As Mann's meticulous history of state power demonstrates, in terms of how the state actually grew, this is not the case. Though the state did eventually become bigger and more powerful, it went through cycles of relative weakening, especially in the nineteenth century when its actual expenditures are compared to the overall national economic activity. For an account of this, see Mann, *Sources Vol. II*, chs 11–14.
52. Tilly, 'War Making'. Tilly outlines an 'ideal sequence' of the classic European state-building experience: Tilly, 'War Making', 183.
53. Tilly, 'War Making', 181.
54. Howard, *War in European History*, 49. An obvious caveat is that the process is highly generalized by Tilly. Tilly updated this account in *Coercion, Capital and European States*, where two logics of accumulation – coercive-intensive and capital-intensive – co-exist and interrelate to develop particular forms of state (capital-intensive; coercion-intensive; and capitalized coercion). That outcomes were contingent on the interaction of these logics accounted for the diverse state forms seen in early modern Europe (to the present). Similarly, but from different foundations, Anderson's account also notes a divide between Western and Eastern approaches to state formation in the Absolutist period; Anderson, *Lineages*. For other accounts, see Brian Downing, *The Military Revolution and Political Change: Origins of Democracy and Autocracy in Early Modern Europe* (Princeton, NJ: Princeton University Press, 1992); Thomas Ertman, *Birth of the Leviathan: Building States and Regimes in Medieval and Early Modern Europe* (Cambridge: Cambridge University Press, 1997); and Victoria Tin-bor Hui, *War and State Formation in Ancient China and Early Modern Europe* (Cambridge: Cambridge University Press, 2005); Bruce Porter, *War and the Rise of the State: The Military Foundations of Modern Politics* (New York: Free Press, 1994).
55. Mann, *Sources Vol. II*, 370 and 375.
56. Van Creveld, *Rise and Decline of the State*, 142–3.
57. Mann, *Sources Vol. II*, 479.
58. Mann, *Sources Vol. II*, 375.
59. Van Creveld, *Rise and Decline of the State*, 217.
60. Van Creveld, *Rise and Decline of the State*, 218–19. See also Christopher Pierson, *Beyond the Welfare State?: The New Political Economy of Welfare*, 2nd ed. (Cambridge: Polity, 1998), ch. 4.
61. See McNeill, *Pursuit of Power*, ch. 4; and Van Creveld, *Rise and Decline of the State*, 155–70.
62. Howard, *War in European History*, ch. 4.
63. For an account of this development, see Deborah Avant, 'From Mercenary to Citizen Armies: Explaining Change in the Practice of War', *International Organization* Vol. 54, No. 1 (2000): 41–72. Barkawi notes that there is often a misconception that this meant that no 'foreign' nationals were utilized. But as he decisively demonstrates, the period of intense imperialism in the nineteenth and early twentieth centuries led to all sorts of colonial conscripts, who cannot be neatly slotted into national frameworks. See Barkawi, *Globalization and War*.

64. Mann, *Sources Vol. II*, 410; and Hsi-Huey Ling, *The Rise of Modern Police and the European States System from Metternich to the Second World War* (Cambridge: Cambridge University Press, 1992). This is something that may be changing in the present day, as national militaries are beginning to provide policing functions. See, for example, Peter Andreas and Richard Price, 'From War Fighting to Crime Fighting: Transforming the American National Security State', *International Studies Review* Vol. 3, No. 3 (2001): 31–52.
65. Mann, *Sources Vol. II*, 20.
66. Stephen Hobden, 'Can Historical Sociology be Critical?', *Alternatives* Vol. 24, No. 3 (1999): 406.
67. See Giddens for an account of the connection between these three dimensions of the state. Giddens, *Nation-State and Violence*, 212–21.
68. Mann, *Sources Vol. II*, 251.
69. Giddens, *Nation-State and Violence*, 221.
70. Howard, *War in European History*, 110.
71. Hobden, 'Can Historical Sociology be Critical?', 403.
72. This description has been borrowed from Giddens, though with a slightly different purpose in mind. As Giddens states, 'the welfare state originated as a "security state" and was actually called such in some countries. It was the socialised, public counterpart to private insurance.' Anthony Giddens, 'Affluence, Poverty and the Idea of a Post-Scarcity Society', in Ken Booth (ed.), *Statecraft and Security: The Cold War and Beyond* (Cambridge: Cambridge University Press, 1998), 314.
73. For a classic analysis that puts war at the centre of changing ideas about social policy, see Richard Titmuss, 'War and Social Policy', in *Essays on 'The Welfare State'* (London: Unwin University Books, 1963). It is certainly not the case that war itself created rights. However, the simplification is made here to demonstrate the connection between state and society in terms of rights and infrastructural power. For a critical analysis of Titmuss, see Pat Thane, *Foundations of the Welfare State*, 2nd ed. (Harlow: Longman, 1996), ch. 7.
74. McNeill, *Pursuit of Power*, 317. The impact of the rapid development of mass production of armaments in Germany and Britain (it had already been a trend in US manufacturing since the War of 1812) was also profound. See McNeill, *Pursuit of Power*, 330–1. Also see Mark Roseman, 'War and the People: The Social Impact of Total War', in Charles Townshend (ed.), *The Oxford History of Modern War* (Oxford: Oxford University Press, 2000), 284–5.
75. Eric Hobsbawm, *Age of Extremes: The Short Twentieth Century, 1914–91* (London: Abacus, 1995), 44–9; Alan S. Milward, *War, Economy and Society 1939–1945* (London: Allen Lane, 1977), ch. 2; Roseman, 'War and the People', 283–5.
76. Milward, *War, Economy and Society*, ch. 4.
77. Brian Bond, *War and Society in Europe, 1870–1970*, 2nd ed. (Stroud, Gloucestershire: Sutton Publishing, 1998), 174.
78. Milward, *War, Economy and Society*, 116.
79. Bond, *War and Society*, 175–6; Milward, *War, Economy and Society*, 111.
80. Milward, *War, Economy and Society*, 111.
81. Bond, *War and Society*, 178; Sherry, *In the Shadow of War*, 69–71.
82. Wars had increasingly been a decisive factor in centralizing power in the federal government in the US: after each major war starting with the Civil

War, federal bureaucracy expanded substantially. See Michael J. Hogan, *A Cross of Iron: Harry S. Truman and the Origins of the National Security State, 1945–1954* (Cambridge: Cambridge University Press, 2000); Paul A. C. Koistinen, *Arsenal of World War II: The Political Economy of American Warfare, 1940–1945* (Lawrence: University Press of Kansas, 2004); Sherry, *In the Shadow of War*; and Stephen Skowronek, *Building a New American State: The Expansion of National Administrative Capacities, 1877–1920* (Cambridge: Cambridge University Press, 1982).

83. Titmuss, 'War and Social Policy', 85.
84. Roseman, 'War and the People', 285–7.
85. Mark Mazower, *Dark Continent: Europe's Twentieth Century* (London: Penguin Books, 1999), 304.
86. Mazower, *Dark Continent*, 304. For an excellent overview, see Pierson, *Beyond the Welfare State?* ch. 4.
87. Hay, *Re-Stating*, 29.
88. See Hay, *Re-Stating*, 55; Bond, *War and Society*, 199.
89. For an account of the impact of the war on domestic programmes, see Bartholomew H. Sparrow, *From the Outside in: World War II and the American State* (Princeton, NJ: Princeton University Press, 1996).
90. Quoted in Sherry, *In the Shadow of War*, 47.
91. Sherry, *In the Shadow of War*, 47–8.
92. Sherry, *In the Shadow of War*, 78.
93. Quoted in Sherry, *In the Shadow of War*, 79.
94. Hogan, *A Cross of Iron*.
95. Mazower, *Dark Continent*, 303. Also see Mann's account of the different kinds of state strategies pursued to this end, which demonstrates well that the 'trade-off' played differently in different types of state regimes, but was important in all of them. Michael Mann, 'Ruling Class Strategies and Citizenship', in *States, War and Capitalism* (Oxford: Basil Blackwell, 1988).
96. T. H. Marshall, 'Citizenship and Social Class', in *Sociology at the Crossroads* (London: Heinemann, 1963), 99.
97. Titmuss, 'War and Social Policy', 82.
98. Sherry, *In the Shadow of War*, 112. See also Daniel Kryder, *Divided Arsenal: Race and the American State During World War II* (Cambridge: Cambridge University Press, 2002); and Margret Randolph Higonnet et al. (eds), *Behind the Lines: Gender and the Two World Wars* (New Haven, CT: Yale University Press, 1987).
99. For more on the latter, particularly in terms of the decreased demands of both left and right, see Charles S. Maier, 'The Two Postwar Eras and Conditions for Stability in Twentieth Century Western Europe', *American Historical Review* Vol. 86, No. 2 (1981): 328–33.
100. This is also reflected in Poggi's discussion of the 'serviceable state' and the 'invasive state'. Poggi, *The State*, 113–27. Marshall accounted for the development of rights through a gradual development of civil, political and social rights, the last of which sees its final development in the welfare states of the twentieth century; see Marshall, 'Citizenship and Social Class'.
101. Marshall saw these developments in a kind of evolutionary framework; however, there have been many criticisms of this, primarily due to Marshall's

narrow focus on Britain, and the lack of interaction between the different bundles of rights. For criticism of Marshall, see Giddens, *Nation-State and Violence*, 202–5; Hay, *Re-Stating*, 68–70; Mann, *Sources Vol. II*, 19–20; and Mann, 'Ruling Class Strategies'.

102. See, for example, Bernard Brodie, *Strategy in the Missile Age* (Princeton, NJ: Princeton University Press, 1965); Robert Jervis, *The Meaning of the Nuclear Revolution* (Ithaca, NY: Cornell University Press, 1989); and Michael Mandelbaum, *The Nuclear Revolution: International Politics Before and After Hiroshima* (Cambridge: Cambridge University Press, 1981).

103. This is given brief outline in McNeill, *Pursuit of Power*, 354–6. For further comments on the 'Victory Program', see Milward, *War, Economy and Society*, 51–2. McNeill also interestingly notes that Jean Monnet was a key figure involved with convincing US policymakers to draw up a wartime mobilization plan in 1941. McNeill, *Pursuit of Power*, 355, fn 88. Transnationalism was less pronounced in the Axis powers, who remained to a large degree, autarkic, except to a limited degree in the case of Japan's Co-Prosperity Sphere. See McNeill, *Pursuit of Power*, 353; Milward, *War, Economy and Society*, 52; and Giddens, *Nation-State and Violence*, 240.

104. McNeill, *Pursuit of Power*, 356.

105. Giddens, *Nation-State and Violence*, 240; also see Clark, *Globalization and Fragmentation*, 115. This is not say that nationalism and the nation-state were principles that were abandoned in the post-war period, for it is more accurate to say that the war promoted both nationalism and internationalism, creating some of the main problems of the latter half of the twentieth century. See Clark, *Globalization and Fragmentation*, 117.

106. John Gerard Ruggie, 'International Regimes, Transactions, and Change: Embedded Liberalism in the Postwar Economic Order', *International Organization* Vol. 36 (1982): 195–231. Clark's discussion of the 'broker state' is also in line with this account. See Clark, *Globalization and International Relations Theory*, 62–5. Also see Robert Latham, *The Liberal Moment: Modernity, Security, and the Making of Postwar International Order* (New York: Columbia University Press, 1997).

107. Simon Dalby, 'Contesting an Essential Concept: Reading the Dilemmas in Contemporary Security Discourse', in Keith Krause and Michael C. Williams (eds), *Critical Security Studies: Concepts and Cases* (London: UCL Press, 1997), 21. Yergin notes that the term 'national security' had only become utilized in policymaking circles during the 1940s. Daniel Yergin, *Shattered Peace: The Origins of the Cold War and the National Security State* (Boston: Houghton Mifflin, 1977), 194–5.

108. McSweeeny, *Security, Identity and Interests*, 28.

109. In a sense it was peculiar, after the relative failure of the nation-state in the inter-war period.

110. The claim of interdependence is common in the globalization literature, but is also becoming more common in the historical literature on the Cold War. For examples of both, see Clark, *Globalization and Fragmentation*, ch. 6; Geir Lundestad, 'The American "Empire" 1945–1990', in *The American 'Empire'* (Oxford: Oxford University Press, 1990); and Held et al., *Global Transformations*.

111. G. John Ikenberry, *After Victory: Institutions, Strategic Restraint, and the Rebuilding of Order After Major Wars* (Princeton, NJ: Princeton University

Press, 2001); Latham, *Liberal Moment*; Dani Rodrik, 'Sense and Nonsense in the Globalization Debate', *Foreign Policy* No. 107 (Summer 1997): 19–36; and Ruggie, 'International Regimes'.

112. The comparison between contemporary globalization and the structures of empires is quite important in this context. See Niall Ferguson, *Empire* (London: Penguin, 2003); and Hopkins, *Globalization in World History*. Barkawi also gives a more specific argument about the transnational organization of military force that has been present for much of world history: Barkawi, *Globalization and War*.

113. For some accounts from a variety of standpoints, see Andrew Bacevich, *American Empire: The Realities and Consequences of US Diplomacy* (Cambridge: Harvard University Press, 2002); Ian Clark, *The Post-Cold War Order: The Spoils of Peace* (Oxford: Oxford University Press, 2001); James E. Cronin, *The World the Cold War Made* (London: Routledge, 1996); Ikenberry, *After Victory*, ch. 6; and John Gerard Ruggie, *Winning the Peace: America and World Order in the New Era* (New York: Columbia University Press, 1996).

114. See Fred Halliday, 'The Cold War as Inter-Systemic Conflict: Initial Theses', in Mike Bowker and Robin Brown (eds), *From Cold War to Collapse: Theory and World Politics in the 1980s* (Cambridge: Cambridge University Press, 1993).

115. For accounts of these debates see Robert Jervis, 'Realism, Neoliberalism and Cooperation: Understanding the Debate', *International Security* Vol. 42, No. 1 (Summer 1999): 42–63; Robert Keohane, 'International Institutions: Two Approaches', *International Studies Quarterly* Vol. 32 (December 1989): 379–96; and James G. March and Johan P. Olsen, 'The Institutional Dynamics of International Political Orders', *International Organization* Vol. 52, No. 4 (1998): 943–69. The overall view taken here is more in line with the 'historical institutionalism', exemplified by the work of Ikenberry. See Ikenberry, *After Victory*, ch. 1.

116. For an account of the development of Bretton Woods, see Fred L. Block, *The Origins of International Economic Disorder* (London: University of California Press, 1977), ch. 2. For more on the specifics of the arrangements, with some detailed evaluations, see Barry Eichengreen, *Globalizing Capital: A History of the International Monetary System* (Princeton, NJ: Princeton University Press, 1996), ch. 4, especially 96–102.

117. See Ikenberry's description of the competing ideas for the post-war order between the State Department, the economic planners (and Keynesian 'new dealers'), and their equivalents in Britain. G. John Ikenberry, 'Creating Yesterday's New World Order: Keynesian "New Thinking" and the Anglo-American Postwar Settlement', in Judith Goldstein and Robert O. Keohane (eds), *Ideas and Foreign Policy* (Ithaca, NY: Cornell University Press, 1993), 66.

118. Of course this is a simplification: the various twists and turns in the world economy did not necessitate a 'victory' for liberal internationalism. The main point is that despite changes and problems within the global political economy, the institutionalization of the liberal, internationalist global economy remained (and remains) intact. Succinct overviews of the Cold War global political economy in the context of globalization can be found in: Clark, *Globalization and Fragmentation*, ch. 7; Eichengreen, *Globalizing Capital*, chs 4–5; and Held et al., *Global Transformations*, chs 3–5.

119. Townsend Hoopes and Douglas Brinkley, *FDR and the Creation of the United Nations* (New Haven, CT: Yale University Press, 1997).
120. All of which are spelt out in Chapter I of the UN Charter.
121. Ikenberry, *After Victory*, 41. Also see Robert B. McCalla, 'Nato's Persistence after the Cold War', *International Organization* Vol. 50, No. 3 (1996): 445–75; and Paul W. Schroeder, 'Alliances, 1815–1945: Weapons of Power and Tools of Management', in Klaus Knorr (ed.), *Historical Dimensions of National Security Problems* (Lawrence: University Press of Kansas, 1975), 227–63.
122. Ikenberry, *After Victory*, 233–9. Also see the accounts in Thomas Risse-Kappen, 'Collective Identity in a Democratic Community: The Case of NATO', in Peter J. Katzenstein (ed.), *The Culture of National Security* (New York: Columbia University Press, 1996), 357–99; and Michael C. Williams and Iver B. Neumann, 'From Alliance to Security Community: NATO, Russia, and the Power of Identity', *Millennium* Vol. 29, No. 2 (2000): 357–87.
123. On the UN's post-Cold War record, see Michael W. Doyle, 'War Making and Peace Making: The United Nations' Post-Cold War Record', in Crocker, Hampson and Aall, *Turbulent Peace* (Washington, DC: United States Institute of Peace Press, 2001). On the UN's contemporary role, see Adam Roberts and Benedict Kingsbury (eds), *United Nations, Divided World*, 2nd ed. (Oxford: Clarendon Press, 1993); and Thomas G. Weiss, David P. Forsythe and Roger A. Coate, *The United Nations and Changing World Politics*, 3rd ed. (Boulder, CO: Westview Press, 2001).
124. For the decision to expand in the context of US foreign policy, see James M. Goldgeier, *Not Whether but When: The U.S. Decision to Enlarge NATO* (Washington, DC: Brookings, 1999). For NATO's new role see Williams and Neumann, 'From Alliance to Security Community'; and David S. Yost, 'The New NATO and Collective Security', *Survival* Vol. 40, No. 2 (1998): 135–60.
125. Paul Cornish, 'NATO: The Practices and Politics of Transformation', *International Affairs* Vol. 80, No. 1 (2004): 63–74; Astri Suhrke, 'A Contradictory Mission?: NATO from Stabilization to Combat in Afghanistan', *International Peacekeeping* Vol. 15, No. 2 (2008): 214–36.
126. G. John Ikenberry, 'Institutions, Strategic Restraint, and the Persistence of American Postwar Order', *International Security* Vol. 23, No. 3 (1998): 54–7.
127. John Lewis Gaddis, *We Now Know: Rethinking Cold War History* (Oxford: Oxford University Press, 1997), 39; Charles S. Maier, 'Alliance and Autonomy: European Identity and U.S. Foreign Policy Objectives in the Truman Years', in Michael J. Lacey (ed.), *The Truman Presidency* (Cambridge: Cambridge University Press, 1989), 273–98, 273–6; and Bruce Cumings, 'Still the American Century', *Review of International Studies* Vol. 25, special issue (1999): 271–99.
128. Lundestad, 'The American "Empire"', 39.
129. Ikenberry, 'Persistence of Postwar Order', 65. Also see Cumings, 'Still the American Century', 285–90.
130. There is of course some question of whether American international legitimacy is being eroded due to the perceived flaunting of international order under the Bush administration. For a useful account, see Robert W. Tucker and David C. Hendrickson, 'The Sources of American Legitimacy', *Foreign Affairs* Vol. 83, No. 6 (2004): 18–32.

131. The revisionist literature is well represented by William Appleman Williams, *The Tragedy of American Diplomacy*, new ed. (New York: W. W. Norton, 1988); and Gabriel Kolko and Joyce Kolko, *The Limits of Power: The World and United States Foreign Policy, 1945–1954* (New York: Harper & Row, 1972). Bacevich has also noted the work of Charles Beard, which predated the Cold War, effectively arguing for the expansionary nature of US foreign policy, starting with the Spanish-American War: Bacevich, *American Empire*, ch. 2. For some of the problems with this scholarship, see Geir Lundestad, 'Moralism, Presentism, Exceptionalism, Provincialism, and Other Extravagances in American Writings on the Early Cold War Years', in *The American 'Empire'* (Oxford: Oxford University Press, 1990), 11–29.

132. See, particularly, John Lewis Gaddis, *The United States and the Origins of the Cold War 1941–1947* (New York: Columbia University Press, 1972). For commentary on the radical tradition in Cold War analysis, see Michael Cox, 'Radical Theory and the Cold War', in Mike Bowker and Brown, *From Cold War to Collapse* (Cambridge: Cambridge University Press, 1993).

133. Lundestad, 'The American "Empire"', 31–115; Gaddis, *We Now Know*, especially chs 2 and 3. The use of empire to discuss US foreign policy has become even more pronounced in analysing President Bush's foreign policy. For overviews see Michael Cox, 'The Empire's Back in Town: or America's Imperial Temptation – Again', *Millennium* Vol. 23, No. 1 (2003): 1–27; Bryan Mabee, 'Discourses of Empire: The U.S. "Empire", Globalisation and International Relations', *Third World Quarterly* Vol. 25, No. 8 (2004): 1359–78; and Stein Tønnesson, 'The Imperial Temptation', *Security Dialogue* Vol. 35, No. 3 (2004): 329–43.

134. Fred Halliday, *The Making of the Second Cold War*, 2nd ed. (London: Verso, 1986), 81.

135. See the accounts in: Hobsbawm, *Age of Extremes*, ch. 12; and Gabriel Kolko, *Confronting the Third World: United States Foreign Policy 1945–1980* (New York: Pantheon, 1988); and Odd Arne Westad, *The Global Cold War* (Cambridge: Cambridge University Press, 2005).

136. Tarak Barkawi and Mark Laffey, 'The Imperial Peace: Democracy, Force and Globalization', *European Journal of International Relations* Vol. 5, No. 1 (1999): 414.

137. For a discussion of this point, see McNeill, *Pursuit of Power*, ch. 10.

138. Barkawi and Laffey, 'The Imperial Peace', 410. Also see Mohammed Ayoob, *The Third World Security Predicament: State Making, Regional Conflict, and the International System* (Boulder, CO: Lynne Rienner Publishers, 1995), 95–100; and K. J. Holsti, 'The Coming Chaos? Armed Conflict in the Periphery', in John Hall and T. V. Paul (eds), *International Order and the Future of International Relations* (Cambridge: Cambridge University Press, 1999), 291.

139. Adam Watson, *The Limits of Independence: Relations Between States in the Modern World* (London: Routledge, 1997), 81.

140. Latham, *Liberal Moment*, 5.

2 Globalization and Security

1. For examples, see Thomas Friedman, *The Lexus and the Olive Tree* (New York: HarperCollins, 2000); Ohmae, *The Borderless World*; and Joseph E. Stiglitz, *Globalization and its Discontents* (Harmondsworth: Penguin, 2003).

2. Compare the following: Richard Falk, *Predatory Globalization: A Critique* (Cambridge: Polity Press, 1999); Hirst and Thompson, *Globalization in Question*; Andrew Hurrell and Ngaire Woods, 'Globalisation and Inequality', *Millennium* Vol. 24, No. 3 (1995): 448–54; Stephen D. Krasner, *Sovereignty: Organized Hypocrisy* (Princeton, NJ: Princeton University Press, 1999); James H. Mittelman, *The Globalization Syndrome: Transformation and Resistance* (Princeton, NJ: Princeton University Press, 2000); James N. Rosenau, 'The Dynamics of Globalization: Toward an Operational Formulation', *Security Dialogue* Vol. 27, No. 3 (1996): 247–62; Jan Aart Scholte, 'Beyond the Buzzword: Towards a Critical Theory of Globalisation', in Elenore Kofman and Gillian Youngs (eds), *Globalisation: Theory and Practice* (London: Pinter, 1997); Strange, *Retreat of the State*; Michael Talalay, Chris Farrands and Roger Tooze (eds), *Technology, Culture, and Competitiveness: Change and the World Economy* (London: Routledge, 1997); Kenneth N. Waltz, 'Globalization and American Power', *The National Interest* No. 59 (Spring, 2000): 46–56; Martin Wolf, *Why Globalization Works* (New Haven, CT: Yale University Press, 2005).
3. Scholte, *Globalization*, 1.
4. For good overviews of the literature, see Clark, *Globalization and International Relations Theory*; Held et al., *Global Transformations*; Hirst and Thompson, *Globalization in Question*; and Jan Aart Scholte, *Globalization: A Critical Introduction*, 2nd ed. (London: Palgrave, 2005).
5. See the discussion in Robert Keohane, 'Introduction: From Interdependence and Institutions to Globalization and Governance', in *Power and Governance in Partially Globalized World* (London: Routledge, 2002).
6. Held et al., *Global Transformations*, provides the most comprehensive analysis of the phenomenon.
7. Scholte, 'Beyond the Buzzword', 46.
8. John Gerard Ruggie, 'Territoriality and Beyond: Problematizing Modernity in International Relations', *International Organization* Vol. 47 (1993): 172.
9. This has been well analysed by Justin Rosenberg, in two publications: Justin Rosenberg, *The Follies of Globalization Theory* (London: Verso, 2001); and Rosenberg, 'Globalization Theory', 2–74. Also see the debate surrounding Rosenberg's article: 'Debate: Rosenberg and Globalization', *International Politics* Vol. 42, No. 3 (2005): 353–99.
10. For more see Rosenberg, 'Globalization Theory'; Saskia Sassen, 'From Internationalism to De-Nationalization?: Thinking About the *Manifesto* Today', *Constellations* Vol. 6, No. 2 (1999): 244–8.
11. For example, see Anthony Giddens, *The Consequences of Modernity* (Cambridge: Polity, 1990); and Scholte, *Globalization*.
12. Giddens, *Consequences*, 63.
13. Giddens, *Consequences*, 139.
14. The division of sources of power here is drawn from Mann, and will be discussed further below. Such changes are also underpinned by facilitative technology. Technology plays a large role in many accounts of globalization, many of which are too heavily deterministic, as if technological development existed outside of society. See Michael Talalay, 'Technology and Globalization', in Randall Germain (ed.), *Globalization and Its Critics: Perspectives from Political Economy* (New York, St Martin's Press, 1999), 204–22.

15. For an interesting account along these lines, see Colin Hay, 'Globalisation as a Problem of Political Analysis: Restoring Agents to a "Process without a Subject" and Politics to a Logic of Economic Compulsion', *Cambridge Review of International Affairs* Vol. 15, No. 3 (2002): 379–92.
16. Robertson, *Globalization*, 8.
17. Scholte, *Globalization*, 73.
18. Ulrich Beck, *What is Globalization?* (Cambridge: Polity, 2000), 10. There are more examples: Giddens: 'the reflexivity of modern social life consists in the fact that social practices are constantly examined in the light of incoming information about those very practices, thus constitutively altering their character.' [*Consequences*, 38]; Shaw: 'social relations become global ... when they are significantly and systematically informed by an awareness of the common framework of worldwide human society.' [Martin Shaw, *Theory of the Global State: Globality as an Unfinished Revolution* (Cambridge: Cambridge University Press, 2000), 12]. Cf. Albrow, *Global Age.*
19. The cultural view is most clear in the work of Robertson.
20. Held et al., *Global Transformations*, 28.
21. Mann's approach is developed in Mann, *Sources of Social Power, Vols I and II.* This is not to say that Mann is beyond criticism, but the overall framework he has developed is extremely useful for analysing globalization, and is very much in line with the neo-Weberian account of the state given in the previous chapter. For some excellent critical discussion of Mann, see the contributions to John A. Hall and Ralph Schroeder (eds), *An Anatomy of Power: The Social Theory of Michael Mann* (Cambridge: Cambridge University Press, 2006).
22. Mann, *Sources Vol. I*, 2.
23. Mann, *Sources Vol. I*, 3.
24. Mann, *Sources Vol. I*, 7–9.
25. See generally, Mann, *Sources Vol. I*, 22–8; and Mann, *Sources Vol. II*, 6–10.
26. Mann, *Sources Vol. II*, 7. Also see the critiques from Hobson and Reus-Smit, who both believe Mann's approach to 'ideas' is too 'materialist'. Hobson, 'Mann, the State and War', 120–40.
27. Mann, *Sources Vol. I*, 25.
28. As stated in the previous chapter, distinguishing between political and military power seems more historically accurate, not to mention analytically useful than collapsing the two which has been the Weberian convention. However, Poggi, for one, has criticized the distinction, noting that states always use forms of coercive power to achieve ends. Gianfranco Poggi, 'Political Power Un-manned: A Defence of the Holy Trinity from Mann's Military Attack', in Hall and Schroeder, *Anatomy of Power.* Mann's response to this criticism is also endorsed here, which is that military power is about more than coercion, but the organization of forms of 'lethal violence'. Michael Mann, 'The Sources of Social Power Revisited: A Response to Criticism', in Hall and Schroeder, *Anatomy of Power*, 351. Cf. Giddens, *Nation-State and Violence.*
29. Mann, *Sources Vol. I*, 26.
30. The importance of this to International Relations theorizing has been stressed by Hobson. See John M. Hobson, 'The Historical Sociology of the State and the State of Historical Sociology in International Relations', *Review of International Political Economy* Vol. 5, No. 2 (1998): 287–9.
31. Mann, *Sources Vol. II*, 2.

32. Mann, *Sources Vol. II*, 9.
33. Mann, *Sources Vol. II*, 10.
34. Mann, *Sources Vol. I*, 16.
35. The real strength of Mann's conceptualization is that it stakes out a middle ground between permanent flux and permanent stability.
36. Cf. David Singh Grewal, *Network Power: The Social Dynamics of Globalization* (New Haven, CT: Yale University Press, 2008).
37. Collins, 'Mann's Transformation'.
38. Mann, *Sources Vol. II*, 11.
39. Michael Mann, 'Has Globalisation Ended the Rise and Rise of the Nation-State?', *Review of International Political Economy* Vol. 4, No. 3 (1997): 475. Also see Charles Tilly, 'International Communities, Secure or Otherwise', in Emanuel Adler and Michael Barnett (eds), *Security Communities* (Cambridge: Cambridge University Press, 1998).
40. Mann, 'Globalisation', 476.
41. Mann, 'Globalisation', 481.
42. See generally, Mann, *Sources Vol. II*, chs 4–7.
43. The following is roughly derived from some of Mann's initial formulations of globalization, and my own analyses using his IEMP model. Mann has examined globalization in a few recent writings: Mann, 'Globalization'; and Mann, 'Globalization and September 11'.
44. For good overviews see Jeffry A. Frieden, *Global Capitalism: Its Rise and Fall in the Twentieth Century* (New York: W. W. Norton, 2006); Eichengreen, *Globalizing Capital*; and Eric Helleiner, *States and the Reemergence of Global Finance: From Bretton Woods to the 1990s* (Ithaca, NY: Cornell University Press, 1994).
45. See the discussion in Mark Rupert, *Ideologies of Globalization* (London: Routledge, 2000), especially ch. 3.
46. For example, Louis J. Pauly and Simon Reich, 'National Structures and Multinational Corporate Behaviour: Enduring Differences in the Age of Globalization', *International Organization* Vol. 51, No. 1 (1997): 1–30.
47. Ankie Hoogvelt, *Globalisation and the Postcolonial World: The New Political Economy of Development* (London: Palgrave, 2001); Ray Kiely, *The New Political Economy of Development: Globalization, Imperialism, Hegemony* (London: Palgrave, 2006); Kiely, 'United States Hegemony and Globalisation'; Mann, 'Globalization and September 11'.
48. For general accounts see Held et al., *Global Transformations*; and Scholte, *Globalization*.
49. Held et al., *Global Transformations*; also see Anne-Marie Slaughter, *A New World Order* (Princeton, NJ: Princeton University Press, 2005).
50. See Barkawi, *Globalization and War* . This is discussed in more detail below.
51. Mann, *Sources Vol. II*.
52. Mann posits consumerism and liberal humanism as well. Mann, 'Globalization and September 11'.
53. The tension between these is argued by Benjamin J. Barber, *Jihad Vs. McWorld: How Globalism and Tribalism are Reshaping the World* (New York: Ballantine Books, 1996).
54. For an account of the tensions between liberalism and religion as global ideologies, see Fiona Adamson, 'Global Liberalism Versus Political Islam: Competing

Ideological Frameworks in International Politics', *International Studies Review* Vol. 7, No. 4: 547–69.

55. Again drawing us back to the tension between nationalism and internationalism, or globalization and fragmentation, as indicated in the previous chapter. See Clark, *Globalization and Fragmentation*.

56. However, this interpretation will also be disputed in the rest of the study. Also see Barkawi's critical discussion of this matter in Barkawi, *Globalization and War*. There have also been some recent attempts to examine the regional governance of security, which fit in with ideas about globalization: see Elke Krahmann, 'Conceptualizing Security Governance', *Cooperation and Conflict* Vol. 38, No. 1 (2003): 5–26; and Mark Webber et al., 'The Governance of European Security', *Review of International Studies* Vol. 30, No. 1 (2004): 3–26.

57. See for example Booth, 'Security and Emancipation'; Ken Booth, *Theory of World Security* (Cambridge: Cambridge University Press, 2007); Keith Krause and Michael C. Williams (eds), *Critical Security Studies* (London: UCL Press, 1997); Smith, 'Mature Anarchy, Strong States, and Security'; J. Ann Tickner, 'Re-visioning Security', in Ken Booth and Steve Smith (eds), *International Relations Theory Today* (London: Polity, 1995), 173–97; Richard Wyn Jones, ' "Travel Without Maps": Thinking About Security After the Cold War', in M. Jane Davis (ed.), *Security Issues in the Post-Cold War World* (Cheltenham, UK: Edward Elgar, 1996), 196–218.

58. The analytic purchase of the argument is not meant to deride the normative claims of the critical security studies agenda, but to show ways in which these dynamics are inherent in the historical constitution (or crystallization) of state power.

59. Buzan, *People, States, and Fear*, 18.

60. Buzan, *People, States, and Fear*, 38.

61. It should be noted that Buzan would likely disagree with this. As he further states, 'the link between individual and national security is anyway so partial that variations in the latter should not be expected to produce immediate or dramatic variations in the state as a whole'. Buzan, *People, States, and Fear*, 51. This does in fact relate to a larger historical question about the *kind* of state Buzan is describing, which is more akin to the nation-state.

62. See, for example, Giddens, *Consequences*; David Harvey, *The Condition of Postmodernity: An Inquiry into the Origins of Cultural Change* (Oxford: Blackwell, 1989); Robertson, *Globalization*; Scholte, *Globalization*.

63. See, for example, Albrow, *Global Age*; Robertson, *Globalization*; and Shaw, *Global State*.

64. This view is quite clear in works on economic transnationalism; see, for example, Rodney Bruce Hall and Thomas J. Biersteker (eds), *The Emergence of Private Authority in Global Governance* (Cambridge: Cambridge University Press, 2002). However, broader approaches have also noted this; see Held et al., *Global Transformations*, ch. 1; David Held and Anthony McGrew (eds), *Governing Globalization: Power, Authority and Global Governance* (Cambridge: Polity, 2002); Thomas Risse-Kappen (ed.), *Bringing Transnational Relations Back In* (Cambridge: Cambridge University Press, 1995); James Rosenau and Ernst-Otto Czempiel (eds), *Governance without Government: Order and Change in World Politics* (Cambridge: Cambridge University Press, 1992); Shaw, *Global*

State; and Rorden Wilkinson and Steve Hughes (eds), *Global Governance: Critical Perspectives* (London: Routledge, 2002).
65. Rogers, *Losing Control*.
66. Booth has noted this as well, though his focus is on the marginalized area of peace studies, and other radical approaches to the problems of military force. Ken Booth, 'Security and Self: Reflections of a Fallen Realist', in Keith Krause and Michael C. Williams (eds), *Critical Security Studies: Concepts and Cases* (London: UCL Press, 1997), 87. For a further discussion of the development of the expansion agenda, in its various guises, see McSweeney, *Security, Identity and Interests* .
67. Richard Crockatt, *The Fifty Years War* (London: Rouledge, 1995), 302.
68. Robert O. Keohane and Joseph S. Nye, *Power and Interdependence: World Politics in Transition* (Boston, MA: Little Brown, 1977). Also see Richard Rosecrance, *The Rise of the Trading State: Commerce and Conquest in the Modern World* (New York: Basic Books, 1986).
69. Of course, there has long been a connection between military power and economic issues, but the revival of the economic also entailed a different conception of interstate relations, one where states were further enmeshed in each others' actions. On the historical link between economics and military power, see Edward Meade Earle, 'Adam Smith, Alexander Hamilton, Friedrich List: The Economic Foundations of Military Power', in Peter Paret (ed.), *Makers of Modern Strategy: From Machiavelli to the Nuclear Age* (Princeton, NJ: Princeton University Press, 1986), 217–61. Also see Michael Mastanduno, 'Economics and Security in Statecraft and Scholarship', *International Organization* Vol. 52, No. 4 (1998): 825–54.
70. See Mazower, *Dark Continent*, ch. 10. Also see Kennedy, *Rise and Fall of the Great Powers*.
71. Samuel Huntington, 'The Clash of Civilizations?', *Foreign Affairs* Vol. 72, No. 3, 22–49; Francis Fukuyama, 'The End of History', *The National Interest* No. 16 (Summer 1989): 3–18; and Francis Fukayama, *The End of History and the Last Man* (Harmondsworth: Penguin, 1992). Cf. John Mearsheimer, 'Back to the Future: Instability in Europe After the Cold War', *International Security* Vol. 15, No. 1 (1990): 5–56.
72. For an overview, see Christopher Coker, *Globalisation and Insecurity in the Twenty-first Century: NATO and the Management of Risk*, Adelphi Paper 345 (Oxford: Oxford University Press, 2002), ch. 3; and Rogers, *Losing Control*, ch. 5.
73. Rogers, *Losing Control*, ch. 3. Also see Chapter 3 below.
74. Some perspectives on this issue can be found in Buzan, Waever and de Wilde, *Security*, ch. 6; Christopher Rudolph, 'Globalization and Security: Migration and Evolving Conceptions of Security in Statecraft and Scholarship', *Security Studies* Vol. 13, No. 1 (2003): 1–32; Christopher Rudolph, 'Security and the Political Economy of International Migration', *American Political Science Review* Vol. 97, No. 4 (2003): 603–20; Saskia Sassen, 'The De Facto Transnationalizing of Immigration Policy', in *Globalization and Its Discontents* (New York: The New Press, 1998), 5–30; Saskia Sassen, *Losing Control?: Sovereignty in an Age of Globalization* (New York: Columbia University Press, 1996), ch. 3; Waever et al., *Identity, Migration and the New Security Agenda in Europe*; and Myron Weiner, *The Global Migration Crisis* (New York: HarperCollins, 1995). Also see Chapter 5 below.

75. For some perspectives on this aspect, see Buzan, Waever and de Wilde. *Security*, ch. 4; Held et al., *Global Transformations*, ch. 8; and Rogers, *Losing Control*, ch. 5.
76. Coker, *Globalisation and Insecurity*, 60. For more on risk and globalization, see Ulrich Beck, *World Risk Society* (Cambridge: Polity, 1999); Giddens, *Consequences*.
77. Malcolm Waters, *Globalization* (London: Routledge, 1995), 3.
78. Buzan, *People, States, and Fear*, 331.
79. Held et al., *Global Transformations*, 126.
80. Kirchner and Sperling provide an interesting empirical analysis of how states respond to global threats in: Emil J. Kirchner and James Sperling (eds), *Global Security Governance: Competing Conceptions of Security in the 21st Century* (London: Routledge, 2007).
81. 'Security community' here is meant in the formal sense indicated in the literature, and is more specific than the usage of 'community of security' above. For a good survey, see Emanuel Adler and Michael Barnett (eds), *Security Communities* (Cambridge: Cambridge University Press, 1998); for an analysis of NATO as a security community, see Risse-Kappen, 'Collective Identity'. For a brief analysis of the concept of security communities, see Emanuel Adler and Michael Barnett, 'Security Communities in Theoretical Perceptive', in Adler and Barnett, *Security Communities*.
82. Emanuel Adler and Michael Barnett, 'A Framework for the Study of Security Communities', in Adler and Barnett, *Security Communities*, 30–1.
83. For an analysis along these lines, see James Goldgeier and Michael McFaul, 'A Tale of Two Worlds: Core and Periphery in the Post-Cold War Era', *International Organization* 46: 467–92. Cf. Barkawi and Laffey, 'The Imperial Peace', 403–34.
84. Alexander Wendt, 'Collective Identity Formation and the International State', *American Political Science Review* Vol. 88, No. 2 (1994): 384–96.
85. For example, see Andrew Linklater, 'The Transformation of Political Community: E. H. Carr, Critical Theory and International Relations', *Review of International Studies* Vol. 23, No. 3 (1997): 321–38.
86. See Chris Brown, *International Relations Theory: New Normative Approaches* (Hemel Hempstead: Harvester Wheatsheaf, 1992).
87. Such a divide is substantively played out in the arguments over humanitarian intervention, particularly the division between 'solidarists' and 'pluralists'. For a good overview and analysis: Wheeler, *Saving Strangers*.
88. Rogers, *Losing Control*.
89. Michael MccGwire, 'The Paradigm that Lost Its Way', *International Affairs* Vol. 77, No. 4 (2001): 777–803; and Michael MccGwire, 'Shifting the Paradigm', *International Affairs* Vol. 78, No. 1 (2002): 1–28.
90. As Blair stated, 'just as within domestic politics, the notion of community – the belief that partnership and co-operation are essential to advance self-interest – is coming into its own; so it needs to find its own international echo. Global financial markets, the global environment, global security and disarmament issues: none of these can be solved without intense international co-operation.' Tony Blair, 'The Doctrine of the International Community', Speech to the Economic Club of Chicago, 22 April 1999.

91. Krahmann, 'Conceptualizing Security Governance'. Cf. Anne-Marie Slaughter, 'The Real New World Order', *Foreign Affairs* Vol. 76, No. 5 (1997): 183–97.
92. Governance is juxtaposed with government in terms of the structure of authority. Government is seen as hierarchical, and in terms of exclusive authority, which is exemplified by the state. Governance is seen as being characterized by diffused authority, or overlapping networks of authority. For further discussion, see Held and McGrew *Governing Globalization*; John Pierre (ed.), *Debating Governance: Authority, Steering and Democracy* (Oxford: Oxford University Press, 2000); and R. A. W. Rhodes, 'The New Governance: Governing Without Government', *Political Studies* XLIV (1996): 652–67.
93. Clark, *Globalization and International Relations Theory*, ch. 6; Held et al., *Global Transformations*, ch. 2; Kaldor, *New and Old Wars*.
94. Clark, *Globalization and International Relations Theory*, 108–9. For more on the 'transnationalisation of legitimate violence', see Mary Kaldor, 'Reconceptualizing Organized Violence', in Daniele Archibugi, David Held and Martin Kohler (eds), *Re-imagining Political Community: Studies in Cosmopolitan Democracy* (Cambridge: Polity, 1998), 91–110; and Kaldor, *New and Old Wars*, ch. 1.
95. The example of NATO, discussed in detail in the previous chapter, is one example of this, which blurs the boundaries of an international and trans-national organization for military power. See, for example, Daniel Deudney and G. John Ikenberry, 'The Nature and Sources of Liberal International Order', *Review of International Studies* Vol. 25 (1999): 183; Held et al., *Global Transformations*, 125; Ruggie, *Winning the Peace*, 44–5.
96. Ian Hurd, 'Legitimacy and Authority in International Politics', *International Organization* Vol. 53, No. 2 (1999): 379–408.
97. Hall and Biersteker, *Private Authority in Global Governance*, Part IV.
98. For an overview, see Halliday, *Making of the Second Cold War*, ch. 4; and Kolko, *Confronting the Third World*.
99. Andrew J. Bacevich and Eliot Cohen (eds), *War over Kosovo* (New York: Columbia University Press, 2002); and Wheeler, *Saving Strangers*. For an interesting dissenting view, see David Chandler, 'International Justice', *New Left Review* (II) 6 (November/December 2000): 55–66.
100. Waters, *Globalization*, 122.
101. Mann, *Sources Vol. I*, 16.
102. The account of 'process' follows the usage in: Charles Tilly, 'Mechanisms in Political Processes', *Annual Review of Political Science* Vol. 4 (2001): 21–41.
103. Keohane and Nye, *Power and Interdependence*.
104. Shaw, *Global Society*, 111.
105. Mann, *Sources Vol. I*, 7–8.
106. Weiss, *Powerless State*, ch. 1.
107. Philip G. Cerny, 'Paradoxes of the Competition State: The Dynamics of Political Globalization', *Government and Opposition* Vol. 32 (1997): 251–74.
108. For more on 'scale shift' as a mechanism, see Doug McAdam, Sidney Tarrow and Charles Tilly, *Dynamics of Contention* (Cambridge: Cambridge University Press, 2001).
109. There is a voluminous literature on global governance. Good overviews can be found in: Held et al., *Global Transformations*; Held and McGrew,

Governing Globalization; Rosenau and Czempiel, *Governance without Government*; Slaughter, *A New World Order*; and Wilkinson and Hughes, *Global Governance*.

110. For transnational social movements and global civil society, see Joseph Camilleri and Jim Falk, *The End of Sovereignty* (Aldershot: Edward Elgar, 1992); Richard Falk, 'Evasions of Sovereignty', in R. B. J. Walker and S. H. Mendlovitz (eds), *Contending Sovereignties: Redefining Political Community* (Boulder, CO: Lynne Rienner, 1990), 61–78. McAdam, Tilly and Tarrow have discussed ways in which 'contentious politics' found in transnational activism can lead to scale shift: McAdam, Tarrow and Tilly, *Dynamics of Contention*; and Sidney Tarrow, *The New Transnational Activism* (Cambridge: Cambridge University Press, 2005).

111. For examples, see 'Production and Security'; Leo Panitch, 'The New Imperial State', *New Left Review* (II) 2 (March/April 2000): 5–20; Leo Panitch, 'Rethinking the Role of the State', in James H. Mittleman (ed.), *Globalization: Critical Reflections* (Boulder, CO: Lynne Rienner, 1996), 83–113. For a critique, see Shaw, *Global State*, 84–90.

112. Discussion of a global or world state has mainly been derided in IR, but there are two very strong analyses of the possibility: Shaw, *Global State*; and Alexander Wendt, 'Why a World State is Inevitable', *European Journal of International Relations* Vol. 9, No. 4 (2003): 491–542.

113. Wendt, 'Collective Identity Formation'.

114. Shaw, *Global State*, 190.

115. Shaw, *Global State*, 199.

116. Held et al., *Global Transformations*, 143.

117. Robert Cooper, 'Grand Strategy', *Prospect*, December 2002.

118. Clark, *Globalization and International Relations Theory*, 107–8.

119. For an excellent discussion of the changing nature of the legitimacy of organized violence, see Anna Leander, *Conditional Legitimacy, Reinterpreted Monopolies: Globalisation and the Evolving State Monopoly on Legitimate Violence*, COPRI Working Paper No. 10, 2002.

120. For example, looking at specific forms of linkage between social sites, such as states and global institutions, and the forms of mechanisms causing changes or durability in such linkages.

3 Nuclear Weapons and the Globalization of Threat

1. For example, Barkawi, *Globalization and War*; Held et al., *Global Transformations*, ch. 2; Kaldor, *New and Old Wars*; and Shaw, *New Western Way of War*.

2. Herz, 'Rise and Demise of the Territorial State'. These themes were expanded upon in his later book, *International Politics in the Atomic Age* (New York: Columbia University Press, 1959).

3. Herz, *International Politics*, 41.

4. John Herz, 'The Territorial State Revisited – Reflections on the Future of the Nation-State', in *The Nation-State and the Crisis of World Politics* (New York: David McKay Company, 1976), 226–52. As Herz himself notes, there were several authors who did take an interest in his standpoint. For notable examples,

see Raymond Aron, *Peace and War* (New York: Doubleday, 1966), 395–403; and Klaus Knorr, *On the Uses of Military Power in the Nuclear Age* (Princeton, NJ: Princeton University Press, 1966), 83–4, 174.

5. See, for example, Richard J. Harknett, 'Territoriality in the Nuclear Era', in Elenore Koffman and Gillian Youngs (eds), *Globalisation: Theory and Practice* (London: Pinter, 1996), 138–49; and Daniel Deudney, 'Political Fission: State Structure, Civil Society, and Nuclear Security Politics in the United States', in Ronnie D. Lipschutz (ed.), *On Security* (New York: Columbia University Press, 1995), 87–123. Deudney's modified 'nuclear one-worldism' is also close to an approach to nuclear weapons that touches on globalization, if not explicitly. See Deudney, 'Political Fission', 90–2; and Daniel Deudney, 'Nuclear Weapons and the Waning of the Real-State', *Daedalus* Vol. 124 (1995): 209–31.

6. See, for example, Jervis, *Nuclear Revolution*; and Mandelbaum, *The Nuclear Revolution*.

7. See Herz, 'The Territorial State Revisited', 234–8. Jervis has noted this as part of his analysis of the nuclear revolution. See Jervis, *Nuclear Revolution*, 29–35.

8. Bernard Brodie, 'Implications for Military Policy', in Bernard Brodie (ed.), *The Absolute Weapon: Atomic Power and World Order* (New York: Harcourt, Brace, 1946), 76.

9. For examples of the former, see Robert Jervis, *The Illogic of American Nuclear Strategy* (Ithaca, NY: Cornell University Press, 1984). For the latter, see McGeorge Bundy et al., 'Nuclear Weapons and the Atlantic Alliance', *Foreign Affairs* (Spring 1982): 753–68.

10. For perspectives on nuclear strategy at the end of the Cold War, see the essays in John Baylis and Robert O'Neill (eds), *Alternative Nuclear Futures: The Role of Nuclear Weapons in the Post-Cold War World* (Oxford: Oxford University Press, 2000); and Eric Herring, 'The Decline of Nuclear Diplomacy', in Ken Booth (ed.), *New Thinking about Strategy and International Security* (London: HarperCollins, 1991), 90–109.

11. For Missile Defence see Charles L. Glaser and Steve Fetter, 'National Missile Defense and the Future of U.S. Nuclear Weapons Policy', *International Security* Vol. 26, No. 1 (Summer 2001): 40–92. For preponderance, see Keir A. Lieber and Daryl G. Press, 'The End of MAD? The Nuclear Dimension of U.S. Primacy', *International Security* Vol. 30, No. 4 (2006): 7–44.

12. Sagan discusses a number of reasons why states develop nuclear weapons, including more symbolic rationales: Scott D. Sagan, 'Why Do States Build Nuclear Weapons? Three Models in Search of a Bomb', *International Security* Vol. 21, No. 3 (1996/97): 64–86. For a detailed analysis of India, see David Kinsella and Jugdep S. Chima, 'Military Industrialization and Public Discourse in India', *Review of International Studies* Vol. 27, No. 3 (2001): 353–74.

13. The wider changes inaugurated by the advent of the atomic bomb has been well documented by Beatrice Heuser, *The Bomb: Nuclear Weapons in their Historical, Strategic and Ethical Context* (Edinburgh Gate, Essex: Pearson Education, 2000). Also see McGeorge Bundy, *Danger and Survival* (New York: Random House, 1988).

14. State leaders and policymakers, of course, also recognized the revolutionary nature of the weaponry, though often in a contradictory fashion, oscillating

between ideas of revolution and ideas of conventionalism. For an excellent overview, see John Lewis Gaddis et al. (eds), *Cold War Statesmen Confront the Bomb: Nuclear Diplomacy since 1945* (Oxford: Oxford University Press, 1999).

15. Bernard Brodie (ed.), *The Absolute Weapon: Atomic Power and World Order* (New York, 1946); Jervis has a good discussion of Brodie's influence: see Jervis, *Nuclear Revolution*, ch. 2.

16. Brodie, 'Implications for Military Policy', 71. Also see Thomas Schelling, *Arms and Influence* (New Haven, CT: Yale University Press, 1966).

17. Jervis, *Nuclear Revolution*, 6. Also see Mandelbaum, *Nuclear Revolution*, 14.

18. Jervis, *Nuclear Revolution*, 15.

19. On the idea of friction, see Martin Shaw, *Dialectics of War* (London: Pluto, 1988), 15–17; Michael Howard, *Clausewitz* (Oxford: Oxford University Press, 1983), ch. 4.

20. Carl von Clausewitz, *On War*, ed. and trans. Peter Paret and Michael Howard (Princeton, NJ: Princeton University Press, 1976), 79. Noted by Howard, *Clausewitz*, 70. Rapoport has discussed some of the issues related to the application of Clausewitz to the nuclear era. See Anatol Rapoport, introduction to *On War*, by Carl von Clausewitz (Harmondsworth: Penguin, 1982), 65–9.

21. Wohlstetter has distinguished between these two aspects. See Albert Wohlstetter, 'Bishops, Statesmen, and Other Strategists on the Bombing of Innocents', *Commentary*, June 1983, 21–2.

22. For an overview, see David MacIssac, 'Voices from the Central Blue: The Air Power Theorists', in Peter Paret (ed.), *Makers of Modern Strategy: From Machiavelli to the Nuclear Age* (Princeton, NJ: Princeton University Press, 1986), especially 629–35; and R. J. Overy, 'Air Power and the Origins of Deterrence Theory Before 1939', *Journal of Strategic Studies* Vol. 15, No. 1 (1992): 73–101.

23. For discussions of nuclear weapons in the context of total war, see Kaldor, *New and Old Wars*, 24–30; Latham, 'Re-imagining Warfare', 213–18; and Shaw, *Dialectics of War*, 38–46. For discussions of the development of total war, see Bond, *War and Society*, ch. 6; Howard, *War in European History*, chs 7 and 8; and Richard Overy, 'Total War II: The Second World War', in Charles Townshend (ed.), *The Oxford History of Modern War* (Oxford: Oxford University Press, 2000), 138–57.

24. Brodie, *Strategy in the Missile Age*.

25. Barry Buzan, *An Introduction to Strategic Studies: Military Technology and International Relations* (London: St Martin's Press, 1986), 159–60; Lawrence Freedman, *The Evolution of Nuclear Strategy*, 2nd ed. (London: Macmillan, 1989), ch. 25.

26. Henry A. Kissinger, 'The Unsolved Problems of European Defense', *Foreign Affairs* Vol. 40, No. 4 (July 1962): 526. See Jervis for more comments on the problems of the conventional war-fighting ideas: Jervis, *Nuclear Revolution*, 19.

27. For example, Jervis, *Nuclear Revolution*.

28. On this distinction, see Shaw, *Dialectics of War*, 38.

29. Mandelbaum is an exception to this, as his work draws historical parallels between other changes in military organization, though his study of the impacts on society is limited. See Mandelbaum, *Nuclear Revolution*. The latter problem is well attested to by the dearth of writing on the impact

of nuclear weapons on polity and society, outside of the constraints of the superpower relationship. For an exception, see McNeill, *Pursuit of Power*, ch. 10. Also see the analysis in Creveld, *Rise and Decline of the State*, 337–54.

30. Herz, *International Politics*, 169.
31. On the concept of risk, see Ulrich Beck, *Risk Society: Towards a New Modernity* (London: Sage, 1992); Beck, *What is Globalization?*; and Giddens, *Consequences*.
32. Henry Kissinger, 'Coalition Diplomacy in a Nuclear Age', *Foreign Affairs* Vol. 42, No. 4 (July 1964): 531.
33. John Lewis Gaddis, 'The Insecurities of Victory: The United States and the Perception of Soviet Threat After World War II', in *The Long Peace* (Oxford: Oxford University Press, 1987), 24.
34. Gaddis, 'Insecurities', 24; cf. Melvyn Leffler, 'The American Conception of National Security and the Beginnings of the Cold War', *American Historical Review* Vol. 89, No. 2 (1984): 346–81.
35. The Triad refers to the pursuit of nuclear deterrence through the three-fold combination of ICBMs, Submarine Launched Ballistic Missiles (SLBMs), and nuclear armed long-range bombers.
36. Henry Kissinger, *Nuclear Weapons and Foreign Policy* (London: Oxford University Press, 1957).
37. Herz, *International Politics*, 210.
38. Herz, *International Politics*, 168.
39. Harknett, 'Territoriality in the Nuclear Era', 142.
40. The effects of nuclear weapons on territoriality has also been well analysed by van Creveld in his study of the decline of the state, though not in the terms envisaged by Herz. See van Creveld, *Rise and Decline of the State*, 337–54.
41. This point is seen in the importance arms control played during the Cold War in maintaining parity of weapons to ensure that the superpower relationship remained stable. Arms control, and the doctrine of deterrence that surrounded it, was therefore meant to maintain the contemporary strategic (and political) balance. See the account of arms control in Buzan, *Introduction to Strategic Studies*, ch. 16.
42. Herz, 'Territorial State Revisited'. Herz mainly connects this 'retrenchment' with the problems of extended deterrence, the end of empire and the rise of nationalism and self-determination of nations.
43. For examples, see Giddens, *Consequences*, 75, 124–6; Held et al., *Global Transformations*, 87; Poggi, *The State*, 174–7; Scholte, *Globalization*, 115. Virillio's meditations of the future of military force have some connections to this as well. See, for example, Paul Virilio and Sylvie Lotringer, *Pure War*, trans. Mark Polizzotti (New York: Semiotext(e), 1983).
44. Giddens, *Consequences*, 126.
45. Held et al., *Global Transformations*, 87.
46. Bundy, *Danger and Survival*.
47. Albert Wohlstetter, 'Nuclear Sharing: Nato and the N+1 Country', *Foreign Affairs* Vol. 39, No. 2 (1961): 385.
48. Kenneth N. Waltz, 'Review of Robert Jervis, *The Illogic of American Strategy*', *Political Science Quarterly* Vol. 100, No. 4 (1986–7): 699.
49. Campbell Craig has also persuasively argued for nuclear weapons to have created paradoxes in post-Second World War realists' views on international security. See Campbell Craig, *Glimmer of a New Leviathan: Total War in the*

Realism of Niebuhr, Morgenthau, and Waltz (New York: Columbia University Press, 2003).

50. Colin S. Gray, *Modern Strategy* (Oxford: Oxford University Press, 1999), 302–6.
51. Rapoport, *On War*, 413.
52. As Jervis points out, 'the denial of the adversary's aims that was possible in the past entailed the protection of the state. The fact that the two effects are now severed, the ease with which each superpower can punish the other, the fact that such punishment does not depend on gaining military advantage, and the overwhelming nature of the destruction that is possible, all conspire drastically to alter the role of force between the superpowers.' Jervis, *Nuclear Revolution*, 13.
53. John Lewis Gaddis, 'The Long Peace: Elements of Stability in the Postwar International System', *International Security* Vol. 10, No. 4 (1986): 99–142. Further examples can be found in: Robert Jervis, 'The Political Effects of Nuclear Weapons: A Comment', *International Security* Vol. 13, No. 2 (1988): 80–90; and Kenneth Waltz, 'Nuclear Myths and Political Realities', *American Political Science Review* Vol. 84, No. 3 (1990): 731–45.
54. Barkawi and Laffey, 'The Imperial Peace', 403–34.
55. For example, Buchan points out three options for future Atlantic relations, all of which were in play at some point. Alastair Buchan, 'Multilateral Force: An Historical Perspective', *International Affairs* Vol. 40, No. 4 (1964): 619–37.
56. Kissinger, 'Coalition Diplomacy', 530.
57. One useful early analysis of this phenomenon can be found in Alistair Buchan, *NATO in the 1960s: Implications of Interdependence*, rev. ed. (London: Chatto and Windus, 1963).
58. An example of the importance of this can be seen in Stromseth's overview of the role of nuclear weapons in the NATO alliance in the 1960s. Jane Stromseth, *The Origins of Flexible Response: NATO's Debate over Strategy in the 1960s* (New York: St Martin's Press, 1988), ch. 2.
59. Wohlstetter, 'Nuclear Sharing', 386.
60. Buzan, *Introduction to Strategic Studies*, 152.
61. John Baylis, 'The Evolution of NATO Strategy, 1949–1990', in Colin McInnes, *Strategy After the Cold War* (London: Routledge, 1992), 99.
62. Marc Trachtenberg, 'The Nuclearization of NATO and U.S. – West European Relations', in *History and Strategy* (Princeton, NJ: Princeton University Press, 1991), 165.
63. Shaun Gregory, *Nuclear Command and Control in NATO: Nuclear Weapons Operations and the Strategy Of Flexible Response* (Basingstoke: Macmillan, 1996), 15.
64. On this aspect of changing state power see Clark, *Globalization and International Relations Theory*, 108–9. For more in the context of NATO, see Deudney and Ikenberry, 'Nature and Sources', 44–5.
65. For more on 'empire', see Chapter 1. There has not been much comment about how nuclear weapons fit into the 'empire' concept. For one interesting analysis that focuses primarily on international class conflict, see Mike Davis, 'Nuclear Imperialism and Extended Deterrence', in *Exterminism and Cold War, New Left Review* (London: Verso, 1982), especially 52–60. For some commentary on this approach to analysing the Cold War, see Halliday, *Making of the Second Cold War*, 28–30.

66. Herz, *International Politics*, 177.
67. It is interesting, in this context, that the primary aim of NATO in the post-Cold War period has been about expansion, an extension of the 'Atlantic community'. This has led NATO to move away from emphasizing its military role in the Cold War, to stressing its important cultural and political factors in creating unity. It indicates that, on some level, NATO was always about building a community. On this point, see Williams and Neumann, 'From Alliance to Security Community'. For a sceptical view on the expansive role of NATO, see Richard Rupp, 'NATO 1949 and NATO 2000: From Collective Defense Toward Collective Security', *Journal Of Strategic Studies* Vol. 23, No. 3 (2000): 154–76.
68. Kissinger, 'Coalition Diplomacy', 527.
69. The US certainly opposed this view, believing the more allies that had nuclear weapons under independent control, the more uncertain deterrence would be.
70. For accounts of the British and French approaches to nuclear strategy, see Beatrice Heuser, *NATO, Britain, France, and the FRG: Nuclear Strategies and Forces for Europe, 1949–2000* (Basingstoke: Macmillan, 1997), chs 3 and 4.
71. In this context, the British–US 'special relationship' consisted of a highly interdependent relationship, with the British relying on US technical assistance to maintain its 'independent' deterrent, while the US gained British policy support for its foreign policy decisions. See the analysis in Ian Clark, *Nuclear Diplomacy and the Special Relationship* (Oxford: Oxford University Press, 1994), 8–12.
72. See Hogan, *A Cross of Iron*.
73. Sherry, *In the Shadow of War*, 138
74. Richard J. Aldrich (ed.), *Espionage, Security and Intelligence in Britain 1945–1970* (Manchester: Manchester University Press, 1998), 1–2.
75. Peter Hennessy, *The Secret State: Whitehall and the Cold War* (London: Penguin, 2003).
76. Herz, *International Politics*, 13.
77. Mandelbaum, *Nuclear Revolution*, 4. Giddens makes some interesting criticisms on this kind of perspective, that people do not tend to worry about high-level, low-probability risks in the manner that Mandelbaum is claiming, because it is generally put at the level of fate, something that is out of the reach of action and is therefore not worth dwelling upon at great length. Giddens, *Consequences*, 132–3. As he states, 'the greater the danger, measured not in terms of probability of occurrence but in terms of its generalised threat to human life, the more thoroughly counterfactual it is. The risks involved are necessarily "unreal", because we could only have a clear demonstration of them if events occurred that are too terrible to contemplate.' Giddens, *Consequences*, 134. Russett's overview of public opinion on nuclear weapons policy in the United States is interesting in this context, as it points to the ways in which the fear of nuclear war was indeed perceived in the population at large, but in a manner that impacted on policy, and less on challenging the legitimacy of the state. See Bruce Russett, 'Democracy, Public Opinion, and Nuclear Weapons', in Philip E. Tetlock et al. (eds), *Behavior, Society, and Nuclear War, Vol. 1* (Oxford: Oxford University Press, 1989), 192–8.

78. Jervis, *Nuclear Revolution*, 182. This also has resonance in the arguments surrounding 'existential' deterrence, which was a reassertion of the 'revolutionary' approach to nuclear weapons: that the very idea of the possibility of their use would stop actors from using them. Jervis, *Illogic*.
79. Tickner, 'Re-visioning Security', 177.
80. Buzan, *People, States and Fear*, 49.
81. For example, Deudney and Harknett have both used Herz's arguments to assist their thinking about the role of nuclear weapons and their affects on territoriality and society.
82. Deudney, 'Political Fission', 99.
83. Deudney, 'Political Fission', 92.
84. Knopf's study dealing with the effects of the nuclear freeze movement on US policy provides some evidence that this may have been the case. Jeffrey W. Knopf, *Domestic Society and International Cooperation: The Impact of Protest on US Arms Control Policy* (Cambridge: Cambridge University Press, 1998).
85. See Heuser, *NATO, Britain, France, and the FRG*, chs 3 and 4.
86. Freedman, *Evolution*, 313.
87. Clark, *Nuclear Diplomacy*, 10; Freedman, *Evolution*, 307–12.
88. Deudney, 'Political Fission', 99.
89. This is Deudney's example. See Deudney, 'Political Fission', 104.
90. Deudney, 'Political Fission', 102–4. Lack of information has been one of the prime problems that has plagued public perceptions of nuclear weapons policy. For example, Russett notes that in the early 1980s, a majority of Americans favoured a policy of no first use of nuclear weapons, but that 81 per cent of those polled thought that the United States already had a policy of no first use. Russett, 'Democracy, Public Opinion, and Nuclear Weapons', 192. This points to the continued problem of the lack of information disseminated to the public about nuclear strategy, which is summed up by Russett in his critique of the way discussions of C^3I improvement were kept out of the public sphere, though it was in this area that public knowledge was perhaps most important. See Russett, 'Democracy, Public Opinion, and Nuclear Weapons', 198–200.
91. Philip K. Lawrence, *Modernity and War: The Creed of Absolute Violence* (London: Macmillan, 1997), 93.
92. Lawrence, especially ch. 5. Also see Scott Kirsch, 'Watching the Bombs Go Off: Photography, Nuclear Landscapes, and Spectator Democracy', *Antipode* Vol. 29, No. 3 (1997): 227–55.
93. Guy Oakes, *The Imaginary War: Civil Defense and American Cold War Culture* (Oxford: Oxford University Press, 1994).
94. For an overview of US policy on targeting, see Desmond Ball, *Targeting for Strategic Deterrence*, Adelphi Papers 185 (London: International Institute for Strategic Studies, 1983).
95. Ian Clark, *Waging War: A Philosophical Introduction* (Oxford: Oxford University Press, 1988), 99.
96. Clark, *Waging War*, 101.
97. Clark, *Waging War*, 101; Jervis, *Nuclear Revolution*, 117.
98. Ball, *Targeting for Strategic Deterrence*, 32. He further notes that despite this, population targeting was inevitably part of US strategic plans, as an element of the countervailing strategy. Ball, *Targeting for Strategic Deterrence*, 33.

99. For a discussion, see Jervis, *Illogic*, 66–72.
100. For criticism see Clark, *Waging War*, 102–3; Jervis, *Illogic*, chs 3 and 4.
101. Russett points out that American support of disarmament developed gradually throughout the Cold War period, and the popularity with which Reagan's SDI program was received was a recognition of the unpopularity of the system of deterrence, however unfeasible SDI was. Russett, 'Democracy, Public Opinion, and Nuclear Weapons', 195–6.
102. Quoted in Jervis, *Nuclear Revolution*, 52.
103. Quoted in Freedman, *Evolution*, 48.
104. Martin Shaw, *Post-Military Society: Militarism, Demilitarization and War at the End of the Twentieth Century* (Cambridge: Polity, 1991).
105. Michael Mann, 'The Roots and Contradictions of Modern Militarism', in *States, War and Capitalism* (Cambridge: Blackwell, 1988), 166–87.
106. The recent revival in the US of a missile defence programme, with all of its flaws, demonstrates the frustration with the old system of deterrence. For an overview of US NMD policy, see Leon Fuerth, 'Return of the Nuclear Debate', *Washington Quarterly* Vol. 24, No. 4 (Autumn 2001), 97–108; and Glaser and Fetter, 'National Missile Defense'.
107. Ruggie, 'Territoriality and Beyond', 139–74.

4   The Security State and the Globalization of the Arms Industry

1. Stephen Brooks' excellent book is a recent exception: Stephen Brooks, *Producing Security: Multinational Corporations, Globalization, and the Changing Calculus of Conflict* (Princeton, NJ: Princeton University Press, 2005).
2. Trevor Taylor, 'Defence Industries in International Relations', *Review of International Studies* Vol. 16, No. 1 (1990): 59–73.
3. Recent overviews can be found in: Deborah Avant, *The Market for Force* (Cambridge: Cambridge University Press, 2005); Robert Mandel, *Armies Without States: The Privatization of Security* (Boulder, CO: Lynne Rienner, 2002); and P. W. Singer, *Corporate Warriors: The Rise of Privatized Military Industry* (Ithaca, NY: Cornell University Press, 2003).
4. For more on this distinction, see Eric Fredland and Adrian Kendry, 'The Privatisation of Military Force: Economic Virtues, Vices and Government Responsibility', *Cambridge Review of International Affairs* Vol. 13, No. 1 (1999): 147–64.
5. See UK Ministry of Defence, *Defence Industrial Policy*, MOD Policy Papers no. 5 (London: HMSO, 2002), 11.
6. Giddens, *Nation-State and Violence*, 120.
7. Keith Hayward, 'The Globalisation of Defence Industries', *Survival* Vol. 43, No. 2 (2001): 116. Cf. David Held, Anthony McGrew, David Goldblatt and Jonathan Perraton, *Global Transformations: Politics, Economics and Culture* (Cambridge: Polity, 1999), 143. Also see Tilly, 'War Making and State Making'.
8. See, for example: Giddens, *Nation-State and Violence*; Mann, *Sources of Social Power, Vol. II*; Tilly, 'War Making'.
9. For an overview, see Earle, 'Adam Smith, Alexander Hamilton, Friedrich List'.

10. As Smith stated: 'If any particular manufacture was necessary, indeed, for the defence of the society, it might not always be prudent to depend upon our neighbours for the supply; and if such manufacture could not otherwise be supported at home, it might not be unreasonable that all the other branches of industry should be taxed in order to support it.' Adam Smith, *An Inquiry into the Nature and Causes of the Wealth of Nations,* ed. Edwin Cannan (London: Methuen, 1904), accessed 29 November 2006 from: Library of Economics and Liberty, www.econlib.org/LIBRARY/Smith/smWN15.html. For more details, see Earle, 'Economic Foundations'.

11. Janice E. Thomson, *Mercenaries, Pirates and Sovereigns* (Princeton, NJ: Princeton University Press, 1994); and Singer, *Corporate Warriors,* ch. 2; and Avant, 'From Mercenary to Citizen Armies', 41–72.

12. For overviews, see Keith Krause, *Arms and the State: Patterns of Military Production and Trade* (Cambridge: Cambridge University Press, 1992), ch. 2; McNeill, *Pursuit of Power,* 102–16; and Andrew Moravcsik, 'Arms and Autarky in European History', *Daedalus* (Fall 1991): 24. It should be noted here that the prime difference between this historical era and the present is that the current focus is on the internationalization and globalization of *production,* and not just *trade.* However, the existence of an international market in arms does have important parallels with the contemporary situation, especially since transnationalization tends to foster the diffusion of military technologies in a similar fashion, with similar consequences.

13. Held et al., *Global Transformations,* 116; Krause, *Arms and the State,* 56–61; McNeill, *Pursuit of Power,* ch. 7; Clive Trebilcock, '"Spin Off" in British Economic History: Armaments and Industry 1760–1914', *Economic History Review* Vol. 22, No. 3 (1969): 474–90.

14. Krause, *Arms and the State,* 55.

15. Clive Trebilcock, *The Industrialization of the Continental Powers 1780–1914* (London: Longman, 1981), 282.

16. McNeill, *Pursuit of Power,* ch. 7.

17. McNeill, *Pursuit of Power,* 224. The main difference was the post-Second World War complete domination of the system by two states: the Soviet Union and the United States. While the Soviet arms industry was entirely state-led, in the US there was still some level of autonomy, though initially heavily subsidized by the state. The contrast between Britain and the US is here interesting, with the US (initially, until about the 1970s) putting security ahead of economic interests, and Britain much more interested in commercial ties in order to find some niche market in order to maintain some autonomy in defence production *and* international politics. See Jeffrey A. Engel, *Cold War at 30,000 Feet* (Cambridge, MA: Harvard University Press, 2007).

18. Richard A. Bitzinger, 'The Globalization of the Arms Industry: The Next Proliferation Challenge', *International Security* Vol. 19, No. 2 (1994): 172.

19. Philip Gummett, 'National Preferences, International Imperatives and the European Defence Industry', in Philip Gummett (ed.), *Globalization and Public Policy* (Cheltenham, UK: Croom Helm, 1996), 143–4.

20. Elisabeth Sköns and Herbert Wulf, 'The Internationalization of the Arms Industry', *Annals of the American Academy of Political and Social Sciences* Vol. 535, No. 1 (September 1994): 43–57.

21. For example, see Bitzinger, 'Globalization'; Hayward, 'Globalisation'; Mary Kaldor, Ulrich Albrecht and Genevieve Schmeder (eds), *Restructuring the Global Military Sector, Volume II: The End of Military Fordism* (London: Pinter, 1998); Theodore Moran, 'The Globalization of America's Defense Industries', *International Security* Vol. 15, No. 1 (Summer 1990): 57–99; Sköns and Wulf, 'Internationalization'; Taylor, 'Defence Industries'.

22. Derek J. Neal and Trevor Taylor, 'Globalisation in the Defence Industry: An Exploration of the Paradigm for US and European Defence Firms and the Implications for Being Global Players', *Defence and Peace Economics* Vol. 12, No. 4 (2001): 349–53.

23. This is also referred to in the literature as 'secularization'. See Pierre De Vestel, *Defence Markets and Industries in Europe: Time for Political Decisions?* Challiot Papers no. 21 (Alencon, France: Institute for Security Studies, Western European Union, 1995), 20.

24. Bitzinger, 'Globalization', 181.

25. Held et al., *Global Transformations*; Michael Borrus and John Zysman, 'Industrial Competitiveness and American National Security', in Wayne Sandholtz et al. (eds), *The Highest Stakes: Technology, Economy, and America's Security Policy* (Oxford: Oxford University Press, 1992);, Steven Vogel, 'The Power Behind "Spin-ons": The Military Implications of Japan's Commercial Technology', in *The Highest Stakes*.

26. Hayward, 'Globalisation', 118.

27. 'Building a New Boeing', *The Economist* (12 August 2000): 83.

28. Andrew Latham, 'The Contemporary Restructuring of the US Arms Industry: Toward "Agile Manufacturing"', *Contemporary Security Policy* Vol. 18 (1997): 109–34.

29. John Lovering, 'Government–Company Relationships in the British Arms Industry: A New Era?', in Claude Serfati (ed.), *Government–Company Relationships in the Arms Industry: Between Change and Stability* (Brussels: European Commission, 2000), 18.

30. Moravcsik, 'Arms and Autarky', 41.

31. Cf. Brooks, *Producing Security.*

32. John Lovering, 'The Production and Consumption of the "Means Of Violence": Implications of the Reconfiguration of the State, Economic Internationalization, and the End of the Cold War', *Geoforum* Vol. 25, No. 4 (1994): 481.

33. Taylor, 'Defence Industries', 66.

34. Keohane and Nye, *Power and Interdependence*, 9.

35. Held et al., *Global Transformations*, 147.

36. For typical statements, see William R. Hawkins, 'Homeland Defense: National-Security Resources Should Not Be Manufactured in Foreign Lands', *National Review*, June 25, 2003; Moran, 'Globalization'; Wayne Sandholtz et al., *The Highest Stakes: Technology, Economy, and America's Security Policy* (Oxford: Oxford University Press, 1992).

37. Moran, 'Globalization', 57.

38. Borrus and Zysman, 'Industrial Competitiveness', 49.

39. Borrus and Zysman, 'Industrial Competitiveness', 7.

40. Borrus and Zysman, 'Industrial Competitiveness', 9.

41. Beverly Crawford, 'Hawks, Doves, but No Owls: International Economic Interdependence and Construction of the New Security Dilemma', in Ronnie D. Lipschutz (ed.), *On Security* (New York: Columbia University Press, 1995).
42. Crawford, 'Hawks, Doves, but No Owls', 151.
43. Moran, 'Globalization'.
44. Though Brooks makes a strong case for showing that US globalization was quite advanced in the 1980s; see Brooks, *Producing Security*, ch. 4.
45. This is especially the case at the level of subcontractors. See the diagram in US Department of Defense, Office of the Deputy Under Secretary of Defense (Industrial Policy), *Speech at Navy Gold Coast Conference, Ventura, California*, 7 October 2003.
46. Economist, 'Hands Across the Sea', *Economist* (7 July 2002), 65.
47. Bitzinger, *Towards*, 82.
48. Niccolo Machiavelli, *The Art of War*, ed. and trans. Christopher Lynch (Chicago, IL: University of Chicago Press, 2005). For a further discussion of Machiavelli's views on military matters, see Felix Gilbert, 'Machiavelli: The Renaissance of the Art of War', in Peter Paret (ed.), *Makers of Modern Strategy* (Princeton, NJ: Princeton University Press, 1986).
49. Exemplified in the development of global proliferation networks dealing with nuclear weapons. See the analysis in Alexander Montgomery, 'Ringing in Proliferation: How to Dismantle an Atomic Bomb Network', *International Security* Vol. 30, No. 2 (2005): 153–87.
50. Bitzinger, 'Globalization'; and W. W. Keller and J. E. Nolan, 'Mortgaging Security for Economic Gain: U.S. Arms Policy in an Insecure World', *International Studies Perspectives* Vol. 2, No. 2 (2001): 177–93.
51. For more on liberalism and globalization, see Rupert, *Ideologies of Globalization*.
52. Sköns, and Wulf, 'Internationalization', 43–57.
53. Economist, 'Arms Across the Sea', *The Economist* (3 February 2001): 64–5.
54. John J. Dowdy, 'Winners and Losers in the Arms Industry Downturn', *Foreign Policy* No. 107 (1997): 88–101; Elisabeth Sköns and Julian Cooper, 'Arms Production', *SIPRI Yearbook 1997*: 239–60.
55. For an account of trends in the 1990s, see Neal and Taylor, 'Globalisation', 340–5; and US Department of Defense, Office of the Deputy Under Secretary of Defense (Industrial Policy), *Transforming the Defense Industrial Base: A Roadmap* (February 2003). The example of the 1993 'last supper' for US defence contractors held by then Secretary of Defense Les Aspin is important example of the drastic change in environment. See Terrence Guay and Robert Callum, 'The Transformation and Future Prospects of Europe's Defence Industry', *International Affairs* Vol. 78, No. 4 (2002): 762, n10.
56. Anne Markusen, 'The Rise of World Weapons', *Foreign Policy* No. 114 (Spring 1999): 40–51. For advocacy of increased transatlantic cooperation (and a current overview), see Andrew D. James, 'European Military Capabilities, the Defense Industry and the Future Shape of Armaments Co-operation', *Defense and Security Analysis* Vol. 21, No. 1 (2005): 5–20.
57. Quoted in Economist, 'Arms Across the Sea', *The Economist* (3 February 2001).
58. Thomas Lansford, 'Security and Marketshare: Bridging the Transatlantic Divide in the Defense Industry', *European Security* Vol. 10, No. 1 (2001): 7.

59. See Economist, 'Europe gets a Defence Giant'. *The Economist* (16 October 1999).
60. On BAE's national mergers and other activities, see International Institute for Strategic Studies, *The Military Balance 1999–2000* (Oxford: Oxford University Press, 1999); M. Harrison, 'BAE and Marconi Merge to form £15bn Defence Giant', *The Independent* (London), 19 January 1999. On the JSF, see Ethan B. Kapstein, 'Capturing Fortress Europe: International Collaboration and the Joint Strike Fighter', *Survival* Vol. 46, No. 3 (2004): 137–60.
61. Neal and Taylor, 'Globalisation', 348, Fig. 1; Guay and Callum, 'Transformation', 760.
62. DoD, *Transforming the Defense Industrial Base*; Eugene Gholz and Harvey M. Sapolsky, 'Restructuring the US Defense Industry', *International Security* Vol. 24, No. 3 (Winter 1999/2000): 5–51; Neal and Taylor, 'Globalisation'.
63. DoD, *Transforming the Defense Industrial Base*.
64. There is some argument about the idea of 'tiers', but here refers, in line with Bitzinger, to states that are trying for degrees of autarky, but are in essence somewhat behind the leading edge of technology. Richard A. Bitzinger, *Towards a Brave New Arms Industry?*, Adelphi Paper 356 (Oxford: Oxford University Press, 2003), 6–7.
65. For an excellent overview of trends in the 'second tier', see Bitzinger, *Towards a Brave New Arms Industry?*
66. Lovering, 'Rebuilding the European Defence Industry', 219.
67. Lovering, 'Rebuilding the European Defence Industry', 227.
68. Dowdy, 'Winners and Losers', 99–101; Bryan Bender, 'USA Seeking Solutions to Globalisation Trend', *Jane's Defence Weekly*, 31 March 1999, 20.
69. The overall thrust of this policy was well spelt out in early writings, see, for example, Jacques Gansler, 'Transforming the U.S. Defence Industrial Base', *Survival* Vol. 35, No. 4 (1993–4): 130–46.
70. Jacques Gansler, *The Defense Industrial Structure in the 21st Century*, Speech at AIAA Acquisition Reform Conference, 27 January 2000.
71. The Bush Administration's continued push towards civilianization can be seen in a number of policies, for example in the 2001 QDR: US Department of Defense, *Quadrennial Defense Review Report 2001* (Washington: September 2001). An important statement can also be found in: DoD, *Transforming the Defense Industrial Base*.
72. De Vestel, *Defence Markets*, 37; and Lovering, 'Government–Company Relationships', 11–13.
73. Markusen, 'The Rise of World Weapons', 40–51.
74. For current British policy, see UK Ministry of Defence, *Defence Industrial Policy*.
75. Martin Edmonds, 'Defence Privatisation: From State Enterprise to Commercialism', *Cambridge Review of International Affairs* Vol. 13, No. 1 (1999): 114–19.
76. DoD, *QDR 2001*, 53. It should be noted that less emphasis was placed on this element in the 2006 report.
77. DoD, *QDR 2001*, 53–4.
78. Weiss's discussion of national strategies to cope with globalization is an excellent account of these differing approaches: see Linda Weiss, *The Myth of the Powerless State* (Ithaca, NY: Cornell University Press, 1998).

79. Goldgeier and McFaul, 'A Tale of Two Worlds', 467–92.
80. Karl W. Deutsch et al., *Political Community and the North Atlantic Area: International Organization in the Light of Historical Experience* (Princeton, NJ: Princeton University Press, 1957); Adler and Barnett (eds), *Security Communities.*
81. Barry Buzan and Eric Herring, *The Arms Dynamic in World Politics* (Boulder, CO: Lynne Rienner, 1998), 44.
82. Risse-Kappen, 'Collective Identity'; Wendt, 'Collective Identity Formation'.
83. Lovering, 'Production and Consumption of the "Means of Violence"', 471–86; and Shaw, *Theory of the Global State.*
84. Paul Cornish, *The Arms Trade and Europe* (London: Royal Institute of International Affairs, 1995); and Terrence Guay, *At Arm's Length: The European Union and Europe's Defence Industry* (London: Macmillan, 1998). See Cornish and Edwards for the development of a European 'strategic culture': Paul Cornish and Geoffrey Edwards, 'Beyond the NATO/EU Dichotomy: The Beginnings of an EU Strategic Culture', *International Affairs* Vol. 77, No. 3 (2001): 587–603.
85. De Vestel provides a very good account of the post-war situation, charting the gradual growth of the European industry, the development of European collaboration in order to compete with the US, and the development of national champions in the 1980s. De Vestel, *Defence Markets.* More recently, European governments are seeing the contest between competition and collaboration as a trade-off between a loss of marketshare versus loss of jobs; see Lansford, 'Security and Marketshare'.
86. Ethan B. Kapstein, 'Allies and Armaments', *Survival* Vol. 44, No. 2 (2002): 145. Gholz is sceptical of the poltical benefits of cooperation: Eugene Gholz, 'The Irrelevance of International Defense Industry Mergers', *Breakthroughs* (Spring 2000): 3–11.
87. The US, due to its pre-eminent position, has its own paradox concerning sharing technology: it wants to maintain the NATO alliance structure, but is reluctant to share technology which is needed both in material (i.e. interoperability) and ideational (i.e. demonstrating trust and partnership) terms.
88. See Kapstein, 'Capturing Fortress Europe'.
89. Taylor, 'Defence Industries', 72.
90. Markusen, 'The Rise of World Weapons', 41. Lovering has pointed out, with regard to the British example, why this cannot accurately be characterized as leaving defence procurement up to the market, as decisions are really made by a few players at BAE and GEC, with an eye to government policy. Lovering, 'Government–Company Relationships'.
91. Hayward, 'Globalisation'. More detail on specific cases outside of the US and Western Europe can be found in the following: Julian Cooper, 'Transforming Russia's Defence Industrial Base', *Survival* Vol. 35, No. 4 (1993–4): 147–62; Tim Huxley and Susan Willett, *Arming East Asia*, Adelphi Paper 329 (Oxford: Oxford University Press, 1999); Yudit Kiss, 'Defence Industry Consolidation in East Central Europe in the 1990s', *Europe–Asia Studies* Vol. 53, No. 4 (2001): 595–612; Antonio Sanchez Andris, 'Restructuring the Defence Industry and Arms Production in Russia', *Europe–Asia Studies* Vol. 52, No. 5 (2000): 897–914; Pjer Simunovic, 'Croatian Arms for Sale: The Evolution, Structure and Export Potential of Croatia's Defence Industry', *Contemporary Security Policy* Vol. 19, No. 3 (1998): 128–51.

92. Hayward, 'Globalisation'.
93. This is usually with regard to the US, which has been the primary supplier to the region – also as a consequence of its continued military presence in the region. See John Lovering and Ron Matthews, 'Defence Industry Restructuring in Pacific-Asia', in Mary Kaldor, Ulrich Albrecht and Genevieve Schmeder (eds), *Restructuring the Global Military Sector, Volume II: The End of Military Fordism* (London: Pinter, 1998), 258.
94. Buzan and Herring, *Arms Dynamic*, 45.
95. Brazil provides some evidence for the collapse and readjustment of arms industries due to globalization: see Bitzinger, *Towards a Brave New Arms Industry*, 41–4; and Ken Conca, 'Between Global Markets and Domestic Politics: Brazil's Military-Industrial Collapse', *Review of International Studies* Vol. 24, No. 4 (1998): 499–513.
96. The recent dispute over the granting of military contracts to a partnership of Northrop Gruman and Airbus over Boeing is a case in point. While the heated rhetoric of politicians concerned security (but mainly *economic* security for regions with aerospace industries), the Air Force just wanted a better product. See Dana Hedgpeth, 'A Foreign Air Raid?', *The Washington Post*, 4 March 2008, D01, accessed 4 March 2008 from: www.washingtonpost.com/wp-dyn/content/article/2008/03/03/AR2008030303194.html; and Peter Pae, 'Congress Likely to Examine Air Force Tanker Decision', *Los Angles Times*, 4 March 2008, accessed 4 March 2008 from: www.larimes.com/business/la-fi-tanker4march04,1,2367575.story?ctrack=1&cset=true
97. While not using this language, Brooks makes a strong argument for the difficulty of states withdrawing from the global system of defence production. See Brooks, *Producing Security*, ch. 4.
98. Hall and Biersteker, *Emergence of Private Authority*; Slaughter, *A New World Order*.
99. There are a number of excellent overviews, which can be found in: Abdel-Fatau Musah, 'A Country Under Siege: State Decay and Corporate Intervention in Sierra Leone', in Abdel-Fatau Musah and J. 'Kayode Fayemi, *Mercenaries: An African Security Dilemma* (London: Pluto Press, 2000); David J. Francis, 'Mercenary Intervention in Sierra Leone: Providing National Security or International Exploitation?', *Third World Quarterly* Vol. 20, No. 2 (1999): 319–38; Kevin O'Brien, 'Private Military Companies and African Security 1990–98', in Abdel-Fatau Musah and J. 'Kayode Fayemi (eds), *Mercenaries: An African Security Dilemma* (London: Pluto Press, 2000); and Mandel, *Armies without States*.

    That the use of PMCs raises serious issues in terms of accountability and legitimacy has been emphasized by the *Report by the UN Special Rapporteur on the Use of Mercenaries 1998*. The report indicated that 'hiring private companies providing security and military assistance and advice is no substitute for maintaining a collective regional security system and genuinely professional national armed security forces loyal to the democratic legal order'. 'The Report by the UN Special Rapporteur on the Use of Mercenaries 1998', in Musah and Fayemi, *Mercenaries*, 301.
100. Well described in Singer's account: Singer, *Corporate Warriors*.
101. Singer, *Corporate Warriors*, 151.
102. Shaw, *Post-Military Society*, especially ch. 5.

103. This is by no means a new phenomenon. In the fifteenth century, the development of private armies, that is, professional soldiers who worked for specific rulers, was of prime importance in the development of the Italian city states. See McNeill, *Pursuit of Power*, ch. 3.
104. Lovering, 'Production and Consumption of the "Means of Violence"', 481.

5   Global Migration, Security and Citizenship

1. William H. McNeill, 'Human Migration: A Historical Overview', in William McNeill and Ruth S. Adams (eds), *Human Migration: Patterns and Policies* (Bloomington, IN: Indiana University Press, 1978), 3.
2. Weiner, *Global Migration Crisis*, 25.
3. Weiner, *Global Migration Crisis*, 25.
4. Stephen Castles, and Mark J. Miller, *The Age of Migration: International Population Movements in the Modern World*, 2nd ed. (London: Macmillan, 1998), ch. 5.
5. Held et al., *Global Transformations*, 286.
6. Buzan, Waever and Wilde, *Security*; Jef Huysmans, *The Politics of Insecurity: Fear, Migration and Asylum in the EU* (London: Routledge, 2006).
7. James F. Hollifield, 'The Emerging Migration State', *International Migration Review* Vol. 38, No. 3 (2004): 887.
8. Fiona B. Adamson, 'Crossing Borders: International Migration and National Security', *International Security* Vol. 31, No. 1 (2006): 165–99; Peter Andreas, 'Redrawing the Line: Borders and Security in the Twenty-first Century', *International Security* Vol. 28, No. 2 (2003): 78–111; Huysmans, *Politics of Insecurity*; Rudolph, 'Security and International Migration'.
9. Hollifield, 'Migration State'.
10. Robin Cohen, 'Diasporas, the Nation-State, and Globalisation', in Wang Gungwu (ed.), *Global History and Migrations* (Boulder, CO: Westview, 1997), 117.
11. For an overview of migration theories, see Castles and Miller, *Age of Migration*, ch. 2.
12. Castles and Miller, *Age of Migration*, 24.
13. Castles and Miller, *Age of Migration*, 25.
14. Douglas T. Gurak and Fe Caces, 'Migration Networks and the Shaping of Migration Systems', in Mary M. Kritz, Lin Lean Lim, Hania Zlotnik (eds), *International Migration Systems: A Global Approach* (Oxford: Clarendon Press, 1992), 151.
15. For a discussion of these early forms of migration, see Castles and Miller, *Age of Migration*, ch. 3; and Lydia Potts, *The World Labour Market: A History of Migration* (London: Zed Books, 1990).
16. These are well described by Stephen Castles, 'Contract Labour Migration', in Robin Cohen (ed.), *The Cambridge Survey of World Migration* (Cambridge: Cambridge University Press, 1995); and Mark J. Miller, 'Evolution of Policy Modes for Regulating International Labour Migration', in *International Migration Systems*.
17. Castles and Miller, *Age of Migration*, 76–7.

18. The United Nations Population division defines these two regions as follows: More developed regions comprise all regions of Europe plus Northern America, Australia/New Zealand and Japan; Less developed regions comprise all regions of Africa, Asia (excluding Japan), Latin America and the Caribbean plus Melanesia, Micronesia and Polynesia. Population Division of the Department of Economic and Social Affairs of the United Nations Secretariat, *Trends in Total Migrant Stock: The 2005 Revision*, accessed Monday, 25 August 2008 from http://esa.un.org/migration

19. Mary Kritz and Hana Zlotnik, 'Global Interactions: Migration Systems, Processes, and Policies', in *International Migration Systems*, 4.

20. US Department of Labor, *The Effects of Immigration on the US Economy and Labor Market* (Washington, DC: US Government Printing Office, 1989), 5; cited in Castles and Miller, *Age of Migration*, 165–6.

21. For more details see OECD, *International Migration Outlook* (Paris: OECD, 2006), 42.

22. This is also reflected by the development of global cities, and the accompanying labour market segmentation. Sassen, for example, has argued that the development of such global cities as sites of capital accumulation has increased the need for secondary service industry labour that is primarily obtained through foreign labour. Much of the new globalized streams of migrants are to specific localities, signifying the importance of macro-networks developed by the global economy. Saskia Sassen, *The Global City: New York, London, Tokyo* (Princeton, NJ: Princeton University Press, 1991). Also see Castles and Miller, *Age of Migration*, 170–1; and Aristide Zolberg, 'The Next Waves: Migration Theory for a Changing World', *International Migration Review* Vol. 23, No. 3 (1989): 410.

23. Held et al., *Global Transformations*, 304. For more analysis, see OECD, *Trends in International Migration, Annual Report, 1998* (Paris: OECD, 1998).

24. Russell King, 'Migrations, Globalization and Place', in Doreen Massey and Pat Jess (eds), *A Place in the World?: Places, Culture and Globalization* (Oxford: Oxford University Press, 1995), 24. See the analysis in OECD, *Trends in International Migration* (Paris: OECD, 1999), 24.

25. Allan M. Findlay, 'Skilled Transients: The Invisible Phenomenon?', in *Cambridge Survey of World Migration*, 515.

26. Findlay, 'Skilled Transients', 515.

27. Overview in OECD, *International Migration Outlook*.

28. OECD, *Trends in International Migration 2004*.

29. Castles and Miller, *Age of Migration*, 150.

30. Giovanna Campani, 'Women Migrants: From Marginal Subjects to Social Actors', in Robin Cohen, ed., *Cambridge Survey of World Migration* (Cambridge: Cambridge University Press, 1995), 546.

31. King, 'Migrations, Globalization and Place', 18.

32. Held et al., *Global Transformations*, 314.

33. Monica Boyd, 'Family and Personal Networks in Migration', *International Migration Review* Vol. 23, No. 3 (1989): 641.

34. Helen Pellerin, 'Global Restructuring in the World Economy and Migration', *International Journal* Vol. 48, No. 2 (1993): 251.

35. Pellerin, 'Global Restructuring', 252.

36. Boyd, 'Family and Personal Networks', 651.

37. Boyd, 'Family and Personal Networks', 639. For an update, see OECD, *International Migration Outlook*, 140–61.

38. Boyd, 'Family and Personal Networks', 645.
39. Kritz and Zlotnik, 'Global Interactions', 4.
40. As Weiner notes, in the case of refugee communities, the acceptance of refugee claims provides an implicit condemnation of policies of the home country, which may create problems in foreign policy relations. Weiner, *Global Migration*, 137.
41. Weiner, *Global Migration*, 139.
42. See, for example, Andreas, 'Redrawing the Line'; Cronin, 'Behind the Curve'; Rudolph, 'Security and International Migration'; and John Tirman (ed.), *The Maze of Fear: Security and Migration after 9/11* (New York: Free Press, 2004).
43. Miller points out some of the problems associated with this view, primarily pointing to the difficulties of estimating the numbers of illegal migrants, and also with regard to the term 'illegal immigration' being a 'highly emotive and imprecise term'. Mark J. Miller, 'Illegal Migration', *Cambridge Survey of World Migration*.
44. For examples, see Gil Loescher, 'International Security and Population Movements', in *Cambridge Survey of World Migration*, 557; Stephen Castles, 'Globalization and Migration: Some Pressing Contradictions', *International Social Science Journal* Vol. 50, No. 156 (1998): 181; and Held et al., *Global Transformations*, 321.
45. Weiner, *Global Migration*, 142. For a discussion of political problems surrounding social costs in Europe in the early 1970s, see Paul White, 'International Migration in the 1970s: Revolution or Evolution?', in Allan Findlay and Paul White (eds), *West European Population Change* (Beckenham: Croom Helm, 1986), 60–6.
46. For recent discussions in IR, see Adamson, 'Crossing Borders'; Huysmans, *Politics of Insecurity*; and Rudolph, 'Security and International Migration'.
47. Waever, Buzan and Kelstrup, *Identity, Migration and the New Security Agenda in Europe*.
48. For example, see Castles and Miller, *Age of Migration*, chs 2 and 9.
49. See generally, Peter Andreas and Thomas J. Biersteker (eds), *The Rebordering of North America: Integration and Exclusion in a New Security Context* (New York: Routledge, 2003); Huysmans, *Politics of Insecurity*; Rudolph, 'Security and International Migration'; Tirman, *Maze of Fear*.
50. Zolberg, 'The Next Waves', 405.
51. Marshall, 'Citizenship and Social Class'.
52. Ulrich K. Preuss, 'Migration: A Challenge to Modern Citizenship', *Constellations* Vol. 4, No. 3 (1998): 312–14.
53. Preuss, 'Migration', 315.
54. Bart van Steenbergen, 'The Condition of Citizenship', in Bart van Steenbergen (ed.), *The Condition of Citizenship*, (London: Sage, 1994), 4.
55. Castles and Miller, *Age of Migration*, 39.
56. Martin O. Heisler and Zig Layton-Henry, 'Migration and the Links Between Social and Societal Security', in Waever et al., *Identity, Migration and the New Security Agenda in Europe*, 154.
57. These arguments are primarily discussed in Waever et al., *Identity, Migration and the New Security Agenda in Europe*, chs 2, 3 and 8; and Buzan, Waever and de Wilde, *Security*, ch. 6. Also see Adamson, 'Crossing Borders', 180–5; and Rudolph, 'Security and International Migration'.

58. Heisler and Leighton-Henry, 'Social and Societal Security', 162.
59. John Urry, 'Mediating Global Citizenship', *iichiko intercultural* Vol. 11 (June 1999): 1.
60. David Held, 'Democracy and the Global System', in David Held (ed.), *Political Theory Today* (Cambridge: Polity, 1991), 204.
61. Y. N. Soysal, *The Limits of Citizenship: Migrants and Postnational Membership in Europe* (Chicago, IL: University of Chicago Press, 1994), 3.
62. Urry, 'Mediating Global Citizenship', 3–4.
63. Urry, 'Mediating Global Citizenship', 4. Also see the plea for a globally oriented citizenship from Parekh: Bhikhu Parekh, 'Cosmopolitanism and Global Citizenship', *Review of International Studies* Vol. 29, No. 1 (2003): 3–17. For a critique of this cosmopolitan argument, see David Chandler, 'New Rights for Old?: Cosmopolitan Citizenship and the Critique of State Sovereignty', *Political Studies* Vol. 51, No. 2 (2003): 332–49.
64. Sassen, *Losing Control?*, 89.
65. Soysal, *Limits of Citizenship*, 41–4.
66. Population Division of the Department of Economic and Social Affairs of the United Nations Secretariat, *Trends in Total Migrant Stock: The 2005 Revision*.
67. Article 13 specifies that: i) 'everyone has the right to freedom of movement and residence within the borders of each state'; and 'everyone has the right to leave any country, including his own, and to return to his country'. Article 14 specifies that: i) 'everyone has the right to seek and to enjoy in other countries asylum from persecution'; ii) 'this right may not be invoked in the case of prosecutions genuinely arising from non-political crimes or from acts contrary to the purposes and principles of the United Nations'. United Nations, *Universal Declaration of Human Rights*, 1948.
68. Linda S. Bosniak, 'Human Rights, State Sovereignty and the Protection of Undocumented Migrants under the International Migrant Workers Convention', *International Migration Review* Vol. 25, No. 4 (1992): 740–1.
69. Castles and Miller, *Age of Migration*, 95.
70. Held, 'Democracy', 219. Held also gives the example of the Nuremberg Tribunal, which 'laid down, for the first time in history, that when *international rules* that protect basic humanitarian values are in conflict with *state laws*, every individual must transgress the state laws (except where there is no room for moral choice)'. Held, 'Democracy', 220.
71. Sassen, *Losing Control?*, 93.
72. Sassen, *Losing Control?*, 63.
73. Sassen, *Losing Control?*, 60–1.
74. Bosniak, 'Human Rights', 741.
75. Bosniak, 'Human Rights', 742.
76. Bosniak, 'Human Rights', 753. The European Union has split up policy-making jurisdiction over free movement and immigration. Free movement is regulated transnationally as part of EU law; however, immigration is still done on a national basis. Andrew Geddes, *Immigration and European Integration: Towards Fortress Europe?* (Manchester: Manchester University Press, 2000), 31.
77. For example, see Weiner, *Global Migration*, especially ch. 5; and Christopher Mitchell, 'International Migration, International Relations and Foreign Policy', *International Migration Review* 3 (1989): 681–708.

78. Mitchell, 'International Migration', 682.
79. Kritz and Zlotnik, 'Global Interactions', 14.
80. Zolberg, 'The Next Waves', 407.
81. Weiner, *Global Migration*, 119.
82. Weiner, *Global Migration*, 112.
83. Held et al., *Global Transformations*, 303.
84. See Castles and Miller, *Age of Migration*, 73–4; White, 'International Migration in the 1970s', 59.
85. Roxanne Lynn Doty, 'The Double-Writing of Statecraft: Exploring State Responses to Illegal Immigration', *Alternatives* Vol. 21 (1996): 171–89.
86. Andreas further argues that increases in border control fulfil a similar purpose, 'about recrafting the image of the border and symbolically reaffirming the state's territorial authority'. Peter Andreas, *Border Games* (Ithaca, NY: Cornell University Press, 2000), x.
87. Held et al., *Global Transformations*, 322.
88. Robin Cohen, 'Policing the Frontiers: The State and the Migrant in the International Division of Labour', in Jeffery Henderson and Manuel Castells (eds), *Global Restructuring and Territorial Development* (London: Sage, 1987), 90.
89. Castles, 'Contract Labour Migration', 510.
90. Miller, 'Evolution of Policy Modes', 305.
91. Castles, 'Contract Labour Migration', 511.
92. Miller, 'Evolution of Policy Modes', 306.
93. Castles, 'Contract Labour Migration', 511.
94. Cohen, 'Policing', 90–1.
95. Cohen, 'Policing', 91. Andreas provides a good overview of the issues involving the US–Mexico border: Andreas, *Border Games*, ch. 3.
96. For further discussion, see Castles, 'Contract Labour Migration'; Miller, 'Evolution of Policy Modes'; Rudolph, 'Security and International Migration'.
97. Jef Huysmans, 'The European Union and the Securitization of Migration', *Journal of Common Market Studies* Vol. 38, No. 5 (2000): 751–77.
98. Huysmans, 'EU and Securitization'.
99. Huysmans, 'EU and Securitization', 757.
100. For example, Sassen, *Losing Control*.
101. Rudolph, 'Security and International Migration'.
102. Doty, 'Double-Writing of Statecraft'.
103. Mark J. Miller, 'Illegal Immigration', in Robin Cohen, ed., *The Cambridge Survey of World Migration* (Cambridge: Cambridge University Press, 1995) 537; also see Bosniak, 'Human Rights', 744.
104. Kritz and Zlotnik, 'Global Interactions', 11.
105. Miller, 'Illegal Migration', 538.
106. Findlay, 'Skilled Transients', 521.
107. Andreas has also noted the tension between increased border security and the needs of the global economy: Andreas, 'Redrawing the Line'. For further discussion see, Adamson, 'Crossing Borders'; Bryan Mabee, 'Re-imagining the Borders of US Security after 9/11: Securitization, Risk and the Creation of the Department of Homeland Security', *Globalizations* Vol. 4, No. 3 (2007): 385–97; and Rudolph, 'Security and International Migration'.
108. For discussion of each, see, respectively: Danny Hakim, 'Clerks Balk at Proposal on Licenses', *New York Times*, 28 September 2007; Michael Cooper and Marc Santora, 'Topic of Immigration Animates Testy Republican

Debate', *International Herald Tribune*, 29 November 2007; Robert Pear and Carl Hulse, 'Immigrant Bill Dies in Senate; Defeat for Bush', *New York Times*, 29 June 2007.

109. Demetrios Papademetriou, 'International Migration in a Changing World', in C. W. Stahl (ed.), *International Migration Today: Volume 2: Emerging Issues* (Paris: UNESCO, 1988), 239.

110. Sassen, *Losing Control?*, 74.

111. Hollifield, 'Migration State'.

112. See Geddes, *Immigration*, ch. 2.

113. The OECD reports that much of this outside of the EU has been regulated though bilateral agreements. The example of the US–Canada 'Strategic Vision for Canada–US Border Co-operation', set up in 1997, is one example of such an agreement. OECD, *Trends in International Migration, Annual Report, 1999* (Paris: OECD, 1999).

114. Hollifield, 'Migration State'; Robert A. Pastor, 'North America's Second Decade', *Foreign Affairs* Vol. 83, No. 1 (2004): 124–35.

115. Nikolas Rose, 'The Death of the Social?: Refiguring the Territory of Government', *Economy and Society* Vol. 25, No. 3 (1996): 345. Quoted in: Urry, 'Mediating Global Citizenship', 2.

116. Sassen, *Losing Control?*, 95.

117. Ruggie, 'International Regimes'.

118. Rodrik, 'Sense and Nonsense', 27.

119. John Gerard Ruggie, 'At Home Abroad, Abroad at Home: International Liberalisation and Domestic Stability in the New World Economy', *Millennium* Vol. 24, No. 3 (1995): 524.

6 Conclusion: The Globalization of Security and the Future of the Security State

1. Wallander has noted that NATO is in effect a security institution, rather than an alliance. Celeste Wallander, 'NATO After the Cold War', *International Organization* Vol. 54, No. 4 (2000): 705–36.

2. See the essays in Hopkins, *Globalization in World History*.

3. For some different perspectives on the issue of hierarchy, see Jack Donnelly, 'Sovereign Inequalities and Hierarchy in Anarchy: American Power and International Society', *European Journal of International Relations* Vol. 12, No. 2 (2006): 139–70; John M. Hobson and J. C. Sharman, 'The Enduring Place of Hierarchy in World Politics: Tracing the Social Logics of Hierarchy and Political Change', *European Journal of International Relations* Vol. 11, No. 1 (2005): 63–98; David A. Lake, 'The New Sovereignty in International Relations', *International Studies Review* Vol. 5, No. 3 (2003): 303–23; Mabee, 'Discourses of Empire'; Daniel Nexon and Thomas Wright, 'What's at Stake in the American Empire Debate', *American Political Science Review* Vol. 101, No. 2 (2007): 253–71.

4. US moves towards unilateralism that characterized the approach to the invasion of Iraq have potentially destabilized some of these claims, which is much of the reason for a re-emergence of discussions of US empire. See, for example, Cox, 'The Empire's Back in Town'; G. John Ikenberry,

'America's Imperial Ambition', *Foreign Affairs* Vol. 81, No. 5 (2002): 44–62; Bruce Jentleson, 'Tough Love Multilateralism', *Washington Quarterly* Vol. 27, No. 1 (2004): 7–24; and Tucker and Hendrickson, 'Sources of American Legitimacy'.

5. Robert Kagan, *Paradise and Power: America and Europe in the New World Order* (London: Atlantic Books, 2003); Michael Cox, 'Kagan's World', *International Affairs* Vol. 79, No. 3 (2003): 523–32; Elizabeth Pond, *Friendly Fire* (Washington, DC: Brookings Institution); and William Shawcross, *Allies: The US, Britain, Europe and the War in Iraq* (London: Atlantic Books, 2004). For a take from the perspective of British politics, see Andrew Gamble, *Between Europe and America: The Future of British Politics* (London: Palgrave Macmillan, 2003).

6. For example, Barry Buzan and Ole Waever, *Regions and Powers: The Structure of International Security* (Cambridge: Cambridge University Press, 2004); Peter Katzenstein, *A World of Regions: Asia and Europe in the American Imperium* (Ithaca, NY: Cornell University Press, 2005).

7. This is very much along the lines indicated by Keohane and Nye. Keohane and Nye, *Power and Interdependence*.

8. Anna Leander, *Global Ungovernance: Mercenaries, States and the Control Over Violence*, COPRI Working Paper No. 4, 2002.

9. Rodney Bruce Hall and Thomas J. Biersteker, 'The Emergence of Private Authority in the International System', in Rodney Bruce Hall and Thomas J. Biersteker (eds), *The Emergence of Private Authority in Global Governance* (Cambridge: Cambridge University Press, 2002), 8.

10. For an account of the problem of legitimacy in 'weak' states, especially connected to contemporary warfare, see Kalevi J. Holsti, *The State, War, and the State of War* (Cambridge: Cambridge University Press, 1996).

11. Crisis in these terms is well articulated in: Jurgen Habermas, *Legitimation Crisis* (Heinemann Educational, 1976); and Colin Hay, 'Crisis and the Structural Transformation of the State: Interrogating the Process of Change', *British Journal of Politics and International Relations* Vol. 1, No. 3 (1999): 317–44.

12. Ian Hurd, 'Legitimacy and Authority in International Politics', *International Organization* Vol. 53, No. 2 (1999): 387.

13. Anna Leander, *Conditional Legitimacy, Reinterpreted Monopolies: Globalisation and the Evolving State Monopoly on Legitimate Violence*, COPRI Working Paper No. 10, 2002, 23.

14. Mandel, *Armies Without States*, 81.

Index

France – *continued*
  and migration, 132, 134
  and nuclear weapons, 78, 82, 145

Gaddis, John Lewis, 35, 72, 75
Gansler, Jacques, 100
Germany, 27, 29, 117, 132
Giddens, Anthony, 19, 20, 21,
    25, 26, 43, 74, 166n. 72,
    184n. 77
global governance, 5, 8, 56–7, 61
globalization
  and Cold War, 32–7
  contemporary state of, 48–9
  defined, 5–6, 8, 41–9, 51
  economic, 4, 90–8, 117–21, 139
  and the state, 4, 6–7, 58–62,
    146–9
globalization of security
  defined, 5, 8–9, 51–2
  three facets, 8–9, 51–2, 52–8,
    142–3
Gray, Colin, 75
Gregory, Shaun, 77

Halliday, Fred, 15, 36, 159n. 5
Harknett, Richard, 73
Hay, Colin, 28
Hayward, Keith, 93
hegemony, 35, 76
Heisler, Martin, 126
Held, David, 44, 55, 62, 74, 95,
    114, 121, 127
Herring, Eric, 102, 105
Herz, John, 16, 65–7, 71, 73, 74, 78,
    80, 81, 85
historical sociology
  and international relations, 1, 18,
    156n. 1
  and security, 7–8, 154
  and the state, 17–22
Hobden, Stephen, 25, 26
Hobson, John M., 16
Hollifield, James, 114, 136, 137
Howard, Michael, 25, 69
human rights, 127–30, 131, 138–9
humanitarian intervention, 21
Huysmans, Jef, 134, 135

Ikenberry, G. John, 35, 169n. 117
interdependence, 5, 10, 32, 37,
    38, 53, 59–60, 64, 71–5, 76,
    77, 78, 82, 87, 92, 95–8, 103,
    132, 150–1
international law, 128–9, 130,
    131, 135
internationalization, 2, 14, 27, 30–1,
    32–7, 56–8, 63, 92–3, 94, 103,
    104, 130, 148

Jervis, Robert, 68, 75, 80–1, 183n. 52
Joint Strike Fighter (JSF), 99, 103

Kaldor, Mary, 7
Keohane, Robert, 59, 95
Kissinger, Henry, 70, 71, 73, 76, 78
Kritz, Mary, 122, 135

Laffey, Mark, 36
Latham, Robert, 37
Layton-Henry, Zig, 126
Leander, Anna, 151
legitimacy, 9, 10, 11, 20, 62, 80–5,
    106–9, 149–54
Lipmann, Walter, 84
Lockheed Martin, 98, 99, 104
Lovering, John, 94–5, 100, 111–12,
    191n. 90
Lundestad, Geir, 35

MccGwire, Michael, 55
McNeill, William H., 27, 31
McSweeney, Bill, 18, 31
Machiavelli, Niccolo, 97
Maier, Charles, 35
Mandel, Robert, 152
Mandelbaum, Michael, 75, 80,
    181n. 29, 184n. 77
Mann, Michael, 1, 7, 19, 20–1, 23,
    25, 59, 85, 156n. 2, 173n. 21,
    173n. 28
  interstitial emergence, 46, 59
  organizational outflanking,
    46, 60
  sources of social power, 44–7, 51
  theory of the state, 19–20,
    163n. 41, 165n. 51